CONTINUITY
AND CHANGE
AFTER INDONESIA'S
REFORMS

The ISEAS – Yusof Ishak Institute (formerly Institute of Southeast Asian Studies) is an autonomous organization established in 1968. It is a regional centre dedicated to the study of socio-political, security, and economic trends and developments in Southeast Asia and its wider geostrategic and economic environment. The Institute's research programmes are grouped under Regional Economic Studies (RES), Regional Strategic and Political Studies (RSPS), and Regional Social and Cultural Studies (RSCS). The Institute is also home to the ASEAN Studies Centre (ASC), the Nalanda-Sriwijaya Centre (NSC), and the Singapore APEC Study Centre.

ISEAS Publishing, an established academic press, has issued more than 2,000 books and journals. It is the largest scholarly publisher of research about Southeast Asia from within the region. ISEAS Publishing works with many other academic and trade publishers and distributors to disseminate important research and analyses from and about Southeast Asia to the rest of the world.

CONTINUITY AND CHANGE AFTER INDONESIA'S REFORMS

Contributions to an Ongoing Assessment

EDITED BY
MAX LANE

LSEAS YUSOF ISHAK
INSTITUTE

First published in Singapore in 2019 by
ISEAS Publishing
30 Heng Mui Keng Terrace
Singapore 119614

E-mail: publish@iseas.edu.sg
Website: <http://bookshop.iseas.edu.sg>

The responsibility for facts and opinions in this publication rests exclusively with the authors and their interpretations do not necessarily reflect the views or the policy of the publisher or its supporters.

ISEAS Library Cataloguing-in-Publication Data

Continuity & Change after Indonesia's Reforms : Contributions to an Ongoing Assessment / edited by Max Lane.
  1. Indonesia—Politics and government—1998-
  2. Political parties—Indonesia.
  3. Democracy—Indonesia.
  4. Indonesia—Foreign relations.
  I. Lane, Max, 1951-, editor
DS644.5 C76   February 2019

ISBN 978-981-4843-22-5 (soft cover)
ISBN 978-981-4843-23-2 (E-book PDF)

Typeset by International Typesetters Pte Ltd
Printed in Singapore by Markono Print Media Pte Ltd

CONTENTS

PREFACE

This book is primarily the outcome of a workshop held at the ISEAS – Yusof Ishak Institute, Singapore in March 2018. Thirteen researchers studying contemporary Indonesian politics gathered at the Institute to discuss the extent to which the previous several years had ushered in a "new politics" or whether such a process was indeed evolving. The discussion also involved other researchers from the ISEAS Indonesian Studies Programme acting as discussants to the ideas presented by those who have contributed chapters. As reflected in this volume, the majority of those present were Indonesia-based researchers.

The reason for asking such questions about the extent of political change was that such a discussion was rife among both observers of Indonesian politics as well as actors and participants. In 2014, Joko Widodo, a furniture manufacturer and former mayor of the provincial city of Solo was elected president of Indonesia, defeating Prabowo Subianto, a Soeharto-era general and part of the milieu of conglomerate capital that had been dominant for so long in Indonesia. Was the election of a president from such a different social milieu than that which was seen to be previously dominant a symptom of deeper changes in Indonesian politics? Or was this new development less significant than many thought?

The eleven chapters in this book are a product of the workshop discussion as well as a reflection of the ongoing assessment of the individual authors. The topic is too wide and complex to expect a collection of 11 contributions such as this book to give definitive answers or resolve major issues. Furthermore, the chapters are not meant to reflect a consensual outcome but rather represent 11 individual contributions to a discussion of political developments over the last several years, especially in relation to the issue of the depth and extent of political change. Although with an eye to the question of change versus continuity, these contributions also focus on specific aspects of recent developments. Only the first chapter makes an attempt to give a general picture of developments based on the materials in this book. It is likely that other kinds of summations of this material are also possible.

In any case, what is happening in Indonesia today is still in process. Attempts to sum up these developments in one work or collection while events are still unfolding would be unwise. We hope this book, however, will be a useful and interesting contribution to the ongoing discussion and analysis of current developments.

Max Lane
Yogyakarta, Indonesia
September 2018

ABOUT THE CONTRIBUTORS

Leo Agustino, Senior Lecturer, Faculty of Social and Political Sciences, Universitas Sultan Ageng Tirtayasa

Richard Chauvel, Honorary Fellow, Asia Institute, University of Melbourne

Ulla Fionna, Fellow, ISEAS – Yusof Ishak Institute, Singapore, 2014–18

Max Lane, Visiting Senior Fellow, ISEAS – Yusof Ishak Institute, Singapore

Cornelis Lay, Professor of Politics and Government, Department of Politics and Government, Faculty of Social and Political Sciences, Universitas Gadjah Mada, Yogyakarta

Rizky Alif Alvian, Researcher, Department of International Relations, Faculty of Social and Political Sciences, Universitas Gadjah Mada, Yogyakarta

Yatun Sastramidjaja, Lecturer, Department of Anthropology, University of Amsterdam, The Netherlands

Amalinda Savirani, Head of the Department of Politics and Government, Faculty of Social and Political Sciences, Universitas Gadjah Mada, Yogyakarta

Mada Sukmajati, Lecturer, Department of Politics and Government, Faculty of Social and Political Sciences, Universitas Gadjah Mada, Yogyakarta

Ahmad Rizky Mardhatillah Umar, PhD Candidate, School of Political Sciences and International Studies, University of Queensland, Australia

Wawan Mas'udi, Lecturer, Department of Politics and Government, Faculty of Social and Political Sciences, Universitas Gadjah Mada, Yogyakarta

1

Indonesia's New Politics: Transaction Without Contestation

Max Lane

The period between 1998 and 2014 in Indonesian politics was defined by a political project necessitated by the fall of Soeharto in 1998 and the end of a specific form of political rule: dictatorship. May 1998 did not mark only the end of the overwhelming power of a specific individual – Soeharto – but at the same time the demolition of the whole structure of political rule that existed at that time. Between 1965 and 1998, and especially from 1972, political power had become centralized in one man, with structures that gave reality to that. These included a national military structure and ideology that both gave the army a physical presence at every level of administration, from national to village, and openly legitimized a repressive role for the army in politics. As president, Soeharto was Supreme Commander of the Armed Forces, backed by a loyal network of officers originating from the time when he was still an active officer himself. This centralized mechanism of repression and control was paralleled by a semi-theatrical electoral and representative structure, in which only three political parties, selected by Soeharto, were allowed and in which the repressive apparatus was able to intervene to determine the personnel and policies of all three. The press and civil society were severely restricted.

Following a complicated evolution and growth of an opposition, even in the face of this repression and at some cost to life and liberty, Soeharto was forced to resign. The removal of the linchpin of the system in the face of popular opposition forced a broad coalition of elite politicians and groups that filled the vacuum left by his departure to concede to the demand for political reform. The military's role in repression stopped (except in the provinces of Papua). The electoral and representative system was opened up to more parties — essentially only communist and separatist parties were banned. Most restrictions of the press and civil society were lifted.

The dismantling of the structures of dictatorship required replacement structures. The primary structure that has become the scaffolding of the present system is the electoral and representative systems. Which groups control the national and local government apparatus is now processed through elections. The armed forces are responsible to an elected government and, so far, have challenged this only once since 1998, and that was during the early transition stage. The new structures allow for multiparty elections for representative parliaments as well as for direct election of national and local executive positions.

The period 1998–2002 was primarily one of transition overseen by three presidents — Habibie, Sukarnoputri, and Wahid. While their presidencies were marked by turmoil, reflecting the continuing momentum from the anti-dictatorship movement of the 1990s, they also moved towards the establishment of the new structures. These included formation of a new parliament, the product of free elections in 1999; the end of single state trade unionism and other controls on civil society; recognition of the freedom of the press; and decentralization of budgetary policy to local government. A Corruption Eradication Commission (KPK), with significant investigative and arrest powers, was established in 2002.

The period between 2002 and 2010 was defined by the finalization and consolidation of these new structures as the basis for political and economic stability. This included the refinement of election laws, the introduction of direct elections for national and local executive positions, the further development of decentralization policy, and three national and several local elections. This was the period of two presidential terms of Susilo Bambang Yudhoyono. The finalization and consolidation of these new political structures defined the Yudhoyono period. Within the global economic context, this political process allowed the Indonesian economy to recover from the turmoil of the 1997 Asian financial crisis and to get through the global crisis of 2008. The Indonesian economy experienced relatively steady Gross National Product (GNP) growth during this period, and there was a very high rate of increase in government revenue. This also allowed the Yudhoyono government the possibility of formulating a medium-term development plan during its final years and to make an initial start on it, which primarily focused on a push to build more infrastructure. Economic development, however, was not the project that defined the Yudhoyono period as compared to the consolidation of the new political structures.

2014: Something New?

The election of President Yudhoyono in 2004 ended a period of significant political tensions. The presidencies of Habibie, Wahid and Sukarnoputri were marked by ongoing political conflict, including protests by the various components of the activist anti-dictatorship movement of before 1998. That ended after the election of Yudhoyono, which opened a period of stabilization. Wahid and Sukarnoputri were figures who emerged out of the opposition to Soeharto; Yudhoyono, while abandoning Soeharto in the very end, was a long-term military official of the Soeharto order. However, he accepted the necessity of restructuring stability.

In a period defined by multiparty electoral democracy, Yudhoyono and his supporters needed to establish an electoral vehicle. This was the Partai Demokrat (PD — Democratic Party). At one level, the PD was (and still is) a vehicle for Yudhoyono personally, and now his family. At another level, it was the party of restructuring and consolidation of new political structures while ensuring overall socio-economic stability. The economy created during the Soeharto period was maintained, with only one significant "reform": the de facto abolition of high-level, centralized cronyism. As the incumbent party for ten years, PD has come to represent this orientation.

The PD, however, was not able to solve the problem of succession to Yudhoyono. While there were rumours of the PD possibly putting forward Yudhoyono's wife as a candidate, this never eventuated. It was only in 2017 that the process of preparing Yudhoyono's son as a successor began — but in a very different political climate. The PD was not able to generate any other potential candidates from within its ranks. This was partly caused by Yudhoyono's overwhelming personal dominance of the leadership allowing no space for other figures to emerge. It was also caused, in a more substantial way, by the fact that the project that defined the PD's character had come to an end. By 2014, all the new structures were in place. The main new project that could possibly redefine a ruling party was the planned big new push on the economy, especially through an accelerated infrastructure plan. The chief designer and spokesperson for this plan was Coordinating Minister for Economic Affairs, Hatta Rajasa, who was from the National Mandate Party (PAN), not the PD. Furthermore, in 2014 PAN decided not to continue to align with PD, which had no viable presidential candidate, but rather with Prabowo Subianto, who had established Gerindra and would be a presidential candidate. Rajasa became Subianto's vice-presidential running mate. PD was left without either a candidate or a project.

Subianto and Rajasa lost the 2014 election by a slim margin to Joko Widodo, who was nominated by the Indonesian Democratic Party of Struggle (PDIP). During this 2014 presidential campaign, considerable commentary developed remarking that the candidacy of Joko Widodo pointed to a major change in the Indonesian political terrain (see the chapters by Sukmajati and Mas'udi for more on Widodo's history and ideology). One factor was that Widodo came from a markedly different social milieu than all previous candidates. Habibie, Wahid, Sukarnoputri, and Yudhoyono had all been nationally prominent figures during the New Order. Whether supporters or opponents of the New Order, they were products of that period and of the social world defined by its elite. Widodo, on the other hand, emerged from the petty bourgeoisie of a small city. He was a middle-level furniture exporter driven by personal ambition into politics, eventually attaching himself to the PDIP and being elected mayor of that small city, Solo. He was elected mayor twice, the second time with a record 90 per cent vote.

His popularity in Solo also provoked discussion that he manifested something new. No politician had ever scored so highly in any kind of popularity measure. Additionally, his popularity stemmed from a combination of two features. One was success in implementing specific popular welfare policies, in particular a universal healthcare scheme. The other feature was a campaign style involving frequent well-publicized visits and dialogues with groupings perceived in the political culture to be representative of the "common people", such as street and marketplace vendors. All these contrasted him markedly with the way in which politicians had campaigned previously. The prevalent political style was to present as a leader with considerable official gravitas, whose electability would be strengthened by association with other national elite figures. Widodo cultivated an image of being approachable rather than an authority figure. His prioritization of healthcare and similar policies in Solo, a town of 500,000 people the majority of whom were members of a self-employed, impoverished precariat, meant that his campaign style was seen as genuine, being reflected in policy priorities. He was later elected governor of Jakarta and after a short period resigned from that position to stand for president. During his short period as governor, he was able to maintain the image and momentum that he built as mayor of Solo.

The perception of Widodo's candidacy as a manifestation of new processes unfolding was strengthened by the contrast with his presidential rival, Prabowo Subianto. Prabowo was from an elite, very wealthy New Order family. He had been married to a daughter of Soeharto. He had risen very quickly through the ranks of the army so that by 1998 he headed what was considered a very important command, Kopassus. He tried to project gravitas rather than closeness to the common people in his campaign. He displayed his wealth and social status as part of establishing his credentials as somebody sufficiently above the common person to be their leader. The tone was: do you want a lamb or a lion for a president? This was an image much more associated with the Soeharto period. It made the claim that Widodo manifested something new even more convincing. Widodo also defended the new structures established by Yudhoyono, including direct elections for president and other executive positions. Prabowo called for their abolition and a return to the pre-restructuring system in which the president, governors, *bupatis* and mayors were elected by various representative bodies. This also presented a contrast between a candidate who represented what was new and a candidate who represented the previous order.

Widodo's campaign also played to this perception of newness. There was clearly an assessment by Widodo and his group that such an approach would appeal to a large section of the public. Campaign tactics that emphasized this newness, this difference with an elitist New Order political culture, were emphasized. These tactics included wearing unpretentious and allegedly low-cost clothing, continuing the practice of market vendor and similar visits, and actively relating to the newly expanding Jakarta white collar working class, whose professional and socially active components were labelled "millennials". He attended large meetings of socially and politically liberal intellectuals and former anti-dictatorship activists, some of whom formed organizations to support his campaign. He associated himself with their cultural icons, such as the band Slang and an activity like *Jalan Sehat* ("Walking for Health") on car-free days in central Jakarta. He issued a "manifesto", the Nawacita, that reflected this "millennial", liberal sentiment.

When Widodo was elected, there were expectations of something new. There was expectation of a government of a new type, with Widodo declaring himself and being declared as a "non-transactional" politician of principle rather than the deal-making politician of the past, such as Yudhoyono. It was more than this, however. Many thought that Indonesia itself was changing politically, that Widodo was a symptom or a manifestation of deeper changes that had indeed facilitated his candidacy.

Something Old, Something New: Strengthened "Transactional Politics"

Widodo was a symptom of something new, but not exactly what his 2014 campaign tried to project. Indeed not a product of the New Order, he is instead, ironically, a product of the "Yudhoyono" order: that is, of a consolidated multiparty electoral system and decentralized system of governance that was restructured to ensure the stability of the economy and society produced by the New Order. It was the restructuring during the Yudhoyono period, an outcome of the fall of Soeharto, that was new and that had facilitated the emergence of Widodo. It was the politics facilitated by this restructuring that was new, and it preceded Widodo: his campaign did not propose any further new restructuring.

One fundamental consequence of the restructuring from centralized, authoritarian politics to decentralized, multiparty electoralism, given the nature of Indonesia's class structure, was a severe fragmentation of political organizations. The restructuring removed an authoritarian centre that had the capacity to enforce *simplifikasi* of political organizations. Under the New Order, only three selected political parties were allowed. In the first post-dictatorship elections, forty-eight parties put up candidates. A combination of some parties not receiving sufficient support and changes to electoral laws has reduced that number, but still in 2019, twenty parties will field candidates.

The proliferation of parties is not a direct or automatic result of much greater electoral political freedom, except insofar as this greater freedom intersects with the reality that Indonesia's socio-economic development since 1965 has given it a highly fragmented domestic bourgeoisie. This is the only class with the resources necessary to establish and finance electoral political parties, especially given the expenses involved in meeting the registration requirements. On the costs of elections and the issue of corruption see the chapter by Agustino. The Indonesian party system reflects the fragmentation of this class. Other classes, such as the working class, however defined, or peasant farmers had been forcibly excluded from any meaningful political life between 1965 and 1998. Unorganized, dispersed geographically, with extremely meagre material resources and no ideological traditions to draw upon, these classes have no political party of any hue, even after active systematic repression ceased in 1998 and trade unions were allowed.

The proliferation of parties, therefore, is not a reflection of different class representation, but rather of different fragments or factions of the best-resourced class. Thus the fourteen parties are all led and backed by businesspeople or ex-government or military officials with family or personal ties to business. Joko Widodo, from the PDIP, is a businessman. Prabowo, an ex-general, is now a businessman, as is his even richer brother.

This fragmentation of the socio-economic elite and multiplicity of parties are the basis for endemic and deep transactional politics at all levels. The term transactional in this book is taken directly from contemporary practical usage. A part of Widodo's image in 2014 was that he was *anomali politik transaksional*. His campaign promised a cabinet selected purely on the basis of capability and not *transaksional*, that is, not based on deals with other parties. Yudhoyono had based himself on a broad coalition of parties and was criticized for being too *transaksional*. Widodo's campaign counterposed his approach to such transactionalism. Widodo's popularity, flowing from perceptions about his time as mayor of Solo, did enhance his bargaining power and enable him to campaign with less visible reliance on doing deals for support. However, that this could not be sustained was already obvious during the Jakarta gubernatorial elections. He had to ally with a party standing for the opposing style, Gerindra, appearing on platforms, not only with Gerindra's newly recruited and short-lived candidate Basuki Tjahaja Purnama (known as Ahok), but also with Prabowo, Widodo's opponent in 2014.

After he was elected, Widodo almost immediately had to enter into deals to form his cabinet. He was subject to widespread criticism for betraying his promise not to be a transactional politician. In fact, by 2017 he transacted all but three parties in the parliament into his cabinet. Partai Demokrat, headed by Yudhoyono, Gerindra, headed by Prabowo, and the Islamist PKS ended up the only parties outside the government. In exchange for cabinet ministries, parties that had not initially been part of the pro-Widodo coalition — such as Soeharto's former party, Golkar; the Soeharto-era PPP; Hanura, headed by former Soeharto General Wiranto; and PAN, symbolically headed by Amien Rais — all joined the government. These transactions also manifested the absence of serious ideological or programmatic differences between the parties. We might note also that Golkar, Hanura, and PPP all represent continuity with New Order politics and personalities.

Transactional politics is indeed new to modern Indonesia and stands in stark contrast to the authoritarian centralism of the New Order period. Centralism, however, was the feature of the New Order government as it related specifically to the Indonesian elite layers as a whole. The New Order state relationship to non-elite layers, the mass of the population, was not so much centralistic as simply repressive, banning membership of political parties at the village and subdistrict levels, allowing only state-controlled workers' and peasants' unions and banning ideologies advocating class-based resistance to elites. The new transactionalism has been, therefore, essentially an intra-class phenomenon with minimal direct impact on the empowerment of non-elite classes.

The intra-class nature of the new transactionalism is, as mentioned above, also reflected in the relative absence of substantive ideological and programmatic differences among the parties in the current government coalition, and indeed between the government coalition and the parties outside the government. The parliamentary parties are divided into three blocs: the coalition supporting President Widodo; the coalition between Gerindra and PKS; and, standing alone, the

Partai Demokrat. However, we can also note that these parties have rarely voted differently on substantial policy issues (see the chapters by Sukmajati and Fionna). Where there have been debates in the parliament, factions often ended up voting for policies that they had criticized in debates. Even where parties have voted differently, they have not launched systematic ongoing campaigns to win public support for their positions, relying more on manoeuvres and surrendering the issues to undirected social media activities. There have been no particularly visible and clear programmatic dividing lines. This is also reflected in the ease with which local coalitions between parties are formed, often along different alignments from those that prevail at the national level. Opposing parties in the national parliament can be close allies in different provinces, districts, and towns.

Furthermore, as August 2018 approaches for nominations to be made for president and vice-president, transactionalism was further exposed. PAN, a party in the pro-Widodo coalition, joined the pro-Prabowo camp. Partai Demokrat, neutral in the 2014 elections, also reached an agreement with Prabowo and Gerindra to form a coalition and to support Prabowo's presidency. In the process of announcing and explaining this, Yudhoyono also said that Widodo had invited Partai Demokrat to join the government several times and that Partai Demokrat had no objection in principle to doing so. Yudhoyono indicated that Partai Demokrat was unable to do so because of perceived reluctance from some pro-Widodo coalition members. This has been interpreted in the media as a reference to the animosity from Megawati Sukarnoputri, president of PDIP, to working with Yudhoyono. In other words, there are no ideological or programmatic differences that stop the PD, or any other party, working with any other party — only clashes of egos and personal interests. In some districts, even the Islamist PKS has been willing to work with the "secular" PDIP.

This non-programmatic politics was further reinforced on the morning that Prabowo registered his candidacy. After a day of "high drama", when Prabowo made a surprise decision to appoint a Gerindra figure, Sandiaga Uno, and some Democrat figures raised the possibility of breaking the deal, and even supporting Jokowi, the Democrat Party went with Prabowo. The only reason publicly given for going with Prabowo and not Jokowi: "We think he can win."

The Effects of Transactional Politics Without Contestation

This kind of highly opportunistic transactional politics severely hinders or distorts political contestation on two fronts: intra-class and between classes. In both cases, the intersection of the existing political format with political economy provides the ultimate shape to political contestation.

Intra-elite transactionalism and the absence of substantial programmatic differentiation are possible because the different factions of the country's elite share the same basic socio-economic interests and outlook. All factions, represented by the parties, have supported the post-1998 political structures. Even Gerindra, PKS and PAN, which opposed direct elections for executive positions during the 2014 presidential campaign, later supported legislation that codified them. No party has offered any fundamental opposition to the economic strategy embodied in annual budgets, with criticisms aimed only at specific issues, and the government's capacity (*kinerja*) to carry out its policies. All parties support the general priority of accelerating construction of infrastructure. While point-scoring criticisms and general admonishments for greater protection from foreign interests come from Gerindra, no differing overall economic strategy has been offered. There is general consensus on the overall strategy of promoting private sector-led economic growth; seeking foreign investments and aid; increasing state subsidization of infrastructure development; and reducing regulations that are perceived as negatively impacting the freedom to do business. There is general agreement on providing a minimal safety net for those defined as extremely poor while also steadily reducing subsidies for both consumer goods and production inputs. Arguments occur around questions of degree and effectiveness, not over basic direction.

While this general consensus on political and economic directions is real, it is also very true that there is no consensus on who should be president and which groups should control the government. So transactionalism is still indeed marked by contestation. However, the underlying shared interests and outlook mean that the contestation must take on non-programmatic, personal or narrowly "cultural" forms. During 2018, for example, social media contestation between pro-Widodo and pro-Prabowo has reduced to a very low level in content.

Each camp now describes the other as either "tadpoles" (what Prabowo supporters call Widodo supporters) or "bats" (what Widodo supporters call Prabowo supporters). Both sides are on the alert for any incident or "misstatement" that can be turned into a meme or a tweet to attack the image of the other. It could be a policy misstatement, or even the shoes or watch a politician is wearing. It has become a policy-free image battle. Any perceived policy failure by the government is immediately taken up in this image war, but no alternative policies or strategies are proposed. As the process gets closer to a formal start, there are social media posts referring to Prabowo's past record on human rights, and also to the record of Widodo's Coordinating Minister of Political and Security, Wiranto.

Alongside this kind of image war, which has escalated during the course of 2018, another important issue used for contestation has emerged: the status of religion (on the politics of religion see the chapter by Alvian). The emergence of religion as a high-profile political issue is a function of two key features of intra-elite transactionalism. The first is the fairly solid intra-elite ideological and programmatic consensus combined with the specific form taken by the "lack of consensus" on who should be president. The competition is between Widodo–Megawati (PDIP), Yudhoyono and his son (PD), and Prabowo (Gerindra). They are all leaders of parties that oppose the idea of a religious or Islamic state. PDIP is well known for this stance, signified by its support for Pancasila, the code words for a state in which all religions have equal formal status and religious law has no overarching authority. In the press conference that announced cooperation between Gerindra and PD in support of Prabowo's candidacy, Yudhoyono put rejection of the religious state (*negara agama*) on equal status with their rejection of communism. He qualified this only by stating that they were also opposed to Islamophobia. Widodo too has recently been going out of his way to meet religious figures. This situation means, however, that the three main forces opposed to a *negara Islam* are competing against each other. Widodo and PDIP have won the support of three other parties that are also opposed to *negara agama*: Golkar, Nasdem, and the Nahdlatul Ulama-connected National Awakening Party (PKB). In the context of intra-elite transactionalism, politics becomes competition to win the public support of other public actors, namely those parties that more prominently campaign under an Islamic banner. Gerindra has thus oriented to cementing its alliance with the PKS and also seeking to be visibly connected to high-profile extra-parliamentary forces looking for a greater formal status for Islamic religious law and a greater political leadership role for religious clerics.

This alignment became increasingly open during 2017 and into 2018. It has been clearest since the 2017 Jakarta gubernatorial elections. The candidate nominated by the PDIP was the Chinese Christian incumbent, Basuki Tjahaja Purnama, who was accused of "blasphemy" against Islam by hardline Islamic figures associated with the Front Pembela Islam (FPI), whose high-profile spokesperson was Habib Riziek. The FPI formed an alliance with other like-minded groups to campaign for Basuki Tjahaja Purnama's arrest. Their propaganda demanded more implementation of Islamic law in response to increased "liberalism" and a greater role for the *ulama*. As explained later in this book, their propaganda did not argue for an Islamic state and attempted to accommodate the old-style New Order official support for Pancasila, thus making an alignment with Gerindra possible. Prabowo has since then consistently publicly associated himself with a range of figures from the FPI-related alliance that emerged at that time. In the round of transactional meetings undertaken in formalizing a nomination of a vice-presidential candidate, Prabowo also met with an assembly of Islamic figures originating from the 2017 Islamist campaigns, although he declined to appoint a religious figure as his vice-president, unlike Widodo.

Parties as Agents of Transaction

This phenomenon is best understood if we can grasp the reality that political parties in Indonesia are defined by their role as agents of transaction. To the extent they are representative institutions, they represent their leadership constituencies in the processes of transaction. As is described later in this book, Indonesia's political parties allocate relatively small resources to policy development, internal education, membership administration, or recruitment — except recruitment of candidates for local or national parliaments (see the chapter by Fionna).

There is a basic acceptance that each party represents a more or less stable constituency, which can be enlarged only marginally and only via national media propaganda. All parties assume that nobody will get more than 30 per cent of the vote and that most will get between 4 per cent and 20 per cent. This acceptance of the current make-up of representation underpins the whole transactional political system. To be elected president, it is assumed that it is optimal to get support from the maximum number of factions (parties). During July 2018, each coalition had as many public meetings as possible of its component members. The pro-Widodo coalition made a photo opportunity out of a meeting of the six parliamentary parties in the coalition as well as another meeting of nine parties, including three that as yet have no parliamentary representatives. Prabowo did the same with serial meetings with Demokrat, PKS and PAN, as well as his extra-parliamentary Islamic support.

No party prioritizes trying to win votes away from other parties with the aim of winning a majority or close to it;[1] it is assumed this is impossible, for a number of reasons. This assessment by the parties applies, in the first instance, to the local level, and then the national level. First, any attempt to campaign seriously to win away the support of another party immediately puts existing coalitions at risk, which all parties consider to be the most pressing need. Widodo, nominated by the PDIP and emphatically claimed by the PDIP to be as president a *petugas partai*, cannot actively use his incumbency to promote the PDIP. He is in effect a president representing nine parties as well as a large bloc of (at least previously) non-party "volunteers". Second, most parties have primary voter bases in particular regions, with no party having a more or less equal level of support throughout the country. Campaigning to truly expand voter support would mean an escalation of penetration into new regions, requiring networks and resources that many parties do not have. Third, there is the ideological and programmatic issue: on what basis does one party attempt to win people away from the parties they presently identify with, given that there is ideological and programmatic identity? Also, parties that emphasize their religious character can pull people away only from other Islamic parties, and on what basis? Competition to appear "more religious" than competitors infects the atmosphere with a trend to vote based on feelings or religious identity, providing the basis for so-called identity politics. On what ideological and programmatic basis can the PDIP, Gerindra, Nasdem, and Golkar compete with each other? The prevailing consensus prevents populist appeals promising serious redistributive policies, which are outside that consensus. The Gerindra–PKS coalition in the Jakarta gubernatorial coalition did promise some trade unions that it would reform the Widodo government's 2015 wages policy, which slowed real wages growth, but reneged on the promise almost immediately after being installed as governor and vice-governor.

This situation underpins the overwhelming reliance of all parties, at all levels, on choosing candidates who are individual figures, personalities, with a pre-existing popularity on whatever basis. While no party, either locally or nationally, can achieve a majority in an election, sometimes an individual can. Widodo's second election as mayor of Solo is an example, as is the 2017 election of the *bupati* of Kulon Progo. Both won popularity on the basis of their health policies. Parties also choose TV personalities, local religious leaders, and military figures. In the 2017 Jakarta elections, the battle was between PDIP and its party allies and PKS and Gerindra, or between Basuki Tjahaja Purnama and Anies Baswedan and Sadiano Una. Anies was nominated by PKS but was known as somebody who strived to be a presidential candidate for the Partai Demokrat and then, when that did not eventuate, became a very high profile and enthusiastic supporter for Widodo in 2014. He was not known as a spokesperson for PKS and its outlook. While Widodo did make statements using Sukarnoist vocabulary in 2014, such as *Trisakti*, he has not campaigned to win support for a specific PDIP ideology, but rather to popularize his own style, which represents an outlook that is shared beyond the PDIP.

Trapped within a consensus reflecting their real shared general interests, intra-elite contestation remains shallow and opportunistic, relying on personality appeal and, for some, "identity politics". The 2019 presidential election, and as a result the parliamentary elections, much more than a competition between parties and programmes, will be dominated by the competition between Widodo and Prabowo (and the personalities who are their vice-presidential candidates), perhaps with former President Yudhoyono also playing a role in this competition.

New Politics and Policy Reform

State policy in all areas since 2014 has fundamentally been a continuation of pre-2014 policies. The main difference is that, with the political restructuring completed, the current government has been liberated to concentrate on economics. An assessment of the results of the government's economic policies is outside the purview of this book, except insofar as they have had immediate political impacts.

Widodo has faced no serious political disruptions or any new major political projects to undertake. The government, having made promises to some of its supporters, did initially take political initiatives to free political prisoners in Papua, but political liberalization there has mostly stalled since then. Having also made promises to deal with long-standing accusations of human rights violations since 1965, including those that took place in 1965–66, the government also organized a public seminar on the 1965 events, with speakers from all sides. The 2015 public seminar on the 1965 events did elicit considerable opposition, including from Widodo's own defence minister, as well as figures associated with the Islamic right, such as Riziek. Again, movement on this issue has also stalled, although in July and August 2018, as the presidential election campaign had a de facto start, Minister Wiranto announced the formation of a new fact-finding team to investigate all such cases. The government had earlier announced the formation of a National Council for Reconciliation, which was criticized for avoiding the question of bringing perpetrators to justice and steering clear of earlier recommendations for an ad hoc Human Rights Court to be established.

Ambiguity of outcome appears to be a consequence of this kind of transactional politics, which abhors serious contestation. Negotiation — the deal — becomes the primary mode of politics alongside image wars, which affect bargaining positions. Campaigning to convince people of ideological, programmatic, and policy perspectives is not part of a political culture that sees parties as agents of transaction and popularity built on personalities as the key currency in negotiations. In a context of deals of this kind and the absence of the capacity or desire for such contestation, policy reforms or initiatives can easily stall once there is resistance. If the resistance can be overcome only by a campaign of explanation throughout society, the tendency is to seek an accommodation.

In addition to the stalling of liberalization around human rights abuses and also Papua (see the chapter by Chauvel), corruption eradication is another example. The ambiguities of policy formulation and implementation are also reflected in how policies to increase the financial autonomy of villages have been partially negated by national control of project formulation and regional economic development being overdetermined by national decisions on infrastructure development and the consequent commercial ramifications (on centre region relations see the chapter by Lay). Neither does there appear to have been any restructuring of foreign policy (see the chapter by Umar), despite early indications of changes being on the agenda.

Inter-class Relations and Contestation

Describing Indonesia's new politics as "transactional", in contrast to the previous authoritarian centralized politics of the New Order, it retains its efficacy precisely because of the absence of contestation from outside the broad national elite layers, the Indonesian bourgeoisie and petty bourgeoisie. The contestation that can take place within and among this elite, given its shared interests and consensus, is highly opportunistic, shallow as regards substance and narrow as regards issues, relying on clashes of personalities, image wars, and appeals to identity. It locks Indonesia into a process of policy reform that more often than not has ambiguous outcomes. When everything is a transaction among factions of the same elite, policy ambiguity is almost inevitable. This is very debilitating because this ambiguity is in relation to the formulation and implementation of the existing policy consensus — so there are ambiguous outcomes, even in relation to what is generally agreed upon.

The almost total absence of contestation from outside the dominant social layers is not an uncommon phenomenon in countries that have experienced an extended period of totalitarian or nearly totalitarian rule that has prioritized institutionalizing the political passivity of the majority of the population. In such societies, the dominant social class and its immediate apparatus are constituted almost along the lines of castes, as in the Asiatic despotic mode of production. As a caste, they had a hereditary right to participation in political life, including the political life of state rule. The other classes, in the twentieth century mainly proletariat and peasantry, are excluded from political life almost completely. Political as well as social organizations with a potential for political activity are either banned (or sometimes physically exterminated) or kept under tight control by the ruling caste during the totalitarian period.

When such a structure ends after a long period — thirty-three out of forty-eight years of existence in Indonesia's case — only the elite has the resources, ideology, and traditions to be able to organize to represent themselves. Even after repressive restrictions are lifted or reduced, it remains the case that for an extended period only the elite class can organize. This has been the case in Indonesia. All existing political parties have been formed by networks from the elite and are staffed by a middle class, formally educated political caste, whose material conditions are far removed from those of the mass of the population (see the chapter by Savirani). In fact, to become a candidate for election in Indonesia, one needs to have graduated from senior high school, setting a minimum entry into the ruling caste. The need for access to money further limits entry.

From 1998, repressive restrictions on trade unions were lifted. President Habibie's government ratified International Labour Organization (ILO) conventions on the rights of trade unions and later presented legislation to give effect to more trade union freedom. The existing state-controlled union fragmented, giving rise eventually to two separate trade union confederations. Hundreds of new enterprise unions were established, many of which later combined to form new federations and confederations. As of 2018, there were thirteen confederations in addition to numerous federations and unaffiliated unions. This was certainly very new and different from what existed under the New Order: a single dictatorship-controlled union. At the same time, it should be noted that the proportion of the workforce that has become union members is still very small, probably less than 10 per cent.

Moreover, by 2015, the two largest union confederations had been co-opted into intra-elite transactional politics. One confederation had become aligned with the Widodo government. The other confederation, which had previously been the most active and militant campaigner for improvement of conditions, aligned with Gerindra and Prabowo. Other unions remained independent, and even highly critical of both Widodo and Prabowo, and of the leaderships of the two confederations. In terms of members, the two aligned confederations were by far the largest. Alignment with one or the other of these two camps was connected to offers of positions in the government, such as cabinet ministers. The process was captured within the transactional framework.

No other sections of non-elite social layers have come to possess organizations even remotely comparable to the trade unions in size and national spread. There are only scattered and dispersed small campaign organizations.

Post-2014 new politics remains that of intra-elite transactionalism, with no inter-class contestation, either of a social democratic character explicitly campaigning for redistribution of wealth or anything more radical, as had existed on a large scale before 1965. However, it would be an incomplete picture if reference was not made to signs of an embryonic challenge to the absence of contestation.

One indication of potential future contestation from non-elite components was the April 2018 Indonesian Peoples Movement Congress (KGRI). This congress was initiated by five trade unions outside of the major confederations aligned with blocs inside the elite. The largest of these was KASBI, which claims more than 30,000 members. The others were much smaller. At least forty-two democratic and human rights, community development, farmer and urban poor groups and left-oriented human rights organizations, as well as several other trade unions, participated and signed a joint declaration affirming their conclusion that a new alternative political organization was needed — an alternative to those originating within the elite. The KGRI mandated an organizing group:

- To recommend to the individual organizations involved in the conference to discuss building an alternative political force.
- To establish a team to discuss the formation of an alternative political force (an alternative political party or alternative political bloc).

All of the forty-two organizations present have been involved in campaigns raising issues and demands counterposed to the policies of the elite's political blocs. Due to their still small size and operation outside of any united front, they have not yet been able to challenge the general mode of intra-elite transactional politics with no substantive contestation. It is clearly the absence of such contestation and the consequent inability to achieve serious reform that is partly the motivation for this initiative. So too is the fear of the increased resort to identity politics facilitated by intra-elite transactional politics having an impact, winning adherents, among the grassroots membership of trade unions and other grassroots organizations.

The absence of any substantial or sustained contestation, aside from confined skirmishes, from outside the broad political and business elite has been very obvious since 1998. However, the process that drove the unravelling of Soeharto's regime was the escalating mobilization of non-elite class forces, in particular the urban poor and factory workers.

Escalation of these mobilizations, especially after the 1997 economic crisis, sharpened the contradiction within Soeharto's ruling faction, which eventually abandoned him rather than see opposition escalate further. During that 1989–98 period, another social layer also played a key leadership role: youth, and in particular a radicalized minority of university students. Different segments of these students formed several different organizations, the most prominent of which was the People's Democratic Party (PRD). Twenty years later there are former PRD members in almost all of the trade unions involved in the KGRI trade unions, and several of the other organizations.

There has been no large radicalized and mobilizing student movement since 1998. The larger student mobilizations that have taken place have been mostly integrated into intra-elite politics. At the same time, left-oriented student organizations are also involved in KGRI. There are also numerous progressive, left student discussion groups and publications. While there is no guarantee that youth or students will play the same vanguard role they did between 1989 and 1998, it can be noted that a vanguard role of radicalized youth has been the pattern in Indonesia at every major political turning point (see the chapter by Sastramidjaja). The final chapter in this book reviews developments relating to youth and students.

Remembering Political Economy

The chapters in this book reflect analytical approaches coming from political science. Economic structures and how they affect politics have not been a focus. In this chapter, I have pointed out that the fragmented nature of the domestic bourgeoisie, mostly along regional lines, has also meant a fragmented system of parties that all reflect different segments of that domestic bourgeoisie, often with their primary support base in particular regions. The chapter by Savirani points to the middle class economic underpinning of almost all of the country's parliamentarians. The role of commercial interests is touched upon in Lay's chapter on national–local relations.

It has been, however, a proposition of this chapter that the period since 2014 has been one in which all political tasks identified as urgent by the elite as a whole have been completed and that the economy became the primary item on the elite's national agenda.

Widodo's presidency, with his emphasis on infrastructure development, deregulation, and achieving GNP growth targets, and with no cultural or political programmes priority, has very much reflected this. The constrained nature of contemporary transactional politics, because of a general consensus over political restructuring and the economy, has facilitated the emergence of identity politics (flowing from the rivalries between the more "secular" parties) and made the status of religion and religious leaders a significant issue, reflected in the rhetorical contestation between Pancasila and "Islam".

It may turn out, however, to be a mistake to think that issues relating to economic policies and economic development are not and will not be equally, and even more, crucial. The consensus on economic policy may fracture if either the current relative economic stability is disturbed (such as with a further decline in the rupiah) or if cost-of-living pressures worsen. Already in the lead-up to the August presidential nominations, those opposed to Widodo increased their rhetoric on economic policy issues, such as the declining value of the rupiah, increase in foreign debt, increase in electricity prices, and increases in fuel prices. There was also considerable criticism of the government's claim in July 2018 that poverty has fallen below 10 per cent, with critics pointing out that the poverty line was set at a very low 400,000–600,000 rupiah per month.

Conclusion

The chapters in this book by thirteen researchers and analysts look at a range of topics that it is hoped will help readers better understand the more recent developments in Indonesian politics. It does not pretend to be totally comprehensive, with some areas not covered at all, such as the role of the military (except in Papua) or rural politics. The contributors are not attempting to settle on a consensual view, but rather hope to provide insights by looking at specific areas. In this introductory chapter, however, I have tried to make at least an initial argument that, when contrasted with the centralized authoritarian politics of the New Order, the current intra-elite transactional mode of politics, facilitated by the political restructuring carried out under President Yudhoyono, does represent a significant change. I have also argued that this opening up to a multiparty electoral system, with its transactionalism, has not yet overcome the legacy of thirty-three years of centralized authoritarian politics in that the passivity on the non-elite majority of the population, enforced by repression between 1965 and 1998, remains prevalent. Thus the current political mode can be described as transactional politics without substantive contestation, only rhetorical.[2]

NOTES

1. While this is generally the case on a national level as regards to parties, the contradiction is that the same does not apply to the competition between presidential candidates.
2. On rhetorical contestation, see Lane (2019).

REFERENCE

Lane, Max. "Contending Rhetoric in Indonesia's Presidential Elections: An Analysis". *ISEAS Perspective*, 25 January 2019.

2

Indonesian Parties Twenty Years On: Personalism and Professionalization amidst Dealignment

Ulla Fionna

Introduction

Political parties' work is commonly assessed primarily on whether they are developing "policy programs giving voters clear choices in elections" and are "sufficiently disciplined and cohesive in the parliamentary assembly to implement these programs" (Dalton et al. 2011). Based on these criteria, Indonesian parties have performed very poorly. Similarly, as party institutionalization[1] is an integral element to "ensure effective governance" through accountability and stability of interests and broadly targeted programmes, again Indonesian parties are failing (Hicken and Kuhonta 2011, p. 573). While there is a level of agreement among scholars that Indonesia's political parties have made significant progress in building stable roots in society and performing certain functions (Ufen 2010; Mietzner 2013), it is also clear that they remain among the most corrupt institutions in the country. Parties' role in resource distribution and nomination of public positions has often led to graft cases, and party politicians have dominated as corruption suspects. Parties were seen as one of the factors for Indonesia's democratic stagnation (Mietzner 2012). The parties' representatives in the state and local parliaments are also known to be highly inefficient in their work ethics and prone to serving and preserving their own interests, rather than aggregating and accommodating public interests (Sherlock 2010).

Despite these problems, parties have indeed changed since 1998. Indonesia and its parties have dramatically advanced as a vibrant democracy. This chapter assesses the progress of parties twenty years after the fall of authoritarianism in Indonesia. Drawing from the works of various scholars, it synthesizes the arguments to highlight the shifts, adjustments, and adaptations that the parties have undertaken. Factors such as legal and institutional changes, as well as global and national trends, have all played a part in the evolution of parties post-Soeharto. The following discussion outlines these various elements and attaches them to major themes: parties as organizations, in elections, and in government.

It is argued in the following sections that, although parties have progressed in the institutionalization process, there are certain vacuums and perversions of their roles. In performing their primary function as the linkage between voters and government, in simplifying the choices in elections, recruiting and training candidates, organizing the work of government, and implementing policies and organizing governmental administration (Dalton et al. 2011, pp. 6–7), parties have been neither active nor efficient. Parties continue to fail in building clear platforms and programmes, as they continue to rely on patronage for their funding and to attract votes.

To start with, it must be acknowledged that parties' role as the link between voters and government has evolved since 1998. They have had to adjust to certain trends and constraints. The electoral system and its regulations have been influential in shaping parties' behaviour. At the same time, there are other prominent trends such as the growing detachment between parties and voters — parties' institutionalization has been very slow or even discontinued. The following discussion examines the ways in which parties have changed or adapted to certain post-1998 dynamics, and assesses the role they play in contemporary Indonesia.

Party Organization and Systems

With mass organizations as the origins of first parties in the country (Shiraishi 1990), many of the existing parties have some sort of association with some of the biggest mass organizations in Indonesia. Some of Indonesia's largest political parties post-independence either had close links or even evolved from existing mass organizations. For instance, during its heyday Masyumi Party (Partai Majelis Syuro Muslimin Indonesia — Council of Indonesian Muslim Associations) had both Nahdlatul Ulama (NU) and Muhammadiyah (both currently Indonesia's largest Muslim organizations) as members; Partai Sarekat Islam (Islamic Union Party) had originated from Sarekat Islam (Islamic Union) and Sarekat Dagang Islam (Islamists Trade Union). Although Soeharto's depoliticization severed these links and connections, they have been utilized again since the 1999 elections to gain support. The effectiveness of these relations can be seen most clearly in the results of the 2014 elections. For instance, Partai Kebangkitan Bangsa (PKB — National Awakening Party) and Partai Amanat Nasional (PAN — National Mandate Party) have much reason to thank their relationship with NU and Muhammadiyah, respectively.[2] PKB cadres specifically attributed the party's success in the regions to calling on the Nahdliyin (NU supporters/sympathizers) to support the Nahdliyin's party or PKB, which is still seen as the main NU party. Similarly, PAN cadres in the regions credited Muhammadiyah networks for their improvement in the 2014 elections. These networks also work for other parties, although possibly not as strongly or directly. Beyond the relatively stable source of votes, parties have not utilized these network to build a more stable support system, as solidity has continually eroded and effective leadership is hard to find (Tomsa 2010, p. 147).

Instead parties rely mainly on patronage for voters' support, a phenomenon institutionalized during Soeharto's rule, which has further evolved since 1998. Despite the organizational networks and indeed the branches that they have developed across the archipelago, parties as organizations have been accused of being amalgamations of often predatory interests (Hadiz 2004), as can be seen in the seemingly endless string of corruption cases involving party politicians. Yet parties as organizations continue to face trends and regulations that have been more challenging.

To start with, alongside the global trend of "decline of parties" in which parties continue to lose attachment and members,[3] it would be hard to argue that any of the parties in Indonesia are mass parties. Long gone are the days when parties could claim mass membership such as that enjoyed by the banned PKI (Partai Komunis Indonesia — Indonesian Communist Party) before 1965, and even the "forced" association with Golkar that applied to civil servants during the New Order (1966–98). Although some of the current parties have been known to boast membership numbers in the millions, particularly some of them closely associated with mass organizations, in reality there is a severe lack of administrative effort in producing and keeping up parties' membership cards, dues, and activities or any effort to nurture affiliations. Compounded by the lack of recruitment drives (except those done by PKS), membership is weak, superficial, and dwindling.[4]

Problems in developing and maintaining membership can also be traced to decades of heavy government interference. Around the period of the 1955 election, the first after independence, the country had a heavily fragmented multiparty system (Feith 1962) in which support was based on ideological leanings and clientelism (Sugiarto 2006). Sukarno established his "guided democracy" in the late 1950s by heavily regulating the party system under his presidency and in the process also sidelined and eventually diminished the largest Islamic party, Masyumi, while other parties lost influence. The only parties with influence were the PKI, the Partai Nasional Indonesia (PNI) and the Nahdlatul Ulama. The PKI's power was terminated following the aborted coup in 1965 and the mass killings, while the PNI's was curbed after it was purged. Soeharto's New Order regime established institutionalized restriction for the parties through "simplifying" the party system — allowing only government-backed Golkar (Golongan Karya — Functional Group) and two other parties, PDI (Partai Demokrasi Indonesia — Indonesian Democratic Party) and PPP (Partai Persatuan Pembangunan — United Development Party) to compete in elections. In such a system, ordinary citizens were discouraged to be members, especially of the non-Golkar parties. Those who were members were closely monitored to prevent challenges to the authorities or government.

Following the fall of Soeharto, the new parties established in the aftermath brought a multiparty system. The number of parties stabilized over the past few elections, so that by 2014 there were ten parties competing, significantly down from forty-eight in the 1999 elections.

Primarily, this resulted from electoral laws restricting new parties.
While the number of parties has stabilized, the individual parties have
increasingly had to deal with internal splits and factionalism.[5] Yet
results from the 2009 elections (the third since the fall of Soeharto)
showed that the party system has been relatively stable, particularly
as regards to core parties — the handful which have managed to
continually obtain a significant percentage of votes. These parties are:
Partai Golkar (Partai Golongan Karya — Functional Group Party),
Partai Demokrasi Indonesia Perjuangan (PDIP — Indonesian
Democratic Party of Struggle), PPP, PAN, PKB, and Partai Keadilan
Sejahtera (PKS — Prosperous Justice Party) (Mietzner 2009). In the
2014 elections their support slipped, with some parties such as
Partai Demokrat (PD — Democratic Party) and Gerakan Indonesia
Raya Party (Gerindra — Great Indonesia Movement Party) stabilizing
their votes, but they have remained the main vote-getters (see
Table 2.1).

TABLE 2.1
Election Results of Main Parties, 1999–2014 (%)

Party	1999	2004	2009	2014
Golkar	22.4	21.6	14.4	14.75
PDIP	33.7	18.5	14	18.95
PKS	1.4	7.3	7.9	6.79
PAN	7.1	6.4	6	7.59
PPP	10.7	8.2	5.3	6.53
PKB	12.6	10.6	4.9	9.04

Source: KPU.

The establishment of these core parties can be attributed to various
factors. The consistently stable percentage of their votes relies much
on party organization. Studies have shown that parties have generally
been able to establish nationwide branches, but the capacities of these
branches vary widely, with the core parties faring better than those
that are not. Partai Golkar and PKS have consistently been the better
organized, although the difference between parties, and certainly
across different regions, may vary. While coordination among national

networks of branches is crucial for party unity and cohesion, parties' organizational capacity has depended on local leaders and cadres. In cases where these leaders are committed to the parties, the branches are well organized and active. Studies have observed cases where local party leaders show greater commitment to their other occupations, typically as regents or mayors or business owners; in these cases the branches tend to be abandoned and not well looked after, while activities are rare, small and far between. Conversely, when leaders spend more time on the branches, there are more activities and local initiatives from them (Fionna 2013).

So far, because of the changes in party system, parties have been struggling to develop solid organizations and "stable roots in society" as conditions for institutionalization (Mainwaring and Scully 1995). While parties such as PKS and Partai Golkar proved that competence is crucial in sustaining active branches able to organize activities even outside election periods, other parties' success has varied. Parties have varying degrees of electability and popularity, and their status will be tested further in the coming elections as various leaderships and corruption scandals continue to embroil them.

Parties in Elections

Ideally, for elections parties should "react to changes in social and political conditions", "play a dominant role in defining the agenda of campaigns", as the "prime actors in political discourse during elections, through their programs, advertising, and education of the citizenry" (Dalton et al. 2011, p. 7). An integral part of these functions is "candidate recruitment and training as an initial linkage in the party government model" (Dalton et al. 2011, p. 7). These roles require parties to be sensitive to sociopolitical changes, able to translate them into their programmes and election campaigns through their candidates — whom are party representatives in furthering and implementing these programmes when elected to government. In fulfilling this function, Indonesian parties also face organizational requirements and electoral regulations, as well as internal challenges that have shaped their electoral function.

To start, while reformasi's euphoria was initially met with the founding of hundreds of parties, subsequently requirements have developed rapidly to be demanding for new entries. In 1999, a party could be established by at least fifty citizens (this number has been reduced to thirty in the new law) who were at least twenty-one years of age. The party should have the state ideology Pancasila in its articles of association and have an ideology that does not contradict Pancasila. Its name and symbol should not bear resemblance with a foreign state's symbol/flag or those of other existing parties. While the conditions for new parties are low, the organizational requirements to compete in elections were already arduous and have become increasingly so. In general, parties have to register as a legal entity to obtain the right to contest elections. In registering, parties need to meet tough prerequisites, which have been made even more arduous over time. To compete in the 1999 elections, parties had to have regional chapters in 50 per cent of all provinces and 50 per cent of districts/municipalities in the province. Those requirements increased in 2014, to having chapters in 100 per cent of provinces, 75 per cent of districts/municipalities in the provinces, and 50 per cent of subdistricts in the districts/municipalities.

In previous elections (1999 and 2004), parties that did not meet the threshold were still allowed to take up the seats they won in the national parliament, but could not contest election again under the same name. Notably, Partai Keadilan, which failed to meet the electoral threshold in 1999 (with only 1.4 per cent of votes) re-registered as Partai Keadilan Sejahtera in the 2004 elections and has since established itself as a credible party. Since 2009, parties that do not meet the threshold cannot send members to parliament. Consequently, the number of parties competing in elections has been impacted by this regulation. As the threshold kept being increased to the current 3.5 per cent, there were only 10 parties competing in the 2014 elections. Only the mega-rich individual politicians were able to defy these odds and still build new parties, primarily to further their personal ambitions.[6] Between 1999 and 2014, as discussed in the previous section, the number of parties competing in elections has reduced and thus stabilized somewhat as major or core parties have continued to fare well. This trend by no means shows that there have been no internal conflicts or divisions within parties. Instead, it implies that cracks within parties have had to be contained internally. Rather than splits and splinters, parties have expanded their leadership to accommodate officials who harbour ambitions (Fionna and Tomsa 2017), although this strategy has not always worked and has led some party officials to join other parties where they see more opportunities.

Thus it is clear that parties compete in elections carrying their handicaps. It became immediately apparent that some associations with legacy institutions or mass organizations were helpful in building a solid and stable base. A handful of parties that were new legal entities were able to cultivate such support — although, as noted earlier, parties have failed to capitalize on this to build clear platforms. For instance, PKB was the political arm of Nahdlatul Ulama, and PAN had close ties with Muhammadiyah; NU and Muhammadiyah are Indonesia's largest Muslim organizations. PPP and Golkar or Partai Golkar were largely the same parties that operated during the New Order era, with the organizations and foundations that supported them throughout the era. Similarly, PDIP "inherited" most of its organizational structure from the former PDI (Tomsa 2010).[7] Fieldwork findings from 2014–16 during various local elections have also confirmed that these linkages were crucial in translating support into real votes.[8]

Yet subsequently, these parties have failed to cultivate and stabilize these connections with legacy institutions. Links with other organizations are generally only partly called upon during elections, and associations with them typically falter once polling starts because there is no particular effort to engage each other and strengthen these relations. Alongside "seasonal" links to these organizations, many of these parties also suffer from factional frictions and leadership malfunction, as party orientation and policy at times are unclear beyond securing votes and funds. Notably among these parties are PPP and Partai Golkar. PKB also had similar problems, although this seems largely resolved.[9] Having leadership positions contested in the parties causes cadres' confusion, and they may have varying opinions on how to further party interests; such conditions are fertile breeding ground for factionalism and splits.

The lack of unity and cohesion worsens the weak partisanship among voters, and thus support for parties is superficial and voters are easily swayed. Tomsa pointed out that, in contrast to countries with well-institutionalized parties, where voters pay little attention to new or small parties, in Indonesia parties are poorly institutionalized, and both party members and voters shift their loyalty easily (Tomsa 2014, p. 263). Such problems translate into the grassroots/branch level as well, as Aspinall pointed that the absence of cohesion and ideology has led to "party shopping", in which local figures hop from one party to another. Loyalty shifts in voting are clearest in how the newly founded PD and PKS obtained votes in the 2004 elections. Some significant signs of voter dealignment can also be seen in the high proportion of swing voters (Asia Foundation 2003) and weak party identification (Mujani and Liddle 2010, p. 76). For example, in 2004, a significant number of the votes for Yudhoyono (from PD) to become president came from people who voted for other parties in the parliamentary elections (IFES 2004). At the same time, problems with unity continued to embroil parties right up to the lead-up to the 2009 elections (Tomsa 2010, p. 147).

Amidst these internal problems, parties also had to strategize — part of which is to form coalitions in order to meet the requirements to nominate candidates.[10] Coalition is an integral part of electoral strategies because so far, none of the parties have gained enough votes to nominate a candidate single-handedly. Consequently parties have to partner with others to accumulate enough votes/seats for candidate nomination. Various combinations have emerged in local elections, with no apparent motive other than meeting the nomination threshold. One case to note is the coalition of parties that competed in the 2014 presidential elections, Koalisi Merah Putih and Koalisi Indonesia Hebat (discussed later in this chapter). The fluid coalitions formed in the national government in the aftermath of the 2014 elections have changed significantly since (as discussed in the next section). The coalitions formed in local elections continue to be fluid, unpredictable, and bearing no resemblance to the ones formed centrally.

The amalgamation of parties in their bid to nominate a candidate has worsened the lack of ideological identities as distinctive "brands" for parties. After the 1955 election, there emerged distinctive political leanings (aliran),[11] the subsequent de-ideologization and depoliticization under the New Order largely repressed political aspiration and ideology, and forced a focus on the state ideology Pancasila as the all-encompassing national philosophy. The requirements for coalition, according to Tomsa (2010, p. 147), have worsened any ability or initiative of parties to develop a clear ideological platform. Similar tendencies can be seen in cabinet formation, as most parties were included in the cabinet appointments under Yudhoyono and PD. Even the current President Jokowi, who attempted to avoid forming an all-inclusive cabinet, increasingly accommodated more parties in his coalition by allocating ministerial seats for them.

Meanwhile, as aliran are no longer as influential as in the past (Mujani and Liddle 2010), parties have adopted a more catch-all approach by claiming that they are religious-nationalists (Platzdasch 2009), in order to place themselves strategically to attract both the secular and the religious — another proof that parties have continued to ignore their lack of ideology. Post-Yudhoyono's two-term presidency, the lack of ideological platform has been somewhat institutionalized. Coalitions continue to form without any ideological considerations. While the national coalition surrounding Yudhoyono was inclusive in the effort to minimize conflict by co-opting as many parties as possible, local coalitions to nominate regional heads have been based purely on finding and pairing candidates who they think have the highest likelihood of winning. Both nationally and locally, attention to candidates has overshadowed the role of parties. It is no longer important or even feasible for the parties to distinguish themselves from one another.

This growing focus on candidates, as distinct from policies, is a result of the evolution of electoral law. Since the 2009 elections, elections are no longer held within a system in which the parties decide the rank of candidates. Under that system, voters cast their ballots for parties and parties chose the individual who would occupy the seat. The electoral law changed that. In particular, Law No. 10/2008 reduced the maximum number of seats per electoral district from 12 in 2004 to 10, benefitting larger parties at the expense of smaller ones. Based on this law, parties with a vote of less than 2.5 per cent can no longer take up seats in the parliament. Furthermore, the annulment of Article 214 of Law No. 10/2008 meant that parties no longer control the placement of candidates on the ballot paper. Instead, seats are allocated based on the number of votes obtained regardless of the placement of candidates in the list (Schmidt 2010).

Indonesian parties are built mainly for elections and do very little outside them. While they have developed nationwide networks, there is minimal effort or focus on branch and membership requirements, which would have encouraged parties to develop stronger roots (Hicken and Kuhonta 2011, p. 578). Branches are active mainly during election periods; any membership drive is generally minimal, and membership management is almost non-existent.[12]

Even their involvement in elections has also significantly decreased. To start, it is important to consider that, while before the 2009 elections the parties had more influence to determine the placements of candidates on the ballot, this influence had greatly diminished. In previous elections, parties could sell a higher placement to the highest bidders, but the current electoral law has shifted to give voters the power to determine who they vote for, and it does not matter where the candidates are on the paper. This open list means that the candidate(s) with the highest total individual vote on the party list claim the party's seat(s). Therefore candidates concentrate on campaigning for themselves, not their party, often competing ferociously with those from the same party. Parties, meanwhile, take a back seat beyond choosing the most popular candidate, demanding money as compensation for the nomination.

Consequently, instead of being primary actors promoting changes (Dalton et al. 2011, p. 7), the parties have relinquished much authority to the candidates. They have simplified and shifted elections to be a popularity contest between candidates who at times have been headhunted because of their popularity (commonly determined by public opinion surveys), rather than loyal long-term party cadres. Voters often have limited knowledge of candidates and are forced to choose based on generic programmes and platforms. In turn, candidates have been crafted to appeal to voters' emotions, and the employment of money to attract or secure votes has been rampant throughout various elections.[13]

Put in such an alienating position, it is then no wonder that voters' sense of detachment from parties continues to grow. Despite the establishment of the core parties, electoral trends have pointed to an increase of non-voters. While the 1999 election recorded only 7.3 per cent of non-voters, in the 2014 presidential election, more than 29 per cent did not vote. One of the reasons is that there has been a process of dealignment in which voters increasingly detach themselves without defining new preferences (Tomsa 2010, p. 146).

Katz (1980) argues that tactics, methods, and knowledge in elections are the products of the systems within which they are organized. Applying that argument in Indonesia, parties' lack of capacity and the electoral trends have made parties a vehicle for individual politicians. As parties continued with limited capacity, electoral laws increasingly brought personalities to the fore in elections at the expense of parties as institutions or advocates of platforms. Candidates increasingly design and determine the way they campaign, with the help of their teams particularly in legislative rounds.[14] Yet parties remain the main gatekeepers for elections, and of policy-making in the government through the parliament, where they dominate. As such, parties' power continues, while their profile in the actual electoral process is diminished.

This trend has become so prevalent, particularly since the 2014 elections, that parties' role has been reduced to being lenders of paraphernalia to candidates. Many candidates fund their own team, which then decides the schedules and details of the campaign. Parties increasingly rely on survey institutes to gauge which candidates they should support, and these institutes become more important than local party branches. Consequently, parties increasingly choose outside people as candidates, and they are just providers of tickets for nominations, and the handling campaign details is done by political consultants, who have taken over the role of parties (Qodari 2010). There has been a significant degree of professionalization of campaigns, but as an adjunct to parties.

Parties and candidates have gradually relied on polling data when mapping the political terrain and have increasingly hired political consultants to formulate their campaign strategies (Qodari 2010). They increasingly use mass media to reach voters — a function previously performed by the party organization and volunteers. In the first election in 1955, the use of mass media — radio — was very limited (Ufen 2010), but by 2009, parties and politicians were relying heavily on TV, radio and print media advertisements to reach voters (Ufen 2010). Indeed, by the 2009 elections, television had become increasingly central to election campaign strategies (Mujani and Liddle 2010, p. 76). For example, in 2004, political and government advertisement spending was about Rp 746 billion (more than US$56 million), but within five years, the figure jumped to Rp 3.64 trillion (more than US$73 million). By February–March 2014, the yearly figure had reached Rp 1.2 trillion (about US$90 million).

Despite the professionalization and the money splurged during elections, non-voting has increased (see Table 2.2). The trend of non-voting is more straightforward: the percentage of eligible voters who choose not to turn up or deliberately spoil their votes has generally been increasing for both national and local elections. While reasons for non-voting vary, there is a general sense of dissatisfaction with the progress of democratization — whether disappointment with parties, parliament, politicians, or other parts of the state apparatus. Although support for democracy remains high, there is a growing frustration over the persistence of problems such as corruption and slow economic development.

TABLE 2.2
Participation and Non-Voting Rates, 1955–2014 (%)

No.	Election	Participation Rate	Non-Voting Rate
1	1955	91.1	8.6
2	1971	96.6	3.4
3	1977	96.5	3.5
4	1982	96.5	3.5
5	1987	96.4	3.6
6	1992	95.1	4.9
7	1997	93.6	6.4
8	1999	92.6	7.3
9	Legislative election 2004	84.1	15.9
10	Presidential election 2004 (first round)	78.2	21.18
11	Presidential election 2004 (second round)	76.6	23.4
12	Legislative election 2009	70.7	29.3
13	Presidential election 2009	71.7	28.3
14	Legislative election 2014	75.2	24.8
15	Presidential election 2014	70.9	29.1

Source: KPU.

Parties in Government

Because no parties have gained enough votes or seats to nominate a presidential candidate single-handedly, they have had to form coalitions to meet the threshold to nominate. This section demonstrates that, rather than ideology-based, the coalitions are more often than not issue-based, and they lack permanence. Consequently, parties in government have been nothing more than alliances of convenience.

This can clearly be seen in the coalitions in the current government under Jokowi. Jokowi's initial coalition was formed to nominate presidential candidates. The formation and changes of these coalitions indicate how fluid and flexible they are — and thus how easily they fall apart. The flexibility and fragility of these coalitions are due to a lack of ideology that could provide a bond. Although there once was a call (largely ignored by the other parties) from PKS, which had the *dakwah*[15] movements as its origin, to create an Islamic party coalition before the 2009 presidential election, it is hard to identify any specific pattern in the formation of the coalitions, other than similar interests in candidates viewed as electable.

In general, the number of presidential candidate pairings has become smaller since the introduction of direct presidential election in 2004. Taking advantage of a lower presidential threshold of 10 per cent of votes, there were five pairs in 2004: Wiranto–Salahuddin Wahid (Golkar), Megawati–Hasyim Muzadi (PDIP), Amien Rais–Siswono Yudo Husodo (PAN), Susilo Bambang Yudhoyono–Jusuf Kalla (PD, Partai Bulan Bintang [PBB — Crescent Star Party], Partai Keadilan Persatuan Indonesia [PKPI — Justice and Unity Party]), and Hamzah Haz–Agum Gumelar (PPP).[16] In 2009, the presidential threshold doubled to 20 per cent of votes or 25 per cent of seats, shrinking the number of coalitions to three: Megawati–Prabowo Subianto (PDIP, Gerindra), Susilo Bambang Yudhoyono–Boediono (PD), and Jusuf Kalla–Wiranto (Golkar, Hanura). By 2014, there were only two pairs, and the size of the coalitions ballooned. The winning pair, Joko Widodo (Jokowi) and Jusuf Kalla, had the backing of five parties: PDIP, Nasdem Party, PKB, Hanura Party, and PKPI. The other pair, Prabowo Subianto and Hatta Rajasa, was supported by four parties: Gerindra Party, PAN, PKS, and PPP. Notably, the lack of permanence in the coalitions can be seen in how a major party such as PDIP allied with Gerindra in 2009 and was on the opposite side in 2014.

As a case in point, the Jokowi–Prabowo competition in the 2014 elections produced two coalitions. There were nationalist/secular parties in both coalitions as well as Islamic/religious parties. At first, Jokowi was adamant in not utilizing cabinet positions as the carrots to attract parties to his side — as traditionally done by previous presidents. At the beginning of his administration, Jokowi's government coalition was smaller than the opposition's. It had 208 seats in the national parliament (109 PDIP, 36 Nasdem, 47 PKB, 16 Hanura), while the opposition had 291 (73 Gerindra, 39 PPP, 40 PKS, 48 PAN, and 91 Golkar).[17] Yet, as his administration progressed and recognized that a bigger coalition makes it easier to govern, he has employed certain strategies to minimize the risks of resistance from the opposition. Mietzner (2016) argues that Jokowi employed a combination of presidential interference in internal party affairs with the offer of ministerial positions to parties that "cross the floor" to join the government coalition. By January 2016, all but Gerindra had moved to join the government (Mietzner 2016). As a result, by mid-2016 the government coalition had managed to turn from a minority into a 69 per cent majority. PKS, although never officially joining Jokowi's coalition, had signalled a friendlier outlook towards the government alongside a change in leadership, which ran some of the most aggressive attacks on Jokowi during the presidential election (ibid.).

Yet, these coalitions have not always voiced a uniform opinion on various issues in government. This issue-based coalition trend can clearly be seen in how they debate in the national parliament on crucial issues, such as the Pilkada Bill (RUU/Rancangan Undang Undang Pemilihan Kepala Daerah, Bill on Local Elections), RUU KPK (Komisi Pemberantasan Korupsi, Corruption Eradication Commission), Perppu Ormas (Peraturan Pemerintah Pengganti Undang Undang tentang Organisasi Massa, Government Regulation In-lieu or Law on Mass Organization), and the revision of the Election Bill.

The first issue that in many ways demonstrated the fragility of the government coalition was the Pilkada Bill. Citing arguments that simultaneous direct local elections were expensive and prone to corruption, and that they have not helped in screening credible candidates, a coalition emerged in the parliament calling for a return to indirect elections (not the first time there was a campaign to abandon direct elections). Being a decisive issue that developed around the time of the 2014 presidential election, it initially became a symbol of strength of the opposition coalition, particularly as the larger size of the opposition threatened to possibly block every policy initiative of the government. Indeed, only last-minute interference by the former President Yudhoyono — notably in contrast to his own PD's declared support for indirect *pilkada* — secured that direct local election is here to stay.

Beyond the settlement of this bill, alongside the crossover of various parties to join the government coalition, the fragility and uncertainty of the coalitions were exposed. Support for the RUU KPK, an initiative by some parties to revise the law on the institute and implement more stringent checks and balances on the authority of KPK — largely seen as an effort to weaken Indonesia's most publicly trusted institution — showed the gap even between the president and his own coalition. The most prominent campaigner for the revision came from President Jokowi's own PDIP, with the support of all other parties. The only party opposing the bill was opposition party, Gerindra.

Another issue that attracted much attention was the bill on Mass Organization. In the aftermath of a string of public demonstrations spearheaded by hardline Muslim organizations against former Jakarta governor Basuki Tjahaja Purnama (Ahok), which were followed by Ahok's jailing, the government produced a new bill that requires all mass organizations to subscribe to Pancasila as their ideology. This regulation was immediately used to ban Hizbut Tahrir Indonesia — a political organization that refuses to acknowledge the Indonesian state and seeks to form an Islamic caliphate, although it is not known to be violent. Deliberation on the bill revealed that PD had sided with Gerindra, PKS, and PAN. PD has been able to change its position on various issues as it has remained neutral by not formally joining any coalitions. Notably, parties not in favour of the bill are not generally known to be consistently friendly towards democratic values, while it was the pro-democracy activists who have warned of the possibilities of the bill being an instrument to repress civil/mass organizations arbitrarily. The government coalition's action to approve it was partially responding to the string of mass demonstrations by the Islamic hardliner groups. Notwithstanding the discussion about which side of the government this bill should receive support from, this is yet another example of the difficulty of pinning down some sort of common thread that can identify the platform of either side of the parliament.

As analysts predicted, the discussion in the parliament depends on specific issues (*CNN Indonesia* 2015), and the support for these bills proved how fickle these groupings are. There is very little ideological cohesion in the positions taken, even between the leaders and the party ranks. The PDIP, which supported direct elections, supported weakening of the Anti Corruption Commission. Moreover, the president, while outspoken about anti-corruption, had not done anything to lobby his party and the others on a bill that would significantly reduce KPK's authority (*detikNews* 2017). It was Gerindra, which defended the current powers of the KPK, that (initially at least) wanted the shift from direct to indirect elections. Yet Gerindra opposed the regulation that allows the government to ban organizations on ideological grounds. Again, Gerindra had seemingly opposite stances on two issues that were important pillars of Indonesia's democracy. This serves as a clear example of the parties' lack of ideological consistency.

Notably, the debates on various bills demonstrate that — primarily because it is not clear what political beliefs each wing of the ruling parties stands for — checks and balances have not been implemented effectively. Even when the president has stated his stance on crucial issues, his own party has not always acted in accordance with that stance.

Concluding Remarks: Lack of Progress and Diminishing Role

Overall, the parties' progress and role in Indonesian politics have so far left much to be desired. Throughout the 1999, 2004, 2009, and 2014 elections, there have been certain positive trends, such as the progress of network development and the fact that parties have been able to manage both national and regional elections. Yet, two decades after reform, parties are still trapped in incapacity. Not only are they limited in their work and functions, but they have in many ways institutionalized some of the remaining negative New Order influence and practices, such as lack of clear or explicit ideology, money politics, and lethargic parliamentary work. This self-serving behaviour has remained unchecked as parties continue to be the gatekeepers to elections and public positions and as their power in the parliament to be the decision makers on government projects continues.

The introduction of direct election in 2005 (2004 for direct presidential elections) has brought significant and lasting changes to voting behaviour and trends. Several general trends have strengthened in the past decade, which can be synthesized as a growing personalization of votes amongst disillusioned voters. The developing electoral system and trends have converged and resulted in voting behaviour that is demanding on participants yet superficial. It is demanding because votes are financially expensive as electoral competition is increasingly stiff and campaigns have evolved into an industry. At the same time, votes have been obtained for superficial reasons. As campaign programmes are typically generic and shallow, and there is very little differentiation among various candidates, voters' decisions tend to be based on mere familiarity with candidates or even on others' recommendations. The parties have so far served no one other than themselves, and, given the electoral law and system and voting trends, will continue to do so. Parties do very little beyond managing candidates and getting votes during elections. The branding effort during elections is severely limited, and candidates typically offer wide-ranging initiatives for social and infrastructure projects yet no differentiation in their rhetoric. The few achievements in institutionalization (political mobilization and participation) pale in comparison with the failures: never-ending problems of corruption and the shortcuts in political recruitment that parties continue to engage in. Indeed, the problems that we see are mere symptoms of flaws in the system. Corrupt interests continue to play a dominant role in the parties as they serve as the main vehicle to achieve strategic public positions.

While there is no shortcut to overcoming these problems, one small step that could be taken is that Indonesia needs to consider electoral rules that encourage party-based electoral strategies, as opposed to personal voting (Hicken and Kuhonta 2011, p. 578). Picking electable external candidates just for the sake of votes may also be discouraged by a requirement that legislative candidates be party members for a minimum of one year before being nominated. While there have been criticisms of this proposal (*Kompas* 2016), it is also unclear whether this will be effective. In any case, there need to be continued checks and balances in monitoring parties' power and operations. At the moment, state institutions can remedy only some cases of corruption. The bigger problems and symptoms of lack of party institutionalization remain unsolved.

NOTES

1. According to Huntington (1968, p. 12), institutionalization is "the process by which organisations and procedures acquire value and stability".
2. PKB significantly improved its 5 per cent votes in the 2009 elections to slightly more than 9 per cent in 2014. PAN had 6 per cent in 2009 which increased to 7.6 per cent in 2014.
3. For a comprehensive discussion on the decline of parties, see Dalton et al. (2011).
4. This trend can be seen further in national surveys such as that by the ISEAS – Yusof Ishak Institute in May 2017, which demonstrates that party membership is low, with only around 1.1 per cent of respondents being party members. See Fionna (2017).
5. For a full discussion of this, see Fionna and Tomsa (2017).
6. The newly established Partai Solidaritas Indonesia, at least on the surface, seems different, with somewhat clearer direction and an agenda of pluralism and equity. However, little is known about this new party, which will compete in its first general election in 2019.
7. For a full discussion on the splits caused by government interference in PDI during the New Order, see e.g. Aspinall (2004).
8. Author's observation from various elections in East Java, 2014–16.
9. For a detailed discussion, see Fionna and Tomsa (2017).
10. To nominate a candidate, parties need to have 20 per cent of votes or 25 per cent of seats. Therefore, in the overwhelming majority of local and national elections, parties have had to form coalitions.
11. Literally "stream", first developed by anthropologist Clifford Geertz to differentiate the world views of Muslims in Java. See Geertz (1960).
12. Except for PKS, parties do not have membership drives. See Fionna (2013).
13. For the latest detailed analysis on money politics,see Aspinall and Sukmajati (2016).
14. In *pilkada*, particularly for regions strategic for the parties, party leadership is generally much more involved in choosing candidates. This is clearly seen in the 2018 rounds of local elections, particularly in the large provinces in Java which have about 100 million voters in total.
15. Literally means proselytization. In the case of PKS, the word was associated with certain associations of Muslim students in university campuses, whose activities were mainly *pengajian* (Quranic study group). These movements gained popularity and momentum to create the party in the 1999 elections.

16. A second round of voting was needed because none of the pairs gained a majority. Yudhoyono–Kalla won the final round.
17. PD, with 61 seats, had not decided to join either coalition.

REFERENCES

Asia Foundation. "Democracy in Indonesia: A Survey of the Indonesian Electorate 2003". Available at <https://asiafoundation.org/resources/pdfs/democracyinindonesia.pdf>.

Aspinall, Edward. "Parliament and Patronage". *Journal of Democracy* 25, no. 4 (2004): 96–110.

Aspinall, Edward and Mada Sukmajati, eds. *Electoral Dynamics in Indonesia: Money Politics, Patronage and Clientelism and Grassroots*. Singapore: NUS Press, 2016.

CNN Indonesia. "Peta Politik di Parlemen Bakal Dipengaruhi Isu, Bukan Koalisi", 5 November 2015. Available at <https://www.cnnindonesia.com/nasional/20151104212132-32-89534/peta-politik-di-parlemen-bakal-dipengaruhi-isu-bukan-koalisi/> (accessed 1 December 2017).

Dalton, Russell, David M. Farrell, and Ian McAllister. *Political Parties & Democratic Linkage: How Parties Organize Democracy*. Oxford: Oxford University Press, 2011.

detikNews. "Jokowi Diminta Perintahkan Partai Koalisi Mundur dari Angket KPK", 23 November 2017. Available at <https://news.detik.com/berita/d-3528305/jokowi-diminta-perintahkan-partai-koalisi-mundur-dari-angket-kpk>.

Feith, Herbert. *The Decline of Constitutional Democracy in Indonesia*. Ithaca, NY: Cornell University Press, 1962.

Fionna, Ulla. *The Institutionalisation of Political Parties in Post-authoritarian Indonesia: From the Grass-roots Up*. Amsterdam: Amsterdam University Press, 2013.

———. "ISEAS Survey: Passive Indonesian Voters Place Candidate before Party". *ISEAS Perspective*, 30 October 2017.

Fionna, Ulla and Dirk Tomsa. "Parties and Factions in Indonesia: The Effects of Historical Legacies and Institutional Engineering". ISEAS Working Paper Series 2017, no. 1. Available at <https://www.iseas.edu.sg/images/pdf/WorkingPaper2017_1.pdf>.

Geertz, Clifford. *The Religion of Java*. Glencoe, Illinois: Free Press, 1960.

Hadiz, Vedi R. "Decentralization and Democracy in Indonesia: A Critique of Neo-Institutionalist Perspectives". *Development and Change* 35, no. 4 (September 2004): 697–718.

Hicken, Allen and Erik Kuhonta. "Shadows from the Past: Party System Institutionalization in Asia". *Comparative Political Studies* 44, no. 5 (2011): 572–97.

Huntington, Samuel. *Political Order in Changing Societies*. New Haven: Yale University Press, 1968.

International Foundation of Electoral Systems (IFES). "Results from Wave XVIII of Tracking Results", 19 October 2004. Available at <http://www.ifes.org/sites/default/files/2004_tracking_survey_results_wave_xviii_eng_2.pdf>.

Katz, Richard. *A Theory of Parties and Electoral Systems*. Baltimore: Johns Hopkins University Press, 1980.

Kompas. "Caleg Diusulkan Sudah Berstatus Anggota Parpol Setahun Sebelum Dicalonkan", 25 August 2016. Available at <http://nasional.kompas.com/read/2016/08/25/17495381/caleg.diusulkan.sudah.berstatus.anggota.parpol.setahun.sebelum.dicalonkan>.

Mainwaring, Scott and Timothy R. Scully. *Building Democratic Institutions: Party Systems in Latin America*. Stanford: Stanford University Press, 1995.

Mietzner, Marcus. "Indonesia's 2009 Election: Populism, Dynasties and the Consolidation of Party System". *Analysis*. Lowy Institute for International Policy, 2009.

―――. "Indonesia's Democratic Stagnation: Anti-Reformist Elites and Resilient Civil Society". *Democratization* 19, no. 2 (2012): 209–29.

―――. *Money, Power, and Ideology: Political Parties in Post-Authoritarian Indonesia*. Honolulu, Singapore and Copenhagen: Hawaii University Press, NUS Press and NIAS Press, 2013.

―――. "Coercing Loyalty: Coalitional Presidentialism and Party Politics in Jokowi's Indonesia". *Contemporary Southeast Asia* 38, no. 2 (2016): 209–32.

Mujani, Saiful and R. William Liddle. "Personalities, Parties, and Voters". *Journal of Democracy* 21, no. 2 (2010): 35–49.

Platzdasch, Bernhard. *Islamism in Indonesia: Politics in the Emerging Democracy*. Singapore: Institute of Southeast Asian Studies, 2009.

Qodari, Muhammad. "The Professionalisation of Politics: The Growing Role of Polling Organisations and Political Consultants". In *Problems of Democratisation in Indonesia: Elections, Institutions, and Society*, edited by Edward Aspinall and Marcus Mietzner. Singapore: Institute of Southeast Asian Studies, 2010.

Schmidt, Adam. "Indonesia's 2009 Elections: Performance Challenges and Negative Precedents". In *Problems of Democratisation in Indonesia: Elections, Institutions, and Society*, edited by Edward Aspinall and Marcus Mietzner. Singapore: Institute of Southeast Asian Studies, 2010.

Sherlock, Stephen. "The Parliament in Indonesia's Decade of Democracy: People's Forum or Chamber of Cronies?" In *Problems of Democratisation in*

Indonesia: Elections, Institutions, and Society, edited by Edward Aspinall and Marcus Mietzner. Singapore: Institute of Southeast Asian Studies, 2010.

Shiraishi, Takashi. *An Age in Motion: Popular Radicalism in Java, 1912–1926.* Ithaca: Cornell University Press, 1990.

Sugiarto, Bima Arya. "Beyond Formal Politics: Party Factionalism and Leadership in Post-Authoritarian Indonesia". PhD dissertation, Australian National University, Canberra, 2006.

Tomsa, Dirk. "The Indonesian Party System after the 2009 Elections: Towards Stability?" In *Problems of Democratisation in Indonesia: Elections, Institutions, and Society,* edited by Edward Aspinall and Marcus Mietzner. Singapore: Institute of Southeast Asian Studies, 2010.

———. "Party System Fragmentation in Indonesia: The Subnational Dimension". *Journal of East Asian Studies* 14 (2014): 249–78.

Ufen, Andreas. "Electoral Campaigning in Indonesia: The Professionalization and Commercialization after 1998". *Journal of Current Southeast Asian Affairs* 29, no. 4 (2010): 11–37.

3

Ideologies of Joko Widodo and Indonesian Political Parties

Mada Sukmajati

Introduction

Ideology and political actors are two sides of a coin. Ideology guides political actors' attitudes and behaviours. Ideology informs their political world views and how they position themselves among other political actors. As emphasized by Hofmeister and Grabow (2011, p. 24), "[I]deologies are comprehensive visions of societies and social developments, which contain explanations, values, and goals for past, present and future developments. Ideologies inspire and justify political and social action. They are an essential element for political orientation." Conversely, political actors serve as ideological tools, vessels through which ideologies are translated into attitudes and behaviours in the political system. As such, political actors have an important role in translating ideology into political action.

To date, research into ideology and political parties in Indonesia has been limited to how ideology influences policy-making. Several studies, for instance Liddle and Mujani (2007), Slater (2018), Ambardi (2008), and Mietzner (2012), argued that the ideologies of Indonesia's political parties have become increasingly difficult to distinguish from each other. Other studies, such as those by Baswedan (2004) and Mietzner (2012), explained that political parties in Indonesia have maintained their ideologies, at least on strategic issues.

In presidential government systems, the ideologies of political parties are closely linked to the policies implemented by the president. Theoretically, there are two different possible types of relations between presidents and the ideologies of political parties. Firstly, ideologies and political parties may influence the policies enacted by a president. In this assumption, there is no difference between members of parliament and a president working to translate the ideologies and platforms of their supporting parties into public policies. Secondly, the policies adopted by a president may influence the ideologies and programmes of political parties. This has occurred, for example, in the United States, where various policies implemented by the country's president have effected shifts in the programmes of the political party backing him (Lewis 2016).

What, then, is the relationship between the policies of Indonesia's president and the ideologies and programmes of Indonesia's political parties within a multiparty system? Some studies have examined how Joko Widodo (henceforth Jokowi) attempted to implement various policies in the early years of his presidency. Muhtadi (2015), for example, argued that Jokowi was unable to implement proper leadership in the early years of his presidency owing to the shackles of the oligarchs, namely the political elites who have long enjoyed positions of power and who control the material resources of Indonesian politics. This argument was supported by a study by Slater (2018), which found that power was divided intensely and opposition parties were weakened, leading to the creation of a cartel party system. Warburton (2017), meanwhile, describes the policies implemented by Jokowi as "pragmatic", "statist-nationalist", and "conservative", and "oriented towards economic growth". However, we still lack studies that examine the relationship between Jokowi's policies and Indonesia's political parties, both those that supported him and those that opposed him.

This chapter discusses the connection between the policies of candidates in the 2014 presidential election and the ideologies of the parties backing them. It also seeks to explore the relationship between Jokowi's policies between 2014 and 2017 and the ideologies of the parties that backed him and opposed him. This included the response of Prabowo Subianto (henceforth Prabowo), who had run against Jokowi in the 2014 presidential election.

Focusing on the 2016 national budget, infrastructure development, basic services (education and healthcare), direct elections, and community organizations, this chapter argues that there are similarities between Jokowi's policies and the programmes of the Partai Demokrasi Indonesia-Perjuangan (Democratic Party of Indonesia-Struggle). Meanwhile, the ideology offered by Prabowo was similar to the ideology and programmes of the Partai Gerakan Indonesia Raya (Greater Indonesia Movement Party, Gerindra). Furthermore, through the first three years of Jokowi's leadership, the president's relations with his backing political parties were not always harmonious, as Jokowi's policies sometimes ran opposite to their agendas. These policies were also regularly challenged by Prabowo and by those political parties that had backed him.

The Ideologies of Presidential Candidates and Their Political Parties

In Indonesia, "ideology" refers to the visions, missions, and programmes of participants in elections, both presidential and legislative. In presidential elections, each pair of presidential and vice-presidential candidates must submit a vision, mission, and programme plan to the Komisi Penyelenggara Pemilu (General Elections Commission, KPU) as a prerequisite for registration. Similar requirements are enforced for legislative elections; all parties must submit a document containing their visions, missions, and programmes to the KPU as part of the registration process.

During the 2014 presidential campaign, Jokowi and his running mate Jusuf Kalla (henceforth JK) promoted an ideology that they named Nawa Cita. This was formulated within a document titled "Jalan Perubahan untuk Indonesia yang Berdaulat, Mandiri, dan Berkepribadian" (A Path of Change towards an Indonesia of Sovereignty, Independence, and Character). Nawa Cita consisted of nine policies:

1. Ensuring that the state can protect the entire nation and provide a sense of security to all citizens.
2. Ensuring government involvement by promoting clean, effective, democratic, and trustworthy governance.

3. Building up Indonesia from the borders by reinforcing regional villages as part of a unitary republic framework.
4. Turning back the weakening of the state by reforming the legal system and law enforcement practices, ensuring dignity, trustworthiness, and freedom from corruption.
5. Improving the quality of life in Indonesia through education (Kartu Indonesia Pintar, Smart Indonesia Cards [KIP]) and healthcare (Kartu Indonesia Sehat, Healthy Indonesia Cards [KIS])
6. Improving productivity and competitiveness on the international market.
7. Ensuring economic independence by mobilizing strategic domestic economic sectors.
8. Promoting a revolution in the national character.
9. Strengthening diversity and promoting social restoration.

Prabowo and his running mate Hatta Rajasa promoted an ideology that they termed "Agenda dan Program Nyata untuk Menyelamatkan Indonesia" (Real Programme and Agenda for Saving Indonesia). Their vision was "Membangun Indonesia yang Bersatu, Berdaulat, Adil, dan Makmur serta Bermartabat" (Building a United, Sovereign, Just, Prosperous, and Dignified Indonesia). They later translated this vision into eight key policies:

1. Building a powerful, sovereign, just, and prosperous economy.
2. Introducing an economy of the people.
3. Restoring food, energy, and natural resource sovereignty.
4. Improving the quality of human resources through education reform.
5. Improving the quality of social development through healthcare, social, religious, cultural, and sports programmes.
6. Accelerating infrastructure development.
7. Promoting conservation of nature and the environment.
8. Establishing a government that protects the people, is free of corruption, and provides effective service.

Comparing the ideologies of these two pairs of candidates, several similarities can be noted. Where Jokowi was promoting a vision of "an Indonesia of Sovereignty, Independence, and Character", Prabowo envisioned "Constructing a United, Sovereign, Just, Prosperous, and

Dignified Indonesia". Furthermore, there was no significant difference between the missions offered by these candidates and their running mates, whether in the field of politics, economics, society, culture, or basic services (education and healthcare). Their differences were primarily rhetorical. As argued by Mietzner (2015), Jokowi adopted a model of technocratic populism while Prabowo relied on a populism rooted in anti-neoliberalism. Therefore, the differences were manifested simply in one side trying to outbid the other.

For example, both Jokowi and Prabowo were committed to improving Indonesia's infrastructure and building new roads. Where Jokowi offered to build more than 2,000 kilometres of roads, Prabowo offered to build more than 3,000 kilometres of roads and bridges. Another example can be found in the candidates' healthcare policies. Jokowi offered to improve healthcare services through the KIS insurance scheme, which was adapted from a policy he had implemented as governor of Jakarta. Meanwhile, Prabowo offered an insurance scheme based on the existing BPJS Kesehatan (Social Welfare Implementation Agency: Healthcare) programme, which had been implemented under President Susilo Bambang Yudhoyono. For agriculture, Jokowi sought to open one million new hectares of agricultural land outside Java; Prabowo sought to open two million hectares of agricultural land.

TABLE 3.1
Presidential and Vice-Presidential Candidates and the Ideologies of their Backing Parties in the 2014 Presidential Election

Candidates	Backing Parties	Formal Ideology
Prabowo Subianto–Hatta Rajasa	Gerindra	Pancasila
	Demokrat	Pancasila
	PKS	Islam
	PPP	Islam
Joko Widodo–Jusuf Kalla	PDIP	Pancasila
	PKB	Pancasila
	Nasdem	Pancasila
	Hanura	Pancasila
	PKPI	Pancasila
	Golkar	Pancasila
	PAN	Pancasila

As for the ideologies of the political parties backing these candidates, most political parties since the fall of authoritarian regime under Soeharto's New Order have formally been rooted in the ideologies of Pancasila and Islam. Parties that have formally adopted a Pancasila ideology include the Partai Demokrasi Indonesia Perjuangan (Indonesian Democratic Party of Struggle, PDIP), Partai Golkar (Working Groups Party), Gerindra, Partai Demokrat (Democratic Party), Partai Nasional Demokrat (National Democratic Party, Nasdem), Partai Kebangkitan Bangsa (National Awakening Party, PKB), Partai Amanat Nasional (National Mandate Party, PAN), Partai Hati Nurani Rakyat (National Conscience Party, Hanura), and Partai Keadilan dan Persatuan Indonesia (Indonesian Party for Justice and Unity, PKPI). Political parties that have formally adopted Islam as their ideological basis include the Partai Keadilan Sejahtera (Prosperous Justice Party, PKS) and Partai Persatuan Pembangunan (United Development Party, PPP).

There are at least three key differences between the political parties that cite Pancasila as their ideological basis. First, there are those parties that emphasize nationalist values, such as PDIP, Gerindra, Nasdem, Hanura, and PKPI. As the victor of the 1999 and 2004 legislative elections, PDIP models itself as following the concepts introduced by Sukarno, positioning the party as heir to the thoughts of Indonesia's Proclamator (Mietzner 2012). As explicitly written in the party's constitution and by-laws, one of the party's missions is to provide a "Wadah untuk membentuk kader bangsa yang berjiwa pelopor, dan memiliki pemahaman, kemampuan menjabarkan dan melaksanakan ajaran Bung Karno dalam kehidupan bermasyarakat, berbangsa, dan bernegara" (A means for shaping the national character with a pioneering spirit, and with the understandings and abilities necessary to spread and implement the teachings of Bung Karno in social, national, and state life) (PDIP 2016). Gerindra first participated in legislative elections in 2009. Its vision contains nationalist and religious values: "Menciptakan kesejahteraan rakyat, keadilan sosial dan tatanan politik negara yang melandaskan diri pada nilai-nilai nasionalisme dan religiusitas dalam wadah Negara Kesatuan Republik Indonesia" (Creating social welfare, social justice, and national governance within the Unitary Republic of Indonesia based on values of nationalism and religiosity) (Partai Gerindra n.d.).

Second are those political parties that emphasize developmentalism and seek to escape the dichotomy of secular nationalism and Islam, namely Golkar and Demokrat. Golkar, during the post-Soeharto *reformasi* (reform) era, has offered a concept termed "Paradigma Baru" (New Paradigm), with the party positioned as a modern political party no longer rooted in the rule of the New Order. The party has asserted that, following the tenet of sustainability, Golkar is committed to "... kekukuhan Partai GOLKAR untuk tetap berideologi Pancasila" (ensuring that GOLKAR remains rooted in the ideology of Pancasila) (Partai Golkar n.d.). Nonetheless, one point in Golkar's doctrine states that the party is not oriented towards a specific ideology or school. Furthermore, Golkar continues to position itself as oriented towards programmes and problem solving (Tomsa 2012).

Demokrat asserts that the party is based on nationalism, humanism, internationalism, all rooted in religious piety (Partai Demokrat n.d.). The party's stated mission is to reform and renovate all fields to realize values of peace, democracy, and welfare, as well as to continue previous generations' struggles against colonialism and promote equal rights and obligations for all citizens (Honna 2012).

Third are those nationalist political parties that also emphasize Islamic values, namely PKB and PAN. Ideologically, PKB's values are closer to nationalism. This is seen in the party's constitution and by-laws, where its goal is to be "Mewujudkan cita-cita kemerdekaan Republik Indonesia sebagaimana dituangkan dalam Pembukaan Undang-Undang Dasar 1945" (The realization of the values of the Indonesian Republic as ensconced within the Preamble to the 1945 Constitution) (Muktamar PKB 2014). This document does not mention any desire to manifest a *khilafah* (Islamic state, caliphate) or implement sharia law, but rather promotes a democratic national framework rooted in a noble character. This vision has influenced the PKB, which has consistently sought to position itself in elections as embracing moderate Islam (Ufen 2006).

PAN initially placed greater emphasis on nationalism. Over time, particularly under the leadership of Amien Rais, it began to stress Islamic values more intensely. As noted by Bolte et al. (in Woischnik and Muller 2013), when conflict broke out in Maluku, the party controversially urged Muslims to travel there for *jihad*. As a result, more moderate supporters of the party (both Muslim and Christian) left PAN in 2001. PAN's vision is the realization of a civil society informed by the values of Islam: "... Di Dalam Negara Indonesia Yang Demokratis Dan Berdaulat, Serta Diridhoi Allah Swt, Tuhan Yang Maha Esa" (... in an Indonesian State that is Democratic and Sovereign, Blessed by Allah Swt, God Almighty) (PAN n.d.).

The political parties that have formally adopted Islam as their ideology are the PKS and PPP. The former has become increasingly moderate as it has translated its Islamic ideology into its manifesto, while the latter has consistently sought to implement sharia in Indonesia. Despite the fact that PKS cadres were primarily Muslim activists, and although it had massively campaigned to implement sharia during the 2014 election, the party soon abandoned this issue (Woischnik and Muller 2013). The long-term goal of PKS is to "Terwujudnya Masyarakat madani yang adil, sejahtera, dan bermartabat" (Manifest a civil society that is just, prosperous, and dignified) (Majelis Pertimbangan Pusat PKS 2008). Although the vision of a civil society included within the party's *Falsafah Dasar Perjuangan* (Basic Philosophy for Struggle) is modelled on the society of the Prophet Muhammad, and although Islamic terms such as *"ukhuwwah Islamiyyah"* are included in the document, the implementation of sharia is not listed as one of the party's main goals (Buehler 2012). The party has focused primarily on more universal points, such as its three main missions: political reform, poverty eradication, and justice-oriented education (Majelis Pertimbangan Pusat PKS 2008).

PPP, on the other side, has consistently followed an Islamic ideology. In its statutes, PPP states its desire to be pious to Allah SWT and realize a sense of humanity and justice based in Islamic values. Meanwhile, in its mission, the party firmly states its desire to "... berjuang dalam mewujudkan dan membina manusia dan masyarakat yang beriman dan bertakwa kepada Allah SWT" (... fight to realize and create an Indonesian populace that is faithful and devout to Allah SWT) (Partai Persatuan Pembangunan 2016). Even in its more universal missions, such as the promotion of human rights and prosperity, the party has emphasized Islamic values.

Candidacy Process

In the 2014 election, potential presidential and vice-presidential candidates had to have at least 25 per cent of votes at the national level or 20 per cent of all seats in the Indonesian parliament. The parties that backed Joko Widodo and Jusuf Kalla were the PDIP, PKB, Nasdem, Hanura, and PKPI, which controlled 36.46 per cent of parliamentary seats and 40.38 per cent of votes. These parties were joined together in a coalition, the Koalisi Indonesia Hebat (Great Indonesia Coalition, KIH). The parties that backed Prabowo Subianto and Hatta Rajasa were Gerindra, Golkar, Demokrat, PAN, PPP, and PKS, which combined controlled 63.54 per cent of parliamentary seats or 59.52 per cent of the national vote. These parties were united in the Koalisi Merah Putih (Red and White Coalition, KMP).

These parties did not establish coalitions based entirely on their formal ideologies. Although the parties backing Jokowi were those with Pancasila as their formal ideology, Prabowo's backing included both parties with the formal ideology of Pancasila and parties with the formal ideology of Islam.

Initially, Golkar sought to run its own presidential and vice-presidential candidates, seeking a space between Jokowi and Prabowo. However, Aburizal Bakrie — the party's chairman at the time — ultimately decided to support Prabowo, being promised a senior ministerial position in exchange. Furthermore, in the lead up to the presidential and vice presidential candidacies, friction emerged within the PPP between its chairman Suryadharma Ali and secretary Romahurmuziy. Suryadharma Ali was perceived as making an individual decision to support Prabowo, one that diverged from the official decision made by the PPP in its Second National Working Meeting in Bandung. However, in May 2014 a national leadership meeting, involving thirty-three provincial-level administrators, ultimately decided to back Prabowo.

In formulating their ideologies, Jokowi and Prabowo had their own teams. Nawa Cita was formulated by a team of academics, volunteers, community figures, civil society organizations, and political party cadres. These included Anggit Noegroho, a journalist and confidant of Jokowi since his time as mayor of Solo; Andi Widjajanto, an academic with the University of Indonesia; Teten Masduki, an anti-corruption activist; Akbar Faisal, from Nasdem; and Marwan Jafar, from PKB (Dewi and Aritonang 2014). This team worked intensively to finalize Nawa Cita before it was given to the KPU.

Nawa Cita was also formulated based on Jokowi's experiences as mayor of Solo and governor of Jakarta. This is apparent, for example, in Jokowi's healthcare, education, and economic programmes. In the 2014 presidential debates, Jokowi emphasized his success in enacting the KIP and KIS programmes in Jakarta during his gubernatorial term. He promised that, if elected president, he would expand KIP and KIS into national welfare programmes (Widodo 2014). During his presidential campaign, Jokowi also suggested programmes promoting the revitalization of traditional markets as well as the dialogic management of street vendors, similar to those programmes he had enacted while serving as the mayor of Solo (Cusworth 2014; Pratikno and Lay 2011; Mas'udi 2017).

If we compare Nawa Cita with the ideologies of the political parties backing Jokowi, we can see that PDIP's ideological influences were powerful, including the Trisakti taught by Sukarno.[1] For example, the vision and mission document prepared by Jokowi and JK states explicitly that Pancasila and Trisakti would serve as the basis for all national development policies (Widodo and Kalla 2014). Jokowi also focused on three problems facing the Indonesian nation: threats to the authority of the state, weakness in the national economy, and rising intolerance and personality crises among the people. As a solution, he urged that the people return to Trisakti (Sasmita 2014). Several times Jokowi emphasized that the vision, missions, and programmes named Nawa Cita were rooted in Trisakti. Jokowi even wrote an article in the daily *Kompas* titled "Revolusi Mental" (Mental Revolution), using this jargon to refer to "usaha bersama untuk mengubah nasib Indonesia menjadi bangsa yang benar-benar merdeka, adil dan makmur" (a shared endeavour to change the fate of the Indonesian nation [and make it] truly independent, just, and prosperous) (Widodo 2014). In this article, Jokowi underscored the important role of Trisakti in his Mental Revolution.

Some ideological influences also came from Nasdem, which frequently used the slogan "Gerakan Perubahan Restorasi Indonesia" (Movement for Restoring Indonesia). The ideologies of Hanura, PKPI, and PKB were of little influence in the Nawa Cita. Meanwhile, the Islamic elements promoted by PKB were not strongly present in Nawa Cita. Here, it can be seen that, among the parties backing Jokowi and JK, it was the PDIP that enjoyed the greatest bargaining power. The party even claimed, on several occasions, that Jokowi was its party official (*petugas*) in the executive branch of government.

The visions, missions, and programmes of Prabowo Subianto and Hatta Rajasa were formulated entirely by Prabowo himself. Hatta Rajasa, the vice-presidential candidate, had little influence. Prabowo's formulations of his campaign's visions, missions, and programmes were influenced by his lengthy experience on the national political stage, including his time running as Megawati Sukarnoputri's vice-presidential candidate in the 2009 election and his time as chairman of the Himpunan Kerukunan Tani Indonesia (Association of Indonesian Farmers, HKTI). In the 2009 presidential election, using the slogan "Megapro Pro Rakyat" (Megawati and Prabowo Pro-People), Megawati Sukarnoputri and Prabowo Subianto (referred to jointly as Megapro) promoted the vision "Gotong royong membangun kembali Indonesia Raya yang berdaulat bermartabat adil dan makmur" (Working together to restore Greater Indonesia, independent, dignified, just, and prosperous). This vision was translated into three missions: enforcing dignified sovereignty and personality, realizing social welfare through a people's economy, and providing firm and effective governance (Sukarnoputri and Subianto 2009).

The visions, missions, and programmes of this presidential and vice-presidential pair were formulated by a team consisting of politicians from PDIP (such as Theo Syafei), Gerindra (such as Fadli Zon), as well as professionals (such as the economist Iman Sugema of the Institute for Development of Economics and Finance) (*Kompas* 2009). Moerdiono, former State Minister of the Secretariat (1988–98) and adviser to Gerindra, was a key figure in bridging Megawati and Prabowo, uniting the candidates with a shared vision, as well as shared missions and programmes (Hendrajit 2009).

Prabowo later replicated this vision, as well as these missions and programmes, for the 2014 presidential election. For example, as vice-presidential candidate in the 2009 election, Prabowo had emphasized an economy of the people. This same programme was Prabowo's keystone policy during his 2014 presidential campaign (*Metrotvnews* 2014; Subianto and Rajasa 2014). Another example can be seen in the "Revolusi Putih" (White Revolution) programme. In the 2009 presidential election, Megapro had promoted a "white revolution", which would be realized by working together with cattlemen to promote a culture of milk-drinking among schoolchildren (Toriq 2017). This programme was also promoted by Prabowo during his 2014 presidential campaign (Sari 2017).

Furthermore, owing to Prabowo's experiences while serving as chairperson of HKTI (the Association of Indonesian Farmers) between 2004 and 2009, he felt competent to understand the problems being faced by farmers and to claim legitimacy in representing their interests (Chrisnandy and Priamarizki 2014; Aspinall 2015). On one occasion, Prabowo also stated that, as chairperson of HKTI, he had played an important role in the formulation of the Village Law (*Metrotvnews* 2014).

Comparing Prabowo's ideology with those of his backing parties, the influence of Gerindra is readily apparent. This came from Prabowo's status as the party's chairman. The influences of PAN — the party of Hatta Rajasa — Golkar, and Demokrat were not readily apparent. The same is true for the ideologies of the PKS and PPP; the influence of Islam is not apparent in Prabowo's visions, missions, or programmes.

Implementation of Nawa Cita and Political Party Response

Indonesia's parliament became divided into two blocs: KIH and KMP. Such polarization also occurred at the local level in some regions. For example, in the Jakarta parliament, several members from KMP refused to attend the ceremony in which Basuki Tjahaja Purnama, better known as Ahok, was made the capital region's governor in Jokowi's stead (Keteng 2014). A similar incident occurred in the Yogyakarta parliament when its internal structure was being prepared, thereby hindering the parliament's duties and limiting its functions (Anshori 2014). This division was a major reason for Jokowi's failure to achieve his legislative targets for 2015. Of the 37 planned laws, Indonesia's parliament was able to pass only 14. However, the situation began to thaw after Jokowi reshuffled his cabinet on 27 July 2016. In this reshuffle, Jokowi offered space for KMP figures: Golkar's Airlangga Hartanto was chosen as Minister of Industry and PAN's Asman Abnur as Minister of Administrative and Bureaucratic Reform. As stated by Suryadinata (2018), after this reshuffle Golkar exerted considerable influence on Jokowi.

Generally, in Jokowi's first three years as president, he maintained political distance from all political parties — both his backers and his opposition. This can be seen in several of his government's public policies. First is the 2016 national budget, which initially included Rp 40 trillion (US$2.78 billion) for state equity participation (Nugroho 2015). Under this state equity participation scheme, certain state-owned enterprises (SOEs) would receive funds through the national budget that would serve as capital for infrastructure development.

The government also sought to cut Rp 17.1 trillion (US$1.19 billion) in subsidies that directly affected the populace, including subsidies on petrol, liquid petroleum gas, and biofuels. In the 2015 budget, a total of Rp 81.8 trillion (US$5.70 billion) was allocated for such fuel subsidies; this was decreased to Rp 64.7 trillion (US$4.51 billion) in the proposed 2016 budget. The government also planned to reduce subsidies on electricity from Rp 76.6 trillion (US$5.34 billion) in 2015 to Rp 73.1 trillion (US$5.1 billion) in 2016.

These plans received different responses from various political parties, both those backing the government and those forming the opposition. The PDIP stated that, generally, it supported both of the government's plans. However, it opposed the state equity participation scheme, as it viewed Minister of State-Owned Enterprises, Rini Soemarno, as lacking the competence for SOE management (Safitri 2015). PDIP also argued that the budget allocated for this state equity participation scheme could be better allocated for social programmes. Nasdem also accepted both plans, but noted its opposition to funding a proposed constituency development programme (UP2DP) (Ihsanuddin 2015). Golkar initially rejected both government plans, although it ultimately accepted the budget with a note. PAN, likewise, accepted this proposed budget with a note.

Of the parties opposing the government, Gerindra staunchly opposed both plans. This attitude was also taken by Prabowo. The Deputy Chairman of Gerindra, Edhy Prabowo, stated that Prabowo had urged party members to remain staunch in their rejection of this policy, even if their opposition was not supported by other political parties (Zulfikar 2015). PKS generally accepted the proposed budget, giving eighteen key points. Ultimately, after intensive debate, including political lobbying with Gerindra, the government and parliament passed the budget by removing the state equity participation scheme from it (Salim 2015).

Second was the government plan to promote infrastructure development. Infrastructure, particularly toll roads, was the main emphasis of Jokowi. Having set a target of 1,060 kilometres of new roads, by October 2017 the government had opened only 300 kilometres (Mutmainah 2017). Furthermore, the government sought to establish sea tolls to promote trade and ease the distribution of goods between Indonesia's islands. Of the 245 projects and one programme spread across 14 infrastructure sectors, 26 had been completed by 2017 (Chandra 2017).

All of the political parties backing the government readily accepted Jokowi's infrastructure policies. PDIP, for example, stated that the government's infrastructure development plan would improve the efficiency of inter-island connections. Furthermore, various goods could be more easily distributed outside of Java. PDIP praised the sea tolls as a concrete manifestation of the development "revolution" being experienced in the Indonesian archipelago, with development occurring from the country's westernmost point to its eastern borders (Firdaus 2016). Golkar argued that, in Jokowi's three years as president, the government had promoted infrastructure development better and more rapidly than under previous President Susilo Bambang Yudhoyono. This infrastructure was judged as providing an important step to addressing the welfare gap in Indonesia, particularly in the country's eastern reaches. Similar arguments were voiced by Nasdem, PKB, and PAN.

Gerindra criticized many of the government's infrastructure development policies, considering them nothing more than propaganda intended to gain votes during the 2019 election (Supriatin 2017). Gerindra also criticized the fact that the 2015 national budget allocated only 26 per cent for infrastructure, and that the 2016 national budget increased foreign debt and slashed subsidies to fund infrastructure development (Sayidina 2015; Zahro 2017). Furthermore, Gerindra argued that fundamental problems such as economic inequality, reduced purchasing power, and national debt would not improve so long as the government focused on physical infrastructure. A similar argument was made by PKS. According to this party, infrastructure development by the government had to absorb more labour. This party saw unemployment staying high and social welfare decreasing as the government continued promoting infrastructure development. However, these political parties ultimately approved the 2016 national budget, after they succeeded in blocking the planned use of a state equity participation scheme for infrastructure development.

Responding to Jokowi's push for infrastructure development, Prabowo and Susilo Bambang Yudhoyono established what they termed a "moral movement", one point of which was opposition to Jokowi's infrastructure development, which they considered benefitting foreign entrepreneurs and labourers more than the Indonesian people (Partai Gerindra 2017). Both held that infrastructure development should use Indonesian labour or be dedicated towards improving the purchasing power of the Indonesian people, which they considered lacking. However, in their criticism of the government's infrastructure development schemes, neither was able to offer a clear alternative.

The government also implemented a number of programmes related to basic services such as education and healthcare. One of these was the distribution of KIP to 17.9 million beneficiaries. This programme offered Rp 225,000 per student per semester for elementary school students, Rp 375,000 per student per semester for junior high school students, and Rp 500,000 per student per semester for vocational and senior high school students (Iqbal 2015). There was also a proposal for full-day schools based on character education, which was formally in line with Nawa Cita. Through this programme, the government sought to extend school hours from five to eight and to reduce the number of school days from six to five a week (Ihsanuddin 2017). In healthcare, the government sought to implement an insurance scheme through the KIS programme, which was intended primarily to improve the welfare of the poor.

Almost all political parties stated their support for the government's healthcare and education policies. PDIP proudly supported Jokowi's basic service programmes, emphasizing that the KIP and KIS programmes were clear proof of Jokowi's success in extending life expectancy in Indonesia. Likewise, Golkar stated that KIP and KIS were basic service programmes that the party would continue to support and promote as they reflected the pro-people attitudes to which Golkar was committed. PAN supported the full-day school policy because it was certain that many senior high school level institutions had already begun such programmes.

However, opposition to the full-day school programme came from PKB, which even threatened to withdraw its support for Jokowi in the 2019 election if he continued promoting the programme. PKB felt that such a policy would destabilize the traditional education system being managed by the Nahdlatul Ulama (NU), the biggest Islamic organization in Indonesia (Suryowati 2017). Much of the party's base consisted of NU members. Given this response, the government later announced that the full-day school policy would not be compulsory. This announcement, in turn, was sharply criticized by Gerindra, which considered it to indicate the government's inability to create and implement a specific concept and vision for national education (Kumparan 2017).

Two controversial policies received diverse responses from political parties. The first was proposed legislation on indirect regional executive elections, which was submitted by parliament in 2014. Immediately after being inaugurated on 20 October 2014, Jokowi faced the serious challenge of changing Government Regulation in Lieu of Law No. 1/2014, which promoted the indirect election of regional leaders through regional parliaments. This regulation was actually a legal product produced by Susilo Bambang Yudhoyono towards the end of his presidency (Maulidar 2014). In the presidential debates, Jokowi made a commitment to implement simultaneous direct elections as a manifestation of the sovereignty of the people and as a means of ensuring efficient regional elections (Juniardhie 2014). Jokowi thus sought consistency in direct elections (Faqih 2014).

The parties backing the government approved direct elections of regional leaders. PDIP firmly asserted that a return to parliamentary selection of regional leaders would be a step backwards. It also emphasized that direct elections were the only means of ensuring citizens were actively involved in democracy (Sholih 2014). PKB stated that it approved of direct elections because they ensured that regional leaders remained accountable to their constituents. From a technical perspective, PKB agreed with Jokowi's argument that, from a budgeting perspective, simultaneous direct elections would save money (Dewan Pengurus Pusat Partai Kebangkitan Bangsa 2014). For Nasdem, although it recognized that direct elections involved such serious problems as money politics, ideally they would better promote the sovereignty of the people mandated by the constitution (Andriansyah 2014).

Considerable dynamism was evidenced among the parties united within the KMP. When Government Regulation in Lieu of Law No. 1/2014 was approved by Yudhoyono in May 2014, not a single party approved of the selection of regional leaders through regional parliaments (Ihsanuddin 2014). This changed when Jokowi began seeking to preserve direct elections. PKS began opposing direct elections of regional leaders, citing the widespread practice of money politics as detrimental to Indonesian democracy (Akuntono 2014). This opposition was rooted in a desire to take the same position as Gerindra, its ally in the KMP (Munawwaroh 2014). However, when Demokrat stated its support for direct regional elections (Bustan 2014), PKS again changed its position, supporting the direct election of regional leaders.

Gerindra staunchly opposed the direct election of regional leaders, citing the method's many weaknesses, including its potential for corruption (Ihsanuddin 2014). The party argued that the selection of regional leaders by local parliaments would minimize corruption, as the Komisi Pemberantasan Korupsi (Corruption Eradication Commission, KPK) could monitor local parliaments easily (Ihsanuddin 2014). In terms of funding, the party argued that the selection of regional leaders by local parliaments would save the government up to 80 per cent. A similar attitude and motive was given by PAN and by Golkar, which was still part of KMP. These parties argued that direct elections would only waste state funding.

The process through which the Elections Law was prepared was a complicated one. Political parties were divided into two blocs, namely KMP and KIH. Various forms of lobbying were undertaken. However, this brought no compromise. The different parliamentary factions then agreed to a vote, in which Gerindra, PKS, and PPP solidly supported indirect election mechanism. Golkar was fragmented, as a minority of representatives supported direct elections. Demokrat chose to walk out during the vote. Finally, the parties in the KIH bloc voted unanimously for continued direct elections (Suharman 2014).

In Indonesia's administrative system, government regulations, instead of law, are issued when emergency situations force a president to make policy. Such regulations must then be sent to parliament for further consideration, after which they can be formalized as law. The second controversial issue in politics was Government Regulation in Lieu of Law No. 2/2017 regarding community organizations. In this, the government sought to implement stricter regulations regarding community organizations, requiring them to have ideological foundations and goals that were not contrary to Pancasila. This was highly reminiscent of the Single Ideological Foundation policy implemented by the New Order government. Furthermore, according to this regulation, the government — through the Ministry of Law and Human Rights — had the authority to dissolve any community organizations it considered contrary to Pancasila, not through the court system but through the revocation of legal recognition. This regulation was used, for example, to dissolve the Indonesian chapter of Hizbut Tahrir (Hizbut Tahrir Indonesia, HTI), which was seen as opposing to the ideology of Pancasila (Burhani 2017).

TABLE 3.2
Policies of Joko Widodo–Jusuf Kalla and Political Party Response

Policy	Political Party	Support
2016 Budget	PDIP	Support, with Notes
	PKB	Support, with Notes
	PAN	Support, with Notes
	Nasdem	Support, with Notes
	Golkar	Support, with Notes
	Gerindra	Oppose
	PKS	Support, with Notes
Infrastructure Development	PDIP	Support
	PKB	Support
	PAN	Support
	Nasdem	Support
	Golkar	Support
	Gerindra	Oppose
	PKS	Oppose
Education and Healthcare	PDIP	Support
	PKB	Oppose (Education)
	PAN	Support
	Nasdem	Support
	Golkar	Support
	Gerindra	Oppose
	PKS	No Position Found
Government Regulation in Lieu of Law No. 1/2014 regarding Indirect Elections	PDIP	Support
	PKB	Support
	PAN	Oppose
	Nasdem	Support
	Golkar	Oppose
	Gerindra	Oppose
	PKS	Oppose
Government Regulation in Lieu of Law No. 2/2017 regarding Community Organizations	PDIP	Support
	PKB	Support, with Notes
	PAN	Oppose
	Nasdem	Support
	PG	Support
	Gerindra	Oppose
	PKS	Oppose

The political parties backing Jokowi responded to this policy in somewhat different ways. PDIP, Golkar, and Nasdem stated their unconditional support. PKB gave its support, with two conditions: it sought the removal of ambiguous points and the promotion of human rights and legal protections, including a special court system for organizations considered to be incompatible with Pancasila by the government (*Fraksi PKB DPR RI* 2017). On the other side, PAN stated its opposition to the legislation, holding that Law No. 17/2013 already dealt with community organizations and thus new legislation was not necessary; furthermore, it feared that the regulation could potentially result in human rights violations (Sani 2017). Citing a similar rationale, Gerindra and PKS also voiced opposition.

From these points, it is clear that the political parties backing the government did not always support Jokowi's policies. PDIP, which was ideologically close to the Nawa Cita ideology, also rejected parts of the 2016 budget, while PKB opposed the planned full-day school policy, ultimately forcing the government to cancel its plans. This also occurred with Golkar and PAN, which backed Jokowi after the election. Gerindra and PKS, on the other side, consistently opposed government policies. Prabowo unfavourably responded to government policies, as did Fadli Zon of Gerindra and Fahri Hamzah of PKS.

Ideology in Indonesia: Similar, Not the Same

Many lessons can be learned from the ideological dynamics in Jokowi's first term. Jokowi was the first Indonesian president who was not the leader of a political party. In formulating his Nawa Cita, Jokowi relied not only on the ideologies of the political parties backing him, but also on a team he formed himself. This team included members of civil society, academics, and politicians from his backing parties.

Similarly, Prabowo did not rely solely on the ideology of Gerindra when he formulated his ideology during the 2014 campaign. It appears that he relied on his individual experiences on the national political stage, including as Megawati Sukarnoputri's vice-presidential candidate in the 2009 presidential election. It is not surprising that the ideology he promoted in 2009 was similar to the one he used in the 2014 election. As such, Jokowi and Prabowo in the 2014 presidential election presented similar ideologies. In this context, we can argue that there was no ideological contestation in the 2014 presidential election.

A similar phenomenon can be found among the political parties. In Indonesia, although political parties' formal ideologies are broadly divided into two categories — Pancasila (secular nationalism) and Islam — this categorization is not manifested in policy-making. This is a clear indication of how cartel politics have developed. As a result, the polarization and ideological differences that emerged following the 1999 legislative election have begun eroding. Ultimately, ideological contestations have been uncommon in elections.

Among the political parties backing Jokowi, there emerged a clear coalition between parties with a Pancasila ideology: PDIP, PKB, Nasdem, and Hanura, followed by Golkar and PAN. Among the parties backing Prabowo, a coalition emerged based on ideological proximity between the Pancasila-based political parties Gerindra and Demokrat and Islam-based parties PKS and PPP. There was no formal relationship between the Nawa Cita and the ideologies of the political parties backing Jokowi. Likewise, there was no formal connection between the ideology adopted by Prabowo and the ideologies of the political parties backing him.

However, over time, Jokowi attempted to connect his Nawa Cita with PDIP's ideology. Conversely, PDIP frequently claimed that Jokowi was a party official holding executive office. At one event, Megawati Sukarnoputri — the chair of PDIP — stated that every party cadre holding public office was carrying the party banner and representing the party (Fauzi 2017). Strangely, PDIP's claim received no opposition from the other parties backing Jokowi. This shows that, on the one hand, Jokowi's ideology was only close to that of PDIP. On the other hand, this also indicates that political parties did not consider Nawa Cita as an important part of their coalition.

The relationship between Jokowi and PDIP indicates a form of mutualism between non-party and party politicians. Jokowi had the ability to formulate his own policies and concrete development programmes. However, he lacked a strong ideological basis and constituent support. Conversely, PDIP had a strong ideological basis and existing constituents. However, the party lacked cadres with the ability to translate this ideology into policies and programmes. A similar experience was encountered by other political parties, which could not offer an alternative for national leadership.

Unlike Jokowi, Prabowo's ideology was close to that of Gerindra. This was not surprising, as Prabowo had served as the chairman of Gerindra since the party's establishment. However, no explicitly Islamic elements are included in the ideology he used. In this context, as argued by Lane (2017), Prabowo required the support of political parties with Islamic ideologies for his electoral purposes and for mobilizing Muslim groups. However, he did not accommodate Islamic political agendas within his ideology. Rather, parties with Islamic ideologies supported Prabowo because it was difficult for them to form a coalition with such secular nationalist parties as PDIP. Furthermore, their inability to field their own presidential candidate, due to their limited voter base and number of parliamentary seats, forced these parties to join Prabowo's coalition.

Based on membership, Riker (1962) identifies three principles of coalitions: size (electoral victory based on the minimal winning size), strategy (electoral victory based on the minimal winning coalition), and disequilibrium (electoral victory based on selective elimination of coalition members). Examining the coalitions backing the presidential candidates in 2014, the parties backing Jokowi followed the strategic principle. During the lead-up to his candidacy, Jokowi stated that it would be no problem if only one other party joined the PD in a coalition. He also stated that political parties backing him had to be prepared to work together, without expecting a particular share of seats (*detikNews* 2014). A different tendency was exhibited by the parties backing Prabowo, which followed the principle of minimal winning size.

The political parties with Islam as their formal ideology (PKS and PPP) decided to back Prabowo in a coalition. PKB — a political party influenced by Islamic values but taking Pancasila as its formal ideology — chose to form a coalition supporting Jokowi. As discussed above, these political parties did not influence the formulation of Nawa Cita that Jokowi used as an umbrella for his policies. However, these parties played an important symbolic role in mobilizing the electorate. For Jokowi, for example, PKB's involvement in the coalition backing him offered an opportunity to gather the support of moderate Muslims (representing the majority of Indonesian Muslims). Meanwhile, PKS and PPP sought to maintain their position by not working together with secular nationalist parties, particularly PDIP, even as coalitions between Islamic parties and PDIP were common in regional elections.

Another point, no less important, is the response of political parties to Jokowi's policies. As discussed above, political parties backing the government responded to its policies in different ways. Some opposed the policies enacted or planned by the Jokowi government, such as

PDIP in response to the 2016 budget and PKB in response to the full-day school policy and regulation on community organizations. In response to this opposition, the government revised its policies. The opposition, i.e. Gerindra and PKS, consistently opposed Jokowi's policies. However, as explained above, these parties' opposition to Jokowi's policies was not rooted in ideological differences.

We can examine the relationship between Jokowi's Nawa Cita and the ideologies of Indonesia's political parties. Nawa Cita could not readily influence the ideologies of political parties, either those backing Jokowi or the president's opposition. To a limited degree, Jokowi sought to strengthen his ideology by linking it to the ideologies of certain parties, particularly PDIP. Therefore, the parties backing Jokowi still had considerable bargaining power with the president. In dealing with several planned policies, they were capable of forcing the government to delay or even cancel its plans.

Several political parties that had initially opposed Jokowi ultimately began supporting him and his government. Golkar and PAN changed their positions, and thus currently form part of Jokowi's coalition. Aburizal Bakrie, the leader of Golkar's Advisory Council, stated that the party had not backed Jokowi in the 2014 election because it was not familiar with Nawa Cita and had suspected that Jokowi's policies would not reflect the desires of the people. However, as Golkar found similarities between its own activities and Nawa Cita, the party decided to back the Jokowi government (*Bantennews* 2018). In 2017, the party announced that it would back Jokowi in the 2019 election. PAN decided to back the Jokowi government in September 2015 to "demi menjaga stabilitas politik dan pemerintahan, khususnya di tengah situasi ekonomi dunia yang sedang tidak stabil" (maintain political and government stability, particularly in the unstable world economic situation) (Teresia 2015). However, PAN has yet to announce whether it will back Jokowi in 2019.

Gerindra and PKS have consistently opposed the Jokowi government. Neither has received a ministerial position within the cabinet. Gerindra's decision to back Prabowo again in the 2019 election has strongly motivated the party to continue opposing the government. A more ideological reason applies to PKS, which refuses to ally itself with secular nationalist parties such as the PDIP.

In the lead-up to the 2019 legislative election, four new political parties have emerged: Partai Solidaritas Indonesia (Indonesian Solidarity Party, PSI), Partai Garuda (Garuda Party), Partai Berkarya (Working

Party), and Partai Persatuan Indonesia (Indonesian Unity Party, Perindo). Generally, these parties have not offered a new ideology, as all have formally taken Pancasila as their basis. PSI seeks an "Indonesia yang berkarakter kerakyatan, berkeadilan dan berkemajuan" (Indonesia characterized by people power, justice, and progress) (Facebook 2015). Garuda has the short vision of "mewujudkan cita-cita perubahan Indonesia" (realizing change in Indonesia) (Partai Garuda n.d.). Both parties are targeting young voters as their potential constituents (Ihsanuddin 2018; Rahman 2018). Promoting a vision of "membangun Indonesia dengan berkarya" (building Indonesia through work), the developmentalist Berkarya Party has emphasized the perceived glory of the New Order period to gain its constituents' sympathies (Agus 2018). Perindo, after previously taking the form of a community organization, became a political party in 2015 with the vision "mewujudkan Indonesia berkemajuan, adil, dan makmur" (realizing an Indonesia of progress, justice, and prosperity) (Partai Perindo n.d.; Ponge 2018).

Berkarya, Garuda, and Perindo all have historical relations with Golkar and Soeharto's New Order. Tommy Soeharto, the chair of the Berkarya Party, is the son of former President Soeharto and twice (unsuccessfully) ran for Golkar chair (Hidayat 2018). The chair of Garuda, Ahmad Ridha Sabana, had previously received financial support from Siti Hardiyanti Rukmana or Tutut, Soeharto's eldest daughter. Another point, which Sabana denied, was that he had served as the commissary of Televisi Pendidikan Indonesia (Indonesian Education Television, TPI), a private television station owned by Tutut (Wiwoho 2018). In Perindo, although not a Golkar cadre himself, Hary Tanoesoedibjo had held high positions in two parties established by former Golkar elites: Hanura and Nasdem (Wijoto 2018).

These new political parties will not field their own presidential candidates in 2019. PSI and Perindo have pledged their support to Jokowi in the election; PSI has even prepared a cabinet for Jokowi's second term. Garuda and Berkarya have yet to ally themselves with any presidential and vice-presidential candidate.

Concluding Remarks

The presence of Jokowi on the national political stage has been a new phenomenon in the *reformasi* era. A figure who is not a party cadre and who rose from mayor of Solo and governor of Jakarta, Jokowi has undertaken an interesting trajectory. From the above discussion, we can see the various political manoeuvres used by Jokowi when dealing with the multiparty system. Relying on his municipal and provincial leadership experiences and supported by civil society, he formulated his Nawa Cita as an umbrella for his policies. He then attempted to link Nawa Cita with the programmes of various parties, particularly PDIP, seeking to cement his political legitimacy and gain party support. On the other hand, these political parties attempted to integrate Nawa Cita into their ideologies, particularly those involving populist issues such as basic services and economic/development.

After his inauguration as president, Jokowi's relations with political parties were not eased, but rather experienced considerable volatility. Various negotiations occurred between Jokowi and political parties. Negotiations were not only conducted with Jokowi's political opponents, but also with the parties backing him. In some of his policies, Jokowi offered space for compromise, ultimately leading to several planned policies not being implemented. In other policies, Jokowi offered no compromise. This can be seen, for example, in his push to develop infrastructure — roads, bridges, and sea tolls — that had effects that could be felt directly by the populace. For Jokowi, such policies were an important means of gaining popular political legitimacy.

The patterns that emerged during and after the 2014 presidential election appear likely to be repeated in 2019. In his candidacy, Jokowi required the support of political parties. Likewise, in the mobilization of voters, he needed his constituents. Nawa Cita proved important in meeting these needs. In this context, Jokowi did not only depend on his relations with political parties. He used Nawa Cita to connect directly with voters. This differs significantly from *Susilo Bambang Yudhoyono*, whose legitimacy relied strongly on his relationships with his backing parties, without a clear or firm ideology. In the lead-up to the 2019 presidential election, Jokowi's chances of being re-elected appear great. The question now is to what extent he will maintain or change his ideology in dealing with political parties and voters.

NOTE

1. Trisakti is a concept first introduced by Sukarno in his speech "Berdikari" (Standing on One's Own Feet), delivered at the Third General Assembly of the People's Consultative Assembly in 1965. Trisakti consists of three concepts: freedom and independence in politics, a [good/positive] personality in economics, and financial self-determination. PDIP later adopted Trisakti as a central component of its party ideology, together with the speech on the birth of Pancasila (1 June 1945). See, "Anggaran Dasar Anggaran Rumah Tangga PDIP Masa Bakti 2015–2020". Compare with "Pidato Presiden Sukarno 'Nawaksara'".

REFERENCES

Agus, Feri. "Supersemar dan Pengukuhan Tommy Soeharto Jadi Ketum Berkarya" [Supersemar and the Selection of Tommy Soeharto as Head of Berkarya]. *CNN Indonesia*, March 2018. Available at <https://www. cnnindonesia.com/nasional/20180311190511-32-282147/supersemar-dan-pengukuhan-tommy-soeharto-jadi-ketum-berkarya> (accessed 13 April 2018).

Akuntono, Indra. "PKS: Pilkada Lewat DPRD Benahi Pemimpin dan Rakyat" [PKS: Elections through Regional Parliament Improve Leadership and Populace]. *Kompas*, September 2014. Available at <https://nasional. kompas.com/read/2014/09/25/17253401/PKS.Pilkada.lewat.DPRD.Benahi. Pemimpin.dan.Rakyat> (accessed 29 March 2018).

Ambardi, Kuskridho. "The Making of the Indonesian Multiparty System: A Cartelized Party System and Its Origin". PhD dissertation, Department of Political Science, Ohio State University, 2008.

Andriansyah, Moch. "NasDem: Ada Nuansa Dendam Politik Terkait RUU Pilkada" [NasDem: Nuance of Political Vengeance Tainting Planned Election Law]. *Merdeka*, September 2014. Available at <https://www.merdeka.com/politik/ nasdem-ada-nuansa-dendam-politik-terkait-ruu-pilkada.html> (accessed 29 March 2018).

Anshori, Ridwan. "Persaingan KIH–KMP Panas" [Tension between KIH–KMP Escalating]. *Sindonews*, November 2014. Available at <https://daerah. sindonews.com/read/921825/151/persaingan-kih-kmp-panas-1415514704 > (accessed 9 July 2018).

Aspinall, Edward. "Oligarchic Populism: Prabowo Subianto's Challenge to Indonesian Democracy". *Indonesia* 99 (2015): 1–28.

Bantennews. "Program Nawacita Jokowi Diklaim Sesuai dengan Cita-cita Golkar" [Jokowi's Nawacita Programme Claimed to Follow Goals of Golkar], 2017. Available at <https://www.bantennews.co.id/program-

nawacita-jokowi-diklaim-sesuai-dengan-cita-cita-golkar/> (accessed 4 March 2018).

Baswedan, Anies R. "Political Islam in Indonesia: Present and Future Trajectory". *Asian Survey* 44, no. 5 (2004): 669–90.

Buehler, Michael. "Revisiting the Inclusion-Moderation Thesis in the Context of Decentralized Institutions: The Behavior of Indonesia's Prosperous Justice Party in National and Local Politics". *Party Politics* 19, no. 2 (2012): 210–29.

Burhani, Ahmad Najib. "The Banning of Hizbut Tahrir and the Consolidation of Democracy in Indonesia". *ISEAS Perspective*, 19 September 2017.

Bustan, M. Taufan SP. "Tamatnya Pilkada Langsung dan Drama Demokrat" [The End of Direct Elections and the Drama of Democracy]. *Liputan 6*, September 2014. Available at <http://www.liputan6.com/news/read/2111956/tamatnya-pilkada-langsung-dan-drama-demokrat> (accessed 29 March 2018).

Chandra, Ardan Adhi. "Baru 26 dari 245 Proyek Strategis yang Rampung, Ini Penjelasan Pemerintah" [Only 26 of 245 Strategic Projects Completed: This is the Government's Explanation]. *detikFinance*, December 2017. Available at <https://finance.detik.com/infrastruktur/3778377/baru-26-dari-245-proyek-strategis-yang-rampung-ini-penjelasan-pemerintah> (accessed 2 March 2018).

Chrisnandy, Yuddy and Adhi Priamarizki. "Explaining the Trajectory of Golkar's Splinters in Post-Suharto Indonesia". *RSIS Working Paper*, July 2014. Available at <https://www.rsis.edu.sg/wp-content/uploads/rsis-pubs/WP277.pdf> (accessed 6 July 2018).

Cusworth, Catrina Croft. "Prabowo or Jokowi: What's the Policy Difference?". *The Interpreter*, June 2014. Available at <https://www.lowyinstitute.org/the-interpreter/prabowo-or-jokowi-whats-policy-difference> (accessed 5 July 2018).

detikNews. "Jokowi: Bagi-bagi Kursi dan Menteri Itu Tidak Baik" [Jokowi: Distribution of Chairs and Ministries Not Good], April 2014. Available at <https://news.detik.com/berita/2556338/jokowi-bagi-bagi-kursi-dan-menteri-itu-tidak-baik≥ (accessed 3 March 2018).

Dewan Pengurus Pusat Partai Kebangkitan Bangsa. "Sikap Resmi FPKB, Pilkada Langsung Satu Putaran" [Formal Position of FPKB: Direct Elections, One Round], September 2014. Available at <http://dpp.pkb.or.id/sikap-resmi-fpkb-pilkada-langsung-satu-putaran> (accessed 29 March 2018).

Dewi, Sita W. and Margareth Aritonang. "Understanding Jokowi's Inner Circle". *The Jakarta Post*, July 2014. Available at <http://www.thejakartapost.com/news/2014/07/04/understanding-jokowi-s-inner-circle.html> (accessed 3 March 2018).

Downs, Anthony. *An Economic Theory of Democracy*. New York: Harper, 1957.

Facebook. "Visi dan Misi PSI" [Vision and Mission of PSI], October 2015. Available at <https://www.facebook.com/notes/partai-solidaritas-indonesia/visi-dan-misi-psi/545487602265118/> (accessed 13 April 2018).

Faqih, Fikri. "Jokowi Kecewa jika DPR Tolak Perppu Pilkada Langsung" [Jokowi Disappointed if Parliament Rejects Direct Election Plan]. *Merdeka*, October 2014. Available at <https://www.merdeka.com/politik/jokowi-kecewa-jika-dpr-tolak-perppu-pilkada-langsung.html> (accessed 28 March 2018).

Fauzi, Gilang. "Mega Tegaskan Status Presiden Jokowi Tetap Petugas Partai" [Mega Emphasizes that Jokowi as President is still Party Official]. *CNN Indonesia*, July 2017. Available at <https://www.cnnindonesia.com/nasional/20150721180244-32-67479/mega-tegaskan-status-presiden-jokowi-tetap-petugas-partai> (accessed 4 March 2018).

Ferrera, Maurizio. "Ideology, Parties and Social Politics in Europe". *West European Politics* 37, no. 2 (2014): 420–38.

Firdaus, Randy Ferdi. "2 Tahun Jokowi, PDIP banggakan KIP dan Infrastruktur Luar Jawa" [2 Years of Jokowi: PDIP Proud of Education Cards and Infrastructure Outside Java]. *Merdeka*, October 2016. Available at <https://www.merdeka.com/politik/2-tahun-jokowi-pdip-banggakan-kip-dan-infrastruktur-luar-jawa.html> (accessed 2 March 2018).

Fraksi PKB DPR RI. "PKB Akan Menyetujui Pengesahan Perppu Ormas, Ini Alasannya" [PKB to Approve Legislation of Law on Community Organisations, This is Why], October 2017. Available at <https://www.fraksipkb.com/2017/10/23/pkb-akan-menyetujui-pengesahan-perppu-ormas-ini-alasannya/> (accessed 29 January 2018).

Hendrajit. "Persekutuan Mega-Prabowo Kunci Kekuatan Goyang SBY" [Mega-Prabowo Coalition to Overthrow SBY]. *The Global Review*, April 2009. Available at <http://theglobal-review.com/lama/content_detail.php?lang=id&id=152&type=2> (accessed 9 July 2018).

Hidayat, Reja. "Bagaimana Tommy Soeharto Membuat Partai Berkarya" [How Tommy Soeharto Made the Berkarya Party]. *Tirto.id*, April 2018. Available at <https://tirto.id/bagaimana-tommy-soeharto-membuat-partai-berkarya-cHbD> (accessed 13 April 2018).

Hofmeister, Wilhelm and Karsten Grabow. *Political Parties, Functions and Organisation in Democratic Societies*. Singapore: Konrad Adenauer Stiftung, 2011.

Honna, Jun. "Inside the Democrat Party: Power, Politics, and Conflict in Indonesia's Presidential Party". *South East Asia Research* 20, no. 4 (2012): 473–89.

Ihsanuddin. "Tolak Pilkada Langsung, Gerindra Beralasan Rawan Korupsi" [Rejecting Direct Elections, Gerindra claims Rampant Corruption]. *Kompas*,

September 2014. Available at <https://nasional.kompas.com/read/2014/09/05/14175821/Tolak.Pilkada.Langsung.Gerindra.Beralasan.Rawan.Korupsi> (accessed 29 March 2018).

———. "Nasdem: KMP Ingin Sisipkan Dana Aspirasi, RAPBN 2016 Bisa Disandera" [Nasdem: Red–White Coalition Seeking to Include Aspiration Money, 2016 Budget May Be Taken Hostage]. *Kompas*, October 2015. Available at <https://nasional.kompas.com/read/2015/10/23/06531251/Nasdem.KMP.Ingin.isipkan.Dana.Aspirasi.RAPBN.2016.Bisa.Disandera> (accessed 29 January 2018).

———. "Jokowi: Tak Perlu Risau soal 'Full Day School'" [Jokowi: No Need to Worry about "Full Day School"]. *Kompas*, August 2017. Available at <https://nasional.kompas.com/read/2017/08/14/13380931/jokowi--tak-perlu-risau-soal-full-day-school-> (accessed 29 January 2018).

———. "PSI, Grace Natalie, dan Citra Partai Anak Muda" [PSI, Grace Natalie, and the Image of the Youth Party]. *Kompas*, February 2018. Available at <https://nasional.kompas.com/read/2018/02/22/12132451/psi-grace-natalie-dan-citra-partai-anak-muda> (accessed 13 April 2018).

Iqbal, Muhammad. "Setahun Jokowi-JK Gebrakan '3 Kartu Sakti' Jokowi" [One Year of Jokowi and Jusuf Kalla: The '3 Potent Cards' of Jokowi]. *detikNews*, October 2015. Available at <https://news.detik.com/berita/3048571/gebrakan-3-kartu-sakti-jokowi> (accessed 2 March 2018).

Juniardhie, Widyanto. "Debat Perdana Capres Cawapres 2014" [First Vice-Presidential Debate, 2014]. *YouTube*, June 2014. Available at <https://www.youtube.com/watch?v=09TXFbvrslw> (accessed 28 March 2018).

Keteng, Andi Muttya. "Ahok: Saya Senang DPRD DKI Jakarta Tak Dikuasai KMP" [Ahok: I'm Happy that KMP Didn't Control the Regional Legislative]. *Liputan 6*, November 2014. Available at <https://www.liputan6.com/news/read/2133992/ahok-saya-senang-dprd-dki-jakarta-tak-dikuasai-kmp> (accessed 4 July 2018).

Kompas. "Tiga Konsep Visi Misi Mega-Prabowo" [Three Main Concepts of Mega-Prabowo's Vision], n.d. Available at <https://nasional.kompas.com/read/2009/05/22/19262074/tiga.konsep.visi.misi.mega-prabowo> (accessed 6 July 2018).

———. "Tim Mega-Prabowo Diperkuat Profesional" [Mega-Prabowo's Campaign Team Backed-up by the Professionals], May 2009. Available at <https://nasional.kompas.com/read/2009/05/18/17290160/tim.kampanye.mega-prabowo.diperkuat.profesional> (accessed 9 July 2018).

Kumparan. "Gerindra: Jokowi Mau Jadi Pahlawan dengan Membatalkan Sekolah 5 Hari" [Gerindra: Jokowi Wants to Become a Hero by Stopping the Five-Day School Plan], June 2017. Available at <https://kumparan.com/@kumparannews/gerindra-jokowi-mau-jadi-pahlawan-dengan-membatalkan-sekolah-5-hari> (accessed 29 January 2018).

Kurniawan, Haris. "DPR Setujui Perppu Pilkada Langsung" [People's Representative Council Agreed with Local Direct Election Option]. *Sindonews*, January 2015. Available at <https://nasional.sindonews.com/read/953019/12/dpr-setujui-perppu-pilkada-langsung-1421730327> (accessed 4 July 2018).

Lane, Max. "A New Ideological Contestation Emerging in Indonesia?" *ISEAS Perspective*, 19 October 2017.

Lewis, Verlan. "The President and the Parties' Ideologies: Party Ideas about Foreign Policy since 1900". *Presidential Studies Quarterly* 47, no. 1 (2016): 27–61.

Liddle, R. William and Saiful Mujani. "Leadership, Party, and Religion: Explaining Voter Behavior in Indonesia". *Comparative Political Studies* 40, no. 7 (2007): 832–57.

Liputan 6. "Fahri: PKS Tak Masalah Pilkada Langsung atau DPRD, Asal..." [Fahri: PKS Has No Problem with Direct Elections or Parliamentary Selection, So Long As...], December 2014. Available at <http://www.liputan6.com/news/read/2150318/fahri-pks-tak-masalah-pilkada-langsung-atau-dprd-asal> (accessed 29 March 2018).

Majelis Pertimbangan Pusat PKS. *Platform Kebijakan Pembangunan PK Sejahtera* [Basic Philosophy and Development Policy Platform of the PKS]. Jakarta: Majelis Pertimbangan Pusat PKS, 2008.

Mas'udi, Wawan. "Creating Legitimacy in Decentralized Indonesia: Joko 'Jokowi' Widodo's Path to Legitimacy in Solo, 2005–2012". PhD dissertation, Faculty of Arts, University of Melbourne, 2017.

Maulidar, Indri. "Jokowi Janji Perjuangkan Pilkada Langsung" [Jokowi Promises to Fight for Direct Elections]. *Tempo*, December 2014. Available at <https://nasional.tempo.co/read/626385/jokowi-janji-perjuangkan-pilkada-langsung> (accessed 28 March 2018).

Metrotvnews. "[Debat Capres 2014] Pembangunan Ekonomi dan Kesejahteraan Sosial (3)" [Economic Development and Social Welfare (3)]. *Youtube*, June 2014. Available at <https://www.youtube.com/watch?v=ZagoaVmqkJ8> (accessed 29 March 2018).

————. "[Debat Capres 2014] Pembangunan Ekonomi dan Kesejahteraan Sosial (5)" [Economic Development and Social Welfare (5)]. *Youtube*, June 2014. Available at <https://www.youtube.com/watch?v=X-ficy9h6AE> (accessed 29 March 2018).

Mietzner, Marcus. "Ideology, Money, and Dynastic Leadership: The Indonesian Democratic Party of Struggle, 1998–2012". *South East Asia Research* 20, no. 4 (2012): 511–31.

————. *Money, Power, and Ideology: Political Parties in Post-Authoritarian Indonesia*. Singapore: NUS Press, 2013.

————. *Reinventing Asian Populism: Jokowi's Rise, Democracy, and Political Contestation in Indonesia.* Hawaii: East–West Center, 2015.

Muhtadi, Burhanuddin. "Jokowi's First Year: A Weak President Caught between Reform and Oligarchic Politics". *Bulletin of Indonesian Economic Studies* 51, no. 3 (2015): 349–68.

Munawwaroh. "Demi Prabowo, PKS Setuju Pilkada Lewat DPRD" [For Prabowo, PKS Approves of Elections through Regional Parliament]. *Tempo*, September 2014. Available at <https://nasional.tempo.co/read/605467/demi-prabowo-pks-setuju-pilkada-lewat-dprd> (accessed 29 March 2018).

Mutmainah, Dinda Audriene. "Tiga Tahun Jokowi, 300 Kilometer Jalan Tol Baru Terbentang" [Three Years of Jokowi: 300 Kilometers of Toll Roads Built]. *CNN Indonesia*, October 2017. Available at <https://www.cnnindonesia.com/ekonomi/20171018150108-92-249239/tiga-tahun-jokowi-300-kilometer-jalan-tol-baru-terbentang> (accessed 2 March 2018).

Muzayyin, Arif Hulwan. "Prabowo Sebut Infrastruktur Bobrok Karena Uang Rakyat Dicuri" [Prabowo Says Infrastructure in Tatters because the People's Money Stolen]. *CNN Indonesia*, March 2018. Available at <https://www.cnnindonesia.com/nasional/20180330181324-32-287108/prabowo-sebut-infrastruktur-bobrok-karena-uang-rakyat-dicuri> (accessed 31 March 2018).

n.a. *Memperjuangkan Masyarakat Madani: Edisi Gabungan Falsafah Dasar Perjuangan dan Misi, dan Program Aksi Jokowi–Jusuf Kalla 2014* [Building Civil Society: A Combined Philosophy and Mission of Struggle and Action, Jokowi–Jusuf Kalla 2014]. Jakarta: n.a., 2014.

Nugroho, Bagus Prihantoro. "Ini Alasan Jokowi Suntik Modal ke BUMN" [This is Jokowi's Reason for Giving Funds to State Corporations]. *detikFinance*, November 2015. Available at <http://finance.detik.com/berita-ekonomi-bisnis/d-3064661/ini-alasan-jokowi-suntik-modal-ke-bumn> (accessed 29 January 2018).

Partai Amanat Nasional (PAN). "Tentang PAN" [About PAN], n.d. Available at <http://www.pan.or.id/tentang_pan/> (accessed 8 February 2018).

Partai Demokrat. "Visi & Misi" [Vision and Mission], n.d. Available at <http://www.demokrat.or.id/visi-misi/> (accessed 8 February 2018).

Partai Garuda. "Visi dan Misi" [Vision and Mission], n.d. Available at <http://partaigaruda.org/> (accessed 13 April 2018).

Partai Gerindra. *Jalan Perubahan untuk Indonesia yang Berdaulat, Mandiri dan Berkepribadian: Visi Manifesto Perjuangan Partai Gerakan Indonesia Raya* [Gerindra Manifesto]. Jakarta: Partai Gerindra, n.d.

————. "Gerindra Kritik Prioritas Proyek Infrastruktur Jokowi" [Gerinda Critical of Jokowi's Prioritizing Infrastructure Projects], August 2017. Available at <http://partaigerindra.or.id/2017/08/02/gerindra-kritik-prioritas-proyek-infrastruktur-jokowi.html> (accessed 29 January 2018).

Partai Golkar. "Visi & Misi" [Vision and Mission], n.d. Available at <https://partaigolkar.or.id/visi> (accessed 8 February 2018).

Partai Perindo. "Profile Partai PERINDO" [Profile of PERINDO], n.d. Available at <http://partaiperindo.com/?page_id=6> (accessed 13 April 2018).

Partai Persatuan Pembangunan. "Visi dan Misi PPP" [Vision and Mission of PPP], September 2016. Available at <http://ppp.or.id/page/visi-dan-misi-ppp.html> (accessed 8 February 2018).

PDI Perjuangan (PDIP). "Visi dan Misi" [Vision and Mission], January 2016. Available at <https://www.pdiperjuangan.id/article/category/child/27/Partai/Visi-dan-Misi> (accessed 8 February 2018).

Ponge, Aldi. "Sejarah Partai Perindo dan Penantiannya di Pemilu 2019" [History of Perindo Party and its Expectations for 2019 Election]. *Tribunnews*, February 2018. Available at <http://manado.tribunnews.com/2018/02/22/sejarah-partai-perindo-dan-penantiannya-di-pemilu-2019> (accessed 13 April 2018).

Pratikno and Cornelis Lay. "From Populism to Democratic Polity: Problems and Challenges in Surakarta, Indonesia". *Power Conflict Democracy Journal* 3, nos. 1–2 (2011): 33–61.

Rahman, Vanny El. "Mengenal Partai Garuda, Partai yang Digerakkan Millenials" [Regarding the Garuda Party, a Party Motored by Millenials]. *IDN Times*, March 2018. Available at <https://news.idntimes.com/indonesia/vanny-rahman/mengenal-partai-garuda-partai-yang-digerakkan-millennials-1/full#> (accessed 13 April 2018).

Riker, William H. *The Theory of Political Coalitions*. New Haven and London: Yale University Press, 1962.

Safitri, Inge Klara. "Politikus PDIP Terus Hantam Menteri Rini Soemarno" [PDIP Politicians Still Challenging Minister Rini Soemarno]. *Tempo*, October 2015. Available at <https://nasional.tempo.co/read/714771/politikus-pdip-terus-hantam-menteri-rini-soemarno> (accessed 29 January 2018).

Salim, Hans Jimenez. "PMN dalam RAPBN 2016 Dibekukan, PDIP Sindir Menteri Rini" [State Equity Participation in Proposed 2016 Budget Frozen, PDIP Looks to Minister Rini]. *Liputan 6*, October 2015. Available at <http://news.liputan6.com/read/2354019/pmn-dalam-rapbn-2016-dibekukan-pdip-sindir-menteri-rini> (accessed 29 January 2018).

Sani, Ahmad Faiz Ibnu. "PAN Beralasan Menolak Perpu Ormas Justru karena Mendukung Jokowi" [PAN Claims to Reject Law on Community Organizations to Support Jokowi]. *Tempo*, October 2017. Available at <https://nasional.tempo.co/read/1027575/pan-beralasan-menolak-perpu-ormas-justru-karena-mendukung-jokowi> (accessed 29 January 2018).

Sari, Nursita. "'Revolusi Putih' Prabowo yang Akhirnya Dijalankan Anies-Sandi di DKI" [Prabowo's 'White Revolution' Implemented by Anies-Sandi in DKI]. *Kompas*, October 2017. Available at <https://megapolitan.kompas.

com/read/2017/11/24/07443961/revolusi-putih-prabowo-yang-akhirnya-dijalankan-anies-sandi-di-dki> (accessed 9 July 2018).

Sasmita, Ira. "Jokowi–JK Usung Konsep Trisakti" [Jokowi–JK Uphold Trisakti Conception]. *Republika*, May 2014. Available at <https://www.republika.co.id/berita/pemilu/menuju-ri-1/14/05/20/n5upjq-jokowijk-usung-konsep-trisakti> (accessed 9 July 2018).

Sayidina, Rachel Maryam. *Pandangan Umum Fraksi Partai Gerindra tentang Rancangan Undang Undang Anggaran Beserta Nota Keuangannya*. Jakarta: Rachel Maryam Sayidina, 2015.

Schmidt, Vivien. "Discursive Institutionalism: The Explanatory Power of Ideas and Discourse". *Annual Review of Political Science* 11 (2008): 303–26.

Sekretariat Jenderal DPP PKB. *Anggaran Dasar/Anggaran Rumah Tangga (AD/ART) Partai Kebangkitan Bangsa: Hasil Muktamar PKB* [Constitution and By-laws of the National Awakening Party, As Agreed Upon at the Party Caucus]. Jakarta: Sekretariat Jenderal DPP PKB, 2014.

Sholih, Mufti. "Ini Alasan PDIP Ngotot Pilkada Langsung" [This is Why PDIP Insists on Direct Elections]. *Metro TV*, September 2014. Available at <http://news.metrotvnews.com/read/2014/09/13/291008/ini-alasan-pdip-ngotot-pilkada-langsung> (accessed 28 March 2018).

Slater, Dan. "Party Cartelization, Indonesian-Style: Presidential Power-Sharing and the Contingency of Democratic Opposition". *Journal of East Asian Studies* (2018): 1–24.

Subianto, Prabowo and Hatta Rajasa. *Visi, Misi dan Program Bakal Pasangan Calon Presiden dan Wakil Presiden* [Vision, Mission, and Programmes of Prospective Potential Presidential and Vice-Presidential Candidates]. Jakarta: Prabowo Subianto and Hatta Rajasa, 2014.

Suharman, Tri. "Drama Penghapusan Pilkada Langsung" [Abolishing Direct Election]. *Tempo*, September 2014. Available at <https://nasional.tempo.co/read/609808/drama-penghapusan-pilkada-langsung> (accessed 9 July 2018).

Sukarno. "Pidato Presiden Sukarno 'Nawaksara' di depan Sidang Umum ke-IV MPRS pada tanggal 22 Juni 1966" [President Sukarno's Speech "Nawaksara", Delivered on People's Consultative Assembly's Fourth General Session, June 22, 1966]. *Perpustakaan Nasional Republik Indonesia*, n.d. Available at <http://kepustakaan-presiden.pnri.go.id/speech/idx.php?box=list_245&hlm=1&search_tag=&search_keyword=&activation_status=&search_7XX=&search_6XX=&presiden_id=1&presiden=sukarno> (accessed 4 July 2018).

Sukarnoputri, Megawati and Prabowo Subianto. *Visi, Misi dan Program Megawati Soekarnoputri dan Prabowo Subianto* [Vision, Mission, and Programmes of Megawati Sukarnoputri and Prabowo Subianto]. Jakarta: Megawati Sukarnoputri and Prabowo Subianto, 2009.

Supriatin. "Gerindra sebut Jokowi Genjot Infrastruktur untuk Dulang Suara Pemilu 2019" [Gerindra Claims Jokowi Pushing Infrastructure to Gather Voter Support in 2019]. *Merdeka*, October 2017. Available at <https://www.merdeka.com/politik/gerindra-sebut-jokowi-genjot-infrastruktur-untuk-dulang-suara-pemilu-2019.html> (accessed 2 March 2018).

Suriyanto. "Empat Pejabat di *Reshuffle* Kabinet Jilid Tiga Jokowi" [Four Officials Reshuffled in Jokowi's Third Cabinet]. *CNN Indonesia*, January 2018. Available at <https://www.cnnindonesia.com/nasional/20180117091937 -32-269498/empat-pejabat-di-reshuffle-kabinet-jilid-tiga-jokowi> (accessed 8 February 2018).

Suryadinata, Leo. "Golkar's Leadership and the Indonesian President". *ISEAS Perspective*, 26 January 2018.

Suryowati, Estu. "PKB: 'Full Day School' Tidak Realistis!" [PKB: "Full Day School" Not Realistic]. *Kompas*, August 2017. Available at <https://nasional.kompas.com/read/2017/08/08/00321041/pkb--full-day-school-tidak-realistis-> (accessed 29 January 2018).

Teresia, Ananda. "PAN Resmi Bergabung dengan Pemerintahan Jokowi" [PAN Officially Joins Jokowi's Government]. *Tempo*, September 2015. Available at <https://nasional.tempo.co/read/697165/pan-resmi-bergabung-dengan-pemerintahan-jokowi> (accessed 26 January 2019).

Tomsa, Dirk. "Still the Natural Government Party? Challenges and Opportunities for Golkar Ahead of the 2014 Election". *South East Asia Research* 20, no. 4 (2012): 491–509.

Toriq, Ahmad. "Begini Penjelasan soal Gerakan 'Revolusi Putih' Prabowo" [Prabowo's Explanation on 'White Revolution' Movement]. *detikNews*, October 2017. Available at <https://news.detik.com/berita/d-3700634/begini-penjelasan-soal-gerakan-revolusi-putih-prabowo> (accessed 9 July 2018).

Ufen, Andreas. "Political Parties in Post-Suharto Indonesia: Between Politik Aliran and 'Philippinisation'". *GIGA Working Papers*, December 2006. Available at <https://www.giga-hamburg.de/en/publication/political-parties-in-post-suharto-indonesia-between-politik-aliran-and-%E2%80%99philippinisation> (accessed 23 February 2018).

Viva. "Gerindra: Pilkada Lewat DPRD, KPK Tinggal Sadap Anggota Dewan" [Gerindra: Elections through Regional Parliament, Corruption Eradication Agency Need Only Choose Council Members], September 2014. Available at <https://www.viva.co.id/berita/politik/538534-gerindra-pilkada-lewat-dprd-kpk-tinggal-sadap-anggota-dewan> (accessed 29 March 2018).

Warburton, Eve. "Jokowi and the New Developmentalism". *Bulletin of Indonesian Economic Studies* 52, no. 3 (2017): 297–320.

Widodo, Joko. "Revolusi Mental" [Mental Revolution]. *Kompas*, May 2014. Available at <https://nasional.kompas.com/read/2014/05/10/1603015/Revolusi.Mental> (accessed 9 July 2018).

Widodo, Joko and Jusuf Kalla. *Jalan Perubahan untuk Indonesia yang Berdaulat, Mandiri dan Berkepribadian: Visi Misi, dan Program Aksi*. Jakarta: Joko Widodo and Jusuf Kalla, 2014.

Wijoto, Ribut. "Anak-anak Partai Golkar, Perindo Cucunya" [Children of Golkar, Perindo the Grandchild]. *Berita Jatim*, April 2018. Available at <http://beritajatim.com/sorotan/327260/anak-anak_partai_golkar,_perindo_cucunya.html> (accessed 13 April 2018).

Wiwoho, Bimo. "Partai Garuda, Gerak Senyap Parpol Anti-Mainstream" [Garuda Party: The Silent Movement of Anti-Mainstream Political Parties]. *CNN Indonesia*, March 2018. Available at <https://www.cnnindonesia.com/nasional/20180307170753-32-281188/partai-garuda-gerak-senyap-parpol-anti-mainstream> (accessed 13 April 2018).

Woischnik, Jan and Philipp Muller. "Islamic Parties and Democracy in Indonesia: Insight from the World's Largest Muslim Country". *KAS International Reports*, 2013. Available at <http://www.kas.de/wf/doc/kas_35685-1522-2-30.pdf?131015> (accessed 23 February 2018).

Zahro, Moh. Nizar. *Pandangan Umum Fraksi Partai Gerakan Indonesia Raya terhadap Rancangan Undang-undang Tentang Anggaran Pendapatan dan Belanja Negara Tahun Anggaran 2017 berserta Nota Keuangannya*. Jakarta: Moh. Nizar Zahro, 2017.

Zulfikar, Muhammad. "Pesan Prabowo ke Fraksi Gerindra: Jangan Takut Suarakan Rakyat Walau Sendirian" [Prabowo's Mandate to Gerindra: Never Afraid of Defending People's Voice, Even Alone]. *Tribunnews*, October 2015. Available at <http://www.tribunnews.com/nasional/2015/10/30/pesan-prabowo-ke-fraksi-gerindra-jangan-takut-suarakan-rakyat-walau-sendirian> (accessed 5 July 2018).

4

Political Islam Movements and Democracy in Indonesia: A Changing Landscape?

Rizky Alif Alvian

Introduction

Confronted with the gradual advance of democratic discourse and institutions in post-*reformasi* Indonesia, Indonesian political Islam movements — ranging from Front Pembela Islam (Islam Defender Front, FPI), Hizbut Tahrir Indonesia (HTI), Majelis Intelektual dan Ulama Muda Indonesia (Indonesian Council of Young Intellectual and Ulama, MIUMI), Wahdah Islamiyah, to Forum Umat Islam (Islamic Community Forum, FUI) — have been compelled to readjust their strategies to ensure their adaptation to the new political landscape. Although they initially conceived democracy as harmful and incompatible with Islamic faith, political Islam movements have gradually adopted various strategies that enable them to enter the democratic arena and be recognized as legitimate players within it. They have attempted to demonstrate stronger compliance with democratic norms and rules and make several adjustments in their ideological stance —

especially on the relationship between Islam, democracy, pluralism, and the nation-state — to justify those strategies.

However, the desire to retain conservative aspirations — such as the rejection of the election of non-Muslim leaders, support the ban on religious minority groups, and persecution against the LGBTQ+ community — remain strong among political Islam activists. Their strategies mainly revolve around attempts to widen their access to state power or to push the state to create conditions favourable for the growth of conservative ways of life. The tension between political Islam's engagement with democracy and its insistence on a conservative agenda subsequently creates a situation where conservative ideas are increasingly articulated through democratic avenues.

The manoeuvre of political Islam movements to enter the democratic arena is crucial because the groups were previously excluded from the centre of Indonesia's national political arena through the continuous argument by pro-democracy activists, government, and international donors that political Islam threatened democracy, pluralism, and national unity. By implication, so this argument goes, they should not be considered as legitimate players in democratization. The decision of political Islam movements to adopt democratic rhetoric, as part of its efforts to win control over democratic institutions, is intended to overcome its exclusion.

Compared to political Islam's preceding strategies, their recent manoeuvre is relatively novel. Prior to this, the movements tended to distance themselves from the state. It was only during the last decade of Soeharto's administration that these groups acquired a wider access to the state.[1] Prior to the 1990s, political Islam had to avoid political activism due to New Order persecution. On the other hand, in the early stage of democratic reform, political Islam groups detached themselves from the prevailing discourse on liberalization of religious affairs and expressed their discontent with this.

This chapter attempts to capture the dynamics of the strategies of Indonesian political Islam movements prior to and after the beginning of democratic reform. Although the movements remain faithful to their conservative aspirations, they have adopted various strategies that, in turn, depend on the particular context of power relations. However, the main purpose of these strategies is largely similar: the capture of state machinery to advance the interests and conservative ideals of political Islam movements. This chapter specifically inquires into the manner through which political Islam movements create a strategic alliance with the state or distance themselves from it.

The discourse of liberal Islam[2] on freedom of religion, and, later, supporting the war on terrorism have been the main challenge to political Islam's perspectives both before and after *reformasi*. On numerous occasions, this set of discourses has been able to block the access of political Islam to the state and limit their opportunities for politically meaningful manoeuvre. In this regard, political Islam's recent tactical shift is interesting because it no longer rejects the liberal discourse from the outset — but, instead, appropriates aspects of it for its own purposes.

Political Islamic groups have been compelled to adjust their ideological framework by abandoning some elements of their discourse that are incompatible with the prevailing discourses of liberal Islam, freedom of religion, and war on terrorism. These elements, for example, include hostility to the notion of democracy, to pluralism, and to the Pancasila. Since the discourses gain their ascendancy, in part, by framing the demands of political Islam as a threat to democracy, pluralism, and national unity, political Islam movements' abandonment of the anti-liberal elements helps them to avoid exclusion and widen the space for advancing their interests.

This chapter defines political Islam as groups involved in political activities that aim to shape society according to specific interpretations of Islamic teachings. They believe Islam is a "complete, divine system" with "superior political model, cultural codes, legal structure and economic arrangement" (Bayat 2007, p. 14; Ayoob 2004, p. 1). Political Islam, to follow Azca, is usually located between the other two Islamist variants, the "pious" and "jihadi". While the pious Islamists are reluctant to participate in political activism and concerned more with spiritual enrichment, jihadi Islamists believe that violent actions are justified to ensure the establishment of an Islamic system (Azca 2011, pp. 33–34). Political Islam considers political involvement as necessary, yet refuses to engage in extreme violence such as terrorism or armed resistance (Abuza 2007, pp. 9–10; Hiariej et al. 2017, pp. 310–11).

Organizations like Partai Keadilan Sejahtera (Prosperous Justice Party, PKS), Partai Bulan Bintang (Crescent Star Party, PBB), FPI, HTI, MIUMI, Wahdah Islamiyah, and FUI could be classified as parts of political Islam. However, as well noted by Hadiz (2014), even this cluster of organizations differs in preferred strategies. While some are in favour of formal engagement with political institutions — through political parties, for instance — others rely on more informal methods in pursuing their ends (ibid.). This chapter gives a stronger emphasis to specific variants of political Islam that do not employ formal engagement. Consequently, Islamist political parties are not the centre of the analysis in this chapter.

First, this chapter offers a depiction of various movements that are referred to as political Islam groups. The section aims to demonstrate the diversity of the groups in terms of their historical trajectories, ideologies, and strength. Second, this chapter identifies the implications of democratic reform for political Islam's position in Indonesia's political landscape. In this section, the chapter argues that post-*reformasi* political arrangements provide political Islam groups with only limited space for advancing their interests, particularly since the discourse of liberal Islam, freedom of religion, and war on terror have prevailed. Thirdly, this chapter investigates political Islam activists' strategies in dealing with democratic reform and identifies shifts in their approaches. Event though political Islam movements previously remained disengaged from democratic reform, they increasingly try to enter the democratic arena by appropriating its rules for their own interests. This process, the chapter argues, creates a political space in which conservative agendas go hand in hand with democracy.

Political Islam Groups in Indonesia: An Overview

This section discusses the profile of FPI, HTI, MIUMI, Wahdah Islamiyah, and FUI. These organizations are chosen due to their active involvement in national political events in recent years and remarkable influence in shaping the context for the 2019 presidential and parliamentary elections. These groups share a similar conviction on the importance of sharia law. They also demonstrate hostility to ideas that they consider to be "liberal", such as minority rights, gender equality, pluralism, and, to some extent, democracy. It is important to note that the following descriptions aim to capture, primarily, the ideological standpoint of these organizations during their early years, while more recent developments will be discussed later in this chapter.

Front Pembela Islam

FPI was established on 17 August 1998 by the Hadrami and Betawi *habaib, ustadh,* and *ulama.* FPI claimed that it had around 15 million members across the country (Jahroni 2004, p. 223). Several analyses doubt this claim and propose more moderate numbers: around 170,000 in early 2000 (Hiariej 2009, p. 62) and 200,000 in 2014 (IPAC 2018, p. 10).

Indonesian security forces allegedly supported the establishment of FPI, mainly by providing financial resources and training for FPI's paramilitary, Laskar Pembela Islam (Islamic Defender Soldiers, LPI) — which possessed a relatively similar structure with the military (Jahroni 2004, p. 213). Not only were senior military and police officers present during FPI's founding ceremony in Pesantren Al-Umm, Ciputat, but the group also joined the military-backed Pasukan Pengamanan Masyarakat Swakarsa (Voluntary Civilian Security Militia, Pam Swakarsa) that disrupted student demonstrations during Sidang Istimewa MPR (People's Assembly Special Session) in 1998 (IPAC 2018, p. 9) and the drafting of Emergency Situation Law, proposed by the army in 1999 (Siar News Service 2000). Later, a leaked 2006 US cable indicated that FPI had developed a relationship with the national police and intelligence agency as its "attack dog" in exchange for financial resources (Wilson 2014, p. 256; US Embassy, Jakarta, 2006). This report was strongly dismissed by FPI (Hidayatullah, September 2011). However, FPI should not be treated merely as a tool of the military and police (Wilson 2010, pp. 253–54). As stated by Jahroni, FPI basically "never refused to cooperate with other groups, as long as the cooperation was mutually beneficial" (Jahroni 2004, p. 216).

The stated primary mission of FPI is to implement Islamic law in Indonesia (IPAC 2018, p. 11). This demand is grounded on the belief that the application of sharia will enable the country to address its political, societal, and economic crises (ibid., p. 226). After the 2013 Musyawarah Nasional (National Congress, Munas), FPI used "NKRI Bersyariah" (Indonesia with Sharia) as a catchphrase for this argument. It is important to note, however, that FPI does not consider this belief to be contradictory to loyalty to the republic — since FPI's theological position does not require the establishment of an Islamic state to ensure the application of Islamic teachings. Instead, FPI overtly demonstrates its allegiance to the idea of Indonesia (Jahroni 2004,

p. 231; Wilson 2015, p. 3). In FPI's perspective, the notion of Pancasila was actually crafted by the *ulama* (Hidayatullah February 2011) and is thus perfectly compatible with Islamic faith. This compatibility, FPI contends, is reflected in the original text of the Jakarta Charter, in which the first principle of Pancasila, "Ketuhanan Yang Maha Esa" (The Oneness of God), was qualified with "dengan kewajiban menjalankan syariat Islam bagi pemeluknya" (the obligation to follow sharia for Muslims). However, this interpretation has been, in FPI's analysis, sidelined in favour of secular understandings of Pancasila (Syihab 2012, pp. 280–81; Hidayatullah 2017). This point of view encourages FPI to campaign for the restoration of the Jakarta Charter (*Liputan6* 2001; *Tempo* 2003), be involved in vigilante activism to combat vices that contradict Islamic law (*Liputan6* 2002) and fight against religious minority groups that it considers deviant (*detikNews* 2008; *Kompas* 2008; *Tempo* 2011). In Rizieq Shihab's words, Muslims have to assume the task of "interpreting Pancasila according to Islamic teachings, nurturing Pancasila in an Islamic manner" (Hidayatullah 2017).

FPI frequently declares its discontent with the idea and practice of democracy. FPI considers democracy to be alien to Islamic teachings and Indonesia's culture and prefers *musyawarah-mufakat* (deliberation and consensus) as an alternative. Democracy's majoritarian logic, according to FPI, might create law that violates Islamic teachings (Syihab 2012, pp. 56–57; Wilson 2015, pp. 3–4), mainly because the voice of *ulama* and non-*ulama* is considered to be equal, not superior, to that of any other citizen (BBC Indonesia 2017). Despite its reluctance to recognize democracy as a legitimate political form of rule for Indonesia, FPI in 2014 nevertheless encouraged Muslims to vote for Islamic parties (PPP, PKS, and PBB) that campaigned for the implementation of sharia in Indonesia (DPP FPI 2014; Suara Islam 2014).

Hizbut Tahrir Indonesia

HTI is Indonesian branch of Hizbut Tahrir, established in the 1950s in East Jerusalem by Taqiyuddin an-Nabhani (Ward 2009, p. 150). The teaching of Hizbut Tahrir was introduced in Indonesia in the 1980s in Pesantren al-Ghazali, Bogor, by Abdullah bin Nuh, a cleric, and Abdurrahman al-Baghdadi, a member of Lebanon's Hizbut Tahrir who arrived in Indonesia in 1982 (ibid., p. 150; Hiariej 2009, p. 66;

Fealy 2010, p. 155; Muhtadi 2009, p. 626). In its early years, students from universities such as Institut Pertanian Bogor (Bogor Agricultural Institute, IPB), Institut Teknologi Bandung (Bandung Technology Institute, ITB), Universitas Indonesia (Indonesia University, UI), and Universitas Gadjah Mada (Gadjah Mada University, UGM) received HTI training, thanks to the network of Lembaga Dakwah Kampus (Campus Dakwah Organization, LDK) in these institutions (Muhtadi 2009, p. 627; Fealy 2010, p. 156; Hiariej 2009, p. 66). The movement worked clandestinely during the Soeharto regime to avoid intelligence interference and began its overt campaign in 2000 (Fealy 2010, p. 156; Ward 2009, p. 151).

In the late 1990s, HTI claimed that it had ten thousand members in twenty provinces (Hiariej 2009, p. 66). Several estimations indicate that HTI has grown rapidly since the early 2000s. Fealy, for example, estimates that HTI recruited several tens of thousand members in the early 2000s (Fealy 2010, p. 156). According to Muhtadi, this number increased significantly to several hundred thousand members in 2007 (Muhtadi 2009, p. 629). HTI also managed to widen its geographical reach. In an interview in 2017, Ismail Yusanto, HTI's spokesperson, said that HTI has branches in thirty-four provinces and more than 300 districts/cities (*Tirto* 2017).

HTI's status as a provincial branch of Hizbut Tahrir compels the movement to follow Hizbut Tahrir's official discourse, with minor adjustments to contextualize the perspective with Indonesia's situation. According to Fealy, "HTI send all manuscripts [for publication] for vetting. Particular attention is paid to the doctrinal content to ensure conformity with centrally sanctioned views and policies" (Fealy 2010, p. 158; Ward 2009, p. 149, calls HTI a "foreign transplant in Indonesian soil".)

HTI's main goal is to develop a global caliphate that unites Muslims across nation-states' territorial boundaries. Caliphate, according to the teaching of Hizbut Tahrir, is "the executive entity for the rules of Islam and which is a general leadership over all Muslims to govern by Islam internally" (Hizbut Tahrir 2017). It is "a unitary state", writes Ward (2009, p. 154), "in which the caliph would have a very wide range of functions no matter how vast his territory was".

HTI contends that the fall of the caliphate (Osman 2010, p. 749; see also Hizbut Tahrir 2018) has fragmented the Muslim world into multiple nation-states and, subsequently, removed its power as a potential challenger to Western civilization. Muslims' conflicting loyalty between their nation and religion has enabled the West to exploit the Muslim community and put it under its control (Ward 2009, pp. 153–55; Ahnaf 2009, p. 73). In this regard, HTI perceives nationalism not only as an ideal alien to Islam, but also as a form of "tribal fanaticism" that hinders Muslims from realizing their religious unity (Muhtadi 2009, p. 633). In an interview in the early 2000s, Yusanto stated that "nationalism has no basis".[3] This perspective is echoed in Yusanto's interview in HTI's official publication, *Al-Waie*, in 2014. Yusanto argued that "Islam clearly rejects nationalism. Islam considers the propaganda for group-, ethnic-, and fatherland-fanaticism as haram". Against this backdrop, HTI regards the concept of caliphate as an antidote to nationalism. It enables the Muslim community to overcome fragmentation and rebuild its power (*Al-Waie* 2014).

HTI rejects democracy due to its un-Islamic nature. HTI holds that society's life should be regulated by laws derived solely from the Koran and prophetic traditions, while democracy opens the opportunity for society to create laws to regulate life. In this regard, the concept of democracy, according to HTI, violates the basic principles of Islamic teachings.[4] The weakness of democracy makes the system incapable of delivering public goods effectively. Due to the lack of Islamic morality and guidance among candidates in elections, democracy continues to create corrupt officials who harm the interests of the people (Ahnaf 2009, p. 75). It is only by restoring the caliphate that these problems can be addressed.

Majelis Intelektual dan Ulama Muda Indonesia

MIUMI was declared in February 2012, following an earlier discussion among its founders in Bachtiar Nasir's (later MIUMI's general secretary) Al-Quran Learning Centre in January 2012 (Nahdlatul Ulama 2012; *Okezone* 2012).[5] The founding of MIUMI was supported by young Islamic scholars coming from various Sunni backgrounds, ranging from Pesantren Gontor alumni, Dewan Dakwah Islamiyah Indonesia (Indonesia Islamic Dakwah Council, DDII), Persatuan Islam (Islam Union, Persis), and Wahdah Islamiyah, to Muhammadiyah and Nahdlatul Ulama activists (IPAC 2018, p. 7; NU 2012). In recent years, MIUMI has established local branches in Aceh, North Sumatra, West Sumatra, Riau, South Sulawesi, West Java, Central Java, East Java, and Yogyakarta, to mention a few (Hidayatullah, December 2012). Although MIUMI is younger than the other organizations discussed in this section, it gradually moved to the centre of national politics, especially due to the activism of its members — for example, Bachtiar Nasir and Zaitun Rasmin — in the Jakarta gubernatorial election.

Nasir is an important figure within MIUMI. As IPAC's analysis demonstrates, Nasir was influenced by the Sahwa movement in Saudi Arabia, which questioned Saudi's dependence on the United States during the first Gulf War (1990–91). The influence of Sahwa encouraged Nasir to conceive the suffering of the Muslim community as the result of "a global secularist conspiracy" that could be addressed through "the broadening of clergy's role into social and political affairs" (IPAC 2018, p. 5). This tone of analysis is widely shared within the movement and visible in MIUMI's positions on numerous issues.

MIUMI is not a mass organization. Its movement is intellectual in nature. It targets specifically young Islamic scholars and *ulama* and aims to re-establish the authority of *ulama* in order to make them a point of reference for public debate and policy-making (Hidayatullah, March 2012). In this regard, MIUMI claims that it does not attempt to contest the authority of established Islamic organizations in Indonesia (NU 2012; *Okezone* 2012) — including Majelis Ulama Indonesia (Indonesian Council of Ulama, MUI) — but instead tries to foster the brotherhood of Muslims in Indonesia, to unite the "spirit of umma" (Hidayatullah 2018).

MIUMI's discourse, however, bears a strong resemblance to other mass-based political Islam organizations. In its declaration, MIUMI identifies "the strong wind of liberalization and varying deviant religious teachings which threaten aqidah and unity of the ummah" as Indonesia's main problem (MIUMI n.d.). In the words of Fahmi Salim, MIUMI's vice-general secretary, MIUMI's activists are "anti-liberal, anti-Shia, and anti-deviant sects" (Hidayatullah, March 2012). Therefore, MIUMI actively participates in conservative campaigns against Shia (Hidayatullah, March 2012), pluralism (Hidayatullah, August 2012; Hidayatullah 2015), gender equality (Hidayatullah 2014), minority rights (*Republika* February 2015), and sexual minorities (*Voa Islam* 2016).

MIUMI counterposes democracy to Islam. Hamid Zarkasyi, head of MIUMI, contends that Islam believes, not in democracy, but in *musyawarah*. He further believes that liberal democratic reform has severely degraded the authority of *ulama* in Indonesia and created a moral uncertainty in the nation (*Muslim Daily* March 2013; *Arrahmah* 2013*a*). On the other hand, Bachtiar Nasir cautions that democracy — which has "colonized" Indonesia (*Arrahmah* 2013*b*) — could potentially be the "new idol" that makes people "infidels" who believe in its supremacy (TVOne 2014). Although MIUMI does not advocate a complete withdrawal from democratic mechanisms, MIUMI's suspicion of democracy encourages it to retain the primacy of *musyawarah* in understanding elections. This is well reflected in Nasir's speech on the 2018 local elections. He recommended deliberations among *ulama* to decide which candidates Muslims should vote for to ensure that the vote was made in accordance with Islamic teachings of *musyawarah* (Kiblat TV 2018; *Republika* 2018).

Other Organizations: Wahdah Islamiyah and Forum Umat Islam

Wahdah Islamiyah's (in outlining the history of Wahdah, I rely on Chaplin 2018) genesis was related to the application of Asas Tunggal[6] in 1985, which triggered dissatisfaction among Muhammadiyah activists in Makassar. After establishing the Fathul Muin Foundation in 1988, these activists received scholarships from Lembaga Ilmu Pengetahuan Islam dan Arab (Islamic and Arabic College of Indonesia), bringing them closer to Salafi doctrine. The organization formally became an Organisasi Masyarakat (Community Organization, Ormas) in 2002 with the name of Wahdah Islamiyah. In 2012, Wahdah had 70 branches across Indonesia. The number increased significantly in 2016 to 120 branches. This rapid expansion was a part of Wahdah's efforts to increase its leverage in national politics.

Wahdah opposes the idea of democracy. In an article written in 2009, Wahdah accused democracy of being a system that might result in the adoption of laws that violate Islamic teachings (*Al Balagh* 2009). The reasoning behind this position was relatively similar to other political Islam movements. For example, democracy enables people with different levels of expertise in religious teachings to influence legislation. For Wahdah, this feature might result in the adoption of laws that are in conflict with Islamic principles. Wahdah, however, did not prescribe disengagement from the democratic system since that might worsen Muslims' mission to advance the implementation of sharia. Wahdah, therefore, identifies candidates that could contribute to this mission and recommends that Muslims vote for them (ibid.). However, in recent years, Wahdah has coined the term *"wasathiyah* democracy", characterized by "balanced and proportional musyawarah" (Wahdah Islamiyah 2016). Although the exact meaning of this term remains vague, Wahdah believes that *wasathiyah* democracy could balance the importance of religious value and freedom of expression (*Republika* 2016). Wahdah's positions on other issues largely resonate with other political Islam movements. Wahdah condemns communism, liberalism, Shia, and Ahmadiyya (Chaplin 2017; Wahdah Islamiyah 2016). Nevertheless, in its 2016 *muktamar* (congress), Wahdah denounced terrorism and radicalism as a "serious threat" to the *umma* and the nation (Wahdah Islamiyah 2016).

Forum Umat Islam (FUI), on the other hand, was established after the fourth Kongres Umat Islam Indonesia (Congress of Indonesian Muslims), organized by the MUI in April 2005 (Munabari 2017, p. 5). The congress concluded with a "Jakarta Declaration" that proposed, among other things, the implementation of sharia. FUI was a forum dedicated to facilitating communication among various Islamist groups in implementing this mission. Among various groups involved in the FUI, the FPI could be considered the most active. FUI possessed a close relationship with HTI prior to the Monas incident in 2008.[7] FUI's involvement in that violent action — with strong support from FPI's militias — triggered HTI to cut off its relationship with FUI.

Interestingly, FUI embraces a similar slogan to FPI, "NKRI Bersyariah". The slogan, it seems, was adopted after a congress in 2013, attended by Rizieq Shihab (*Muslim Daily* August 2013). Accordingly, similar with FPI's perspective on NKRI Bersyariah, FUI does not perceive its commitment to the implementation of sharia to be contradictory with nationalism. Instead, the application of sharia reflects a correct interpretation of the first principle of Pancasila (Munabari 2017, p. 9). In addition, although FUI believes that democracy is alien to Islamic teachings, FUI declares its support to candidates in elections who are considered able to mainstream FUI's agenda of sharia implementation (ibid., p. 10).

Reformasi and the Liberalization of Religion

This section argues that the 1998 *reformasi* was immediately followed by initiatives to liberalize religious affairs by pro-democracy and human rights activists, NGOs, and international donors. The discourse of freedom of religion had a more crucial role in directing religious life in Indonesia. The framework is strongly intertwined with the discourse of liberal Islam — previously sidelined in Soeharto's last years — and the discourse on the war on terror. The emergence of these discourses resulted in the creation of institutions that favoured the interests of the reformists. These discourses framed the demands of political Islam as dangerous for democracy and human rights, theologically deviant, and threatening to national security and unity.

The political turmoil that followed the 1997 financial crisis altered the political configuration of the late Soeharto era. Despite political Islam's endeavours to back Soeharto and B.J. Habibie,[8] the New Order eventually collapsed and liberal Islam's leader, Abdurrahman Wahid, became president. Since the establishment of Ikatan Cendekiawan Muslim Indonesia (Indonesian Association of Muslim Intellectuals, ICMI) (Hefner 1993; Liddle 1996), Wahid had expressed his discontent with Soeharto's late policies on Islam, which he condemned as being sectarian and dangerously putting Indonesia's widely known pluralism in peril. In 1994, Wahid said "some members of ICMI ... are sectarian" (Barton 2002, p. 183). To counter this strategy, Wahid was involved in the creation of Forum for Democracy and led NU to be in opposition to the New Order (ibid., pp. 184–85). Wahid, however, was not a radical reformist. Crouch considers him — as well as Wahid's competitor, Megawati Sukarnoputri — as "moderate opposition" (Crouch 2015, p. 15), or "semi-opposition" according to Aspinall (2005) to the New Order government. During their presidencies, both Wahid and Megawati worked more to secure their political support rather than implementing radical measures to reform Indonesia's political institutions, such as limiting the military's influence in politics.[9]

After the New Order fell, popular forces and student movements, unfortunately, also suffered from dissolution. The radical organizations PRD, for instance, proved unable to compete in elections and further experienced internal rifts that significantly weakened its power (Lane 2008). This situation provided moderate reformists with an opportunity to navigate the crafting of democratic institutions in Indonesia. As observed by Savirani and Tornquist (Savirani and Tornquist 2015, p. 1), in the context of 1998 Indonesia, the idea was "to foster a pact of moderate reformers who could contain both reactionary forces and radical popular movements by combining economic liberties, civil society, free and fair elections and the establishment of institutions (usually defined as rules of the game) with which moderates could live".

These moderate-directed reforms established several political institutions related to the governance of religion in the public sphere. In general, these reforms revolved around attempts to ensure broader religious freedom. This was done by introducing the idea of civil and political rights into the political arena. These instruments were implemented relatively early compared to other democratic institutions (Subono 2007, p. 40). For instance, in 1998, during Habibie's administration, the MPR decided to ratify international human rights instruments, resulting in Law No. 39/1999 on human rights, which formally recognized the rights of Indonesian citizens, including, among others, freedom of belief and religious expression. In 2000, the discourse on human rights — including on religious freedom — was incorporated into the second amendment of Indonesia's constitution, as described below. Indonesia further adopted the International Covenant on Civil and Political Rights and International Covenant on Economic, Social, and Cultural Rights in the following years (Bagir 2013, pp. 1–2).

Fenwick (2016, pp. 72–75) offers an overview on the basic structure of this reform. Article 29 of the constitution — which already instructed the state to protect citizens' "freedom of worship" — was retained. Article 28E, however, was added to further address the issue. Articles 28E(1) and (2) respectively stated that "every person shall be free to choose and to practise the religion of his/her own choice ..." and "every person shall have the right of the freedom to believe his/her faith, and to express his/her views and thoughts, in accordance with his/her conscience". The amended constitution also emphasized that this right is non-derogable via Article 28I. Similar emphasis was previously made in Law No. 39/1999. Article 22 explicated that a citizen holds "the right to freedom to choose his religion and to worship according to the teachings of his religion and beliefs", as well as instructing the state to guarantee such freedom.

The discourse of freedom of religion marked a novel stage in the governance of religion in Indonesia. Bagir considers the concept of freedom of religion as a "new language in the attempt to provide a better framework for the management of the rich diversity of religious expressions in Indonesia" (Bagir 2014, p. 27; see also Hefner 2013). The rise of the concept of freedom of religion was a part of Indonesia's liberalization during *reformasi*. It was indicative of gradual adherence to the prevailing global discourse and legal regimes on religion. The concept of freedom of religion itself was built around the presupposition that individuals' beliefs were decided autonomously and voluntarily in an environment within which multiple religions were available. In such a situation, the primary task of the state was to ensure that this "religious marketplace" — to borrow Hurd's words — prevailed and operated properly (Hurd 2015, p. 54).

Freedom of religion, therefore, required the state to act in a specific manner. It had to refrain from interference into the religious life of citizens, allow the presence of various religious beliefs, provide citizens with protection in expressing their beliefs, prohibit — even with coercion — attempts to limit citizens' freedom, and, most importantly, maintain its "neutrality". Neutrality, in this sense, was supposed to be reflected in the state's avoidance of unequal treatment of different religious beliefs, resulting in the state's withdrawal from religious affairs. By implication, the discourse of freedom of religion actually did not create a completely neutral state. It instead emphasized the importance of capturing state machinery and utilizing it for purposes set by the discourse.

Freedom of religion, however, was not the only discourse animating the reform of the institutions. Liberal Islamic thinking — which was sidelined during the last decade of Soeharto's reign — acquired a crucial role post-*reformasi* and reinforced the message of freedom of religion (see, for example, Rachman 2010*a*; Rachman 2010*b*). Alongside organizations like Yayasan Paramadina (Paramadina Foundation) or Lembaga Kajian Islam dan Sosial (Institute for Islamic and Social Studies), the exponents of Jaringan Islam Liberal (Liberal Islam Network, JIL), a loose network of Islamic scholars and activists, were arguably the most prominent actors in the dissemination of the liberal Islam narrative. As observed by van Bruinessen, JIL was the intellectual "heir" of Nurcholish Madjid and Abdurrahman Wahid, prominent advocates of the compatibility of Islam, nation-state, and democracy during the New Order (van Bruinessen 2013). The discourse of liberal Islam shared some of the basic tenets of the concept of freedom of religion.

For instance, liberal Islam's emphasis on the importance of separating religion from politics went hand in hand with freedom of religion's demand for the withdrawal of the state from religious affairs. More importantly, both of the discourses advocated the neutrality of the state (van Bruinessen 2006, p. 22). Liberal Islam painfully contested argumentations that supported the establishment of an Islamic state by trying to demonstrate that Islam did not offer religious teachings related to politics. This reasoning echoed the spirit of the discourse of freedom of religion, which, as previously discussed, encouraged the state to remain neutral, created an environment supportive of the coexistence of different religions.

In addition to the discourse of freedom of religion and liberal Islam, the discourse of war on terrorism was also influential in crafting the landscape of governance of religion in post-*reformasi* Indonesia. Particularly after the 9/11 attack and a series of terrorist assaults in Indonesia in the early 2000s, the distinction between the "good" and "bad" Muslims began to proliferate (Hiariej et al. 2017, pp. 317–19; see also Mamdani 2005). This distinction relied upon the assumption that terrorism was caused mostly by bad Muslims who were fanatical in their religious understanding. In opposition to this category, the good Muslims were represented as moderates who challenged the influence of bad Muslims. Within this discourse, the role of the state was to counter terrorism to maintain order: to intercept terrorist activities and to curb the spread of terrorist ideology. Although this discourse was not identical with that on freedom of religion and liberal Islam, it shared a similar perspective that countering the radical understanding of religion was necessary. In 2004, Megawati Sukarnoputri asked the Department of Religion to be vigilant toward "fanatics" who considered the annihilation of other religious beliefs as their "holy task" (*Tempo* 2004).

The interplay between the discourse of freedom of religion, liberal Islam, and war on terror became the main force of reform in governance of religion post-*reformasi*. This complex array of discourses brought about initiatives that aimed to engineer religious life according to their ideals. NGOs and academic think tanks — such as the Wahid Institute, Setara Institute, and Centre for Religious and Cross-Cultural Studies at Universitas Gadjah Mada — monitored the state of freedom of religion in Indonesia. Their reports attempted not only to measure the degree of freedom of religion, but also to identify actors responsible for violating that freedom. Interestingly, the reports by the Wahid Institute, for example, placed the state apparatus as one of the most responsible violators. These violations, according to the 2014 report, were mostly conducted by police, local government, and village officials (Wahid Institute 2014, pp. 21–22). The report subsequently proposed that the government — particularly the police — maintain neutrality and ensure that law enforcement was functioning properly against the offenders' freedom of religion (ibid., pp. 35–36). In addition, these actors tried to alter the government's approach by providing the police with training to handle religious conflicts and by conducting research to improve government's performance (see, for example, Panggabean et al. 2014). These efforts were coupled with endeavours to influence the government to adopt regulations to better protect citizens' freedom of religion (Bagir 2014).

There were also campaigns to combat the influence of conservative teachings of religion. These efforts were amplified particularly after the 9/11 attack and series of terrorist assaults in Indonesia. NGOs and academic think tanks attempted to develop an alternative understanding of Islam that might delegitimize conservative teachings. To some extent, these endeavours were similar to previous efforts during the New Order regime, when liberal Islam thinkers tried to counter the demand for an Islamic state. Actors in post-*reformasi* Indonesia still dealt with similar issues and, in several circumstances, took resources from past liberal Islam thinkers. Notable initiatives from the Maarif Institute, for example, attempted to demonstrate that the idea of *kebhinekaan* (diversity) was compatible with Islam — including electing non-Muslims as leaders. The book, *Fikih Kebhinekaan* (The Fiqh [Law] of Diversity), scrutinized the Madinah Charter to show that the concept of *umma* was used to refer to both Muslims and non-Muslims, thus indicating that Islam conceives them as equal (Baidhawy 2015, pp. 135–38). It also proposed theological arguments to denounce teachings that prohibited Muslims from voting for non-Muslim leaders (Dzuhayatin 2015, pp. 310–16). NGOs, like Setara Institute and Wahid Foundation, went further by openly calling political Islam organizations — FPI and HTI for example — "radical" (CNN 2018; *Tempo* January 2017). Setara even accused the Aksi Bela Islam (Action to Defend Islam)[10] as an arena for the revival of *jihadist* groups and terrorism. According to Setara, the presence of Bachtiar Nasir and Zaitun Rasmin — both accused by Setara of being sponsored by Wahhabism — was an important indication of this development (RMOL 2016). This discourse — proposed largely by pro-democracy and human rights as well as liberal Islam activists — not only challenges the conservative teachings promoted by political Islam groups but also signals that political Islam activists are dangerous for national stability, unity, and democracy.

This concern is, interestingly, shared by the government apparatus. Security concerns over the emergence of terrorism in Indonesia have encouraged the state to strengthen its participation in these efforts. The Badan Nasional Penanggulangan Terorisme (National Agency for Combating Terrorism, BNPT), established in 2010, actively engaged in initiatives to disseminate terrorist counter-narratives. BNPT's approach aims to stimulate the growth of "moderate and tolerant understanding" within "the framework of NKRI" while preventing the spread of "radical terrorist ideology" (BNPT n.d.). Understandably, prior to the Aksi Bela Islam in December 2016, the head of BNPT, Suhardi Alius, made a comment similar to that of civil society. He said, for instance, that the demonstration might be "infiltrated by terrorist groups" and asked people to protect national unity and harmonious relationships between religions (*Jawa Pos* 2016; *Kompas* 2016). Besides this similar style of analysis, BNPT also often relies on the discourse of liberal Islam to complement its nationalist discourse to show that a radical interpretation of Islam is erroneous and, subsequently, to scorn people's desire to displace the Indonesian government with an Islamic state or be involved in *jihad* against non-Muslims. BNPT, however, rarely uses the discourse of freedom of religion.

The role of the state in the governance of religion post-*reformasi* is therefore ambiguous. Activists and scholars who strongly believed in freedom of religion and a liberal–progressive interpretation of Islam attempted to use the moment to transform key institutions in this area. They tried to introduce a new conception on how government was supposed to deal with religious affairs. The concept was largely accepted formally, resulting in the creation of several institutions expected to support the conduct of religious affairs in democratizing Indonesia. In his assessment of the progress of democratization, Subono even argued that civil and political rights — including the freedom of religion — developed at a much greater pace than other institutions (Subono 2007, p. 40).

This situation exposes the nature of reform of governance of religion post-*reformasi*. Although institutions were reformed, implementation was largely stalled. Instead, the state's concern over security stimulated a new area of collaboration between the state and activists and scholars. The need to contest the influence of terrorism compelled them to craft a strategic alliance. This collaboration was advantageous for activists since it provided them with the opportunity to further influence state's perspective and approach on religious affairs. It also potentially enabled them to acquire resources to combat political Islam activists. On the other hand, this collaboration was crucial for the state because the activists and scholars provided it with an ideological lexicon that was thought necessary to weaken terrorism. This alliance has proven to be limited, however. Although the activists and the state could work collaboratively in constraining the spread of radical interpretation of Islam, this cooperation did not run very well in areas that were also prioritized by the reformers, such as the protection of minority rights or the retraction of anti-blasphemy law. Understandably, organizations that are supportive of the government's endeavours in countering radicalism also offer scathing criticisms of its performance in protecting freedom of religion. These criticisms are directed, mainly, to the government's tacit involvement in human rights violations and inability to create legal frameworks that are supportive of freedom of religion (*Kompas*, July 2017; *Tribun* 2017).

Despite these limitations, democratic reform has stimulated the formation of political institutions that foster a new pattern of religious life. The combination of discourse of freedom of religion, liberal Islam, and war on terrorism, moreover, results in the negative framing of conservative teaching of Islam. Conservative demands are perceived to be threatening to democracy, theologically deviant, inclined to violence, and incompatible with national unity. Conservative aspiration is, in short, illegitimate in Indonesia's political arena.

Joko Widodo's ascendancy to power is interesting in this context. Compared to his predecessors, Widodo showed a possibility of widening the alliance between activists and the state. His manifesto identified intolerance as one of Indonesia's three main problems. Jokowi further criticized the state's inability to respect and manage differences within society and prevent the growth of hatred, discrimination, and violence against the other (Widodo and Kalla 2014, pp. 1–2). This rhetoric — which could be understood, in part, as an effect of Widodo's close relationship with pro-democracy activists — enabled Jokowi to build an image that emphasized his commitment to Pancasila and diversity during the 2014 presidential election campaign.

This strategy required Widodo to demarcate himself starkly from the conservative groups, including political Islam activists. He was compelled to disseminate a rhetoric that delegitimized the demand of conservative groups. Widodo, for instance, strongly supported NU's "Islam Nusantara" narrative. Islam Nusantara is "an interpretation of Islam that takes into account local Indonesian customs in forming its fiqh [law]" or, to use Faturrahman's words, "Islam yang terindegenisasi" (Islam with indigenization) (Fachrudin 2015; NU April 2015). Widodo frequently associates Islam Nusantara with the idea of "tolerance" and "national unity" (*Republika* June 2015). He also uses the concept to distinguish Indonesia from war-torn Islamic countries like Syria, Iraq, or Libya (NU June 2015). For him, it is the unique nature of Islam in Indonesia that enables the country to avoid violent crisis. In addition to this narrative, Lukman Hakim Saifuddin, the Minister for Religion, also adopted a more empathetic approach to religious minority issues by inviting minority groups for discussion and bolstering the relationship between activists and government on religious harmony issues (*detikNews* 2014).

Widodo's controversial decision to ban HTI could also be read through this perspective. The government decided on the ban in July 2017, although the intention had been publicly declared in May by Wiranto, Coordinating Minister for Political, Legal, and Security Affairs. Wiranto contended that HTI's activities of promoting caliphate threatened "the security and order of society and the unity of NKRI". The purpose of the disbanding was to "protect the unity of the nation, based on Pancasila and Undang-Undang Dasar (National Constitution) 1945" (CNN Indonesia May 2017). Also, a press release by the Ministry of Law and Human Rights stated that HTI violates Indonesian ideology and law. By banning HTI, Widodo aimed to demonstrate his strong allegiance to the idea of Indonesia's pluralism. Furthermore, the action signalled that Widodo perceived HTI's demand — gradually introducing the idea of caliphate to trigger political changes — to be illegitimate. He aimed to show that he closely followed the prescription of pro-*reformasi* activists in dealing with public religious affairs.

Widodo's decision to implement Peraturan Pemerintah Pengganti Undang-Undang tentang Organisasi Kemasyarakatan (Government

Regulation on Community Organization, Perpu Ormas) was also in line with this approach. In adopting the policy, Widodo attempted to limit the movements of political Islam groups while simultaneously demonstrating his commitment to national unity in order to garner wider support. For example, it was through this decision that he secured support from NU (*Tempo* October 2017).

Widodo's manoeuvre strengthened the relationship between the state and activists. He reinforced the opposition to conservative aspirations proposed by the discourse of freedom of religion, liberal Islam, and the war on terror. This strategy, however, was made at the expense of further exclusion of conservative demands from the political arena. This changing strategic context forced political Islam groups to alter their approach.

Overcoming Exclusion: Political Islam's Shift of Strategies

This section is concerned with the way in which political Islam groups responded to the liberalizing of post-*reformasi* Indonesia. It attempts to demonstrate that political Islam activists are generally excluded from the institutions that emerged after *reformasi*. Initially, they tried to contest the transformation by not only being reluctant to comply with the rules, but also by exploiting multiple flaws within institutions to advance their interests. The groups, however, gradually adopted different approaches, resulting in their increasing engagement with democratic rules.

Following the resignation of Soeharto, political Islam activists tried to back Habibie, mainly through ICMI. Although pressure on Habibie was increasing, particularly due to a series of protests conducted by students and popular forces, the groups were reluctant to dissolve their strategic alliance with him. After all, political Islam movements had just acquired access to the state during the last decade of New Order reign after fighting for that status for two decades. Political Islam activists' strategic alliance with the regime had encouraged them to actively spread the view that the New Order's political and economic turmoil was deliberately created by the enemies of Islam. During this short period, the interpretation of Islam proposed by the groups became the "favoured Muslim discourse" (a term coined by van Bruinessen 2009) due to its ability to contest the demands of the pro-democracy movement. As further discussed below, organizations such as MUI and Komite Indonesia untuk Solidaritas dengan Dunia Islam (Indonesian Committee for Solidarity with the Islamic World, KISDI) disputed the growing demand for democratic reform by accusing democracy of being Western-centric.

The failure of political Islam movements to back the New Order and to gain significant representation in the MPR in the following election inevitably altered the situation. Organizations like KISDI or ICMI that were dominant in the last decade of the New Order and even rallied behind Soeharto and Habibie were no longer able to access the state and, consequently, were forced to the margins of the political arena. However, at this moment of democratic transition, various Islamist organizations emerged (for example, FPI and Majelis Mujahidin Indonesia [Indonesian Mujahideen Council] and, later on, FUI), formalized into Ormas (Wahdah Islamiyah), or emerged after ending their clandestine phase (HTI).

Despite their theological differences, these organizations in general aimed to implement their idea of Islamic teachings. Although this standpoint was already present during Soeharto's administration, these groups' overt voicing of their demands was remarkable — something that was unthinkable under the New Order, particularly prior to the 1990s. This trend, in part, could be perceived as a continuation of late developments in the New Order reign, when conservative aspirations were increasingly allowed space by the regime. The discourse proposed by these organizations, for instance, bore a resemblance to the narratives that emerged from the early 1990s until the decline of Soeharto's order, albeit, in several dimensions, they tended to a more radical tone. In this regard, although the organization could not be subsumed under the category of political Islam used by this article, Laskar Jihad was an extreme example (Azca 2011; Hassan 2008). It not only accused the Wahid government of being infidel due to its lack of compliance with an Islamic moral order, but also sent militias to intervene in communal conflicts in Ambon and Poso. The militia recruitment was interesting because Laskar Jihad overtly campaigned through public recitations — even mass gatherings in Jakarta — about the importance of fighting infidels and establishing a fully Islamic order in Indonesia. The example of Laskar Jihad demonstrates that Islamists' political expression was largely unrestrained during the early years of democratic transition: FPI rallied for the restoration of the Jakarta

Charter in 2001, while HTI organized a conference on the restoration of caliphate attended by thousands of people in 2000.

However, there is an important distinction between the discourse promoted by political Islam movements in the early phase of reform and the last years of the New Order. In the last decade of Soeharto, political Islam groups mostly worked to support the interests of the regime. KISDI's campaigns during these years were focused on countering the concept of liberal democracy and human rights by framing them as Western inventions that were not only alien to Islam but also threatening to it. KISDI also propagated that the human rights violation accusations in East Timor against Soeharto were devised by "enemies of Islam" — referring to Western countries, Israel, and Indonesian Chinese and Christians — while a DDII supporter argued that the 1998 financial crisis was actually caused by the "rats", namely the Indonesian Chinese (Hefner 2002, p. 759). MUI even accused anti-Habibie protesters of being communists (ibid.). All of these moves reflected political Islam groups' proximity to the state. In Hefner's words, the moves were a part of "repressive 'scaling down'" of "democratic Islam" (ibid.). It is possible, however, to understand this as a part of Soeharto's strategy for countering the demand for democratic reform.

Compared to that phase, the demands advanced by political Islam movements after *reformasi* indicate considerable distance between them and the state. The groups repetitively argued that the state was not sufficiently committed to addressing problems that threatened the interests of Muslim. FPI's raids, for example, were usually framed as a response to the state's inability to control vices (*Liputan6* 2003). Similar statements were issued by FPI and HTI when the Cikeusik killings — the raid against Ahmadiyya[11] in Banten — occurred in 2011. The state was again portrayed as the main actor that enabled the violence to happen by refusing to disband Ahmadiyya (Hidayatullah February 2011; HTI 2011).

In the midst of this situation, the role of MUI became increasingly crucial for the movements to increase their legitimacy, amplify their voices, and strengthen their leverage. MUI was established in 1975 by Soeharto as a semi-official institution of Indonesian *ulama*. Between 1975 and 2000, MUI saw itself mostly as the *khadim al-hukumah* (servant of the government). It rarely intervened in the public sphere or issued controversial *fatwa*. However, MUI altered its role after 2000. It changed its ideology from Pancasila to Islam, positioned itself as the "servant of the umma", and attributed "the police of aqidah" as its role (Ichwan 2013, p. 61). Moreover, MUI performed as a "tent" — "not only a place for sharing ideas and aspirations but [one that] builds consensus and collective agreement on matters related to the affairs of Muslims" (Hasyim 2016, p. 215).

In 2005, MUI issued a *"haram" fatwa* on "secularism, pluralism, and liberalism", labelled Ahmadiyya as deviant, and asked the state to ban the belief. This shift in MUI could be understood as an effect of growing influence of political Islam movements within the organization. By 2005, for instance, members of HTI and FUI began to be represented within the council (Ichwan 2013, p. 69). The movements — particularly FPI and FUI — also organized multiple rallies to support MUI's *fatwa*, confirming the close links between these organizations and MUI.

Political Islam groups' positions on these issues demonstrated their resistance to the progress of liberalization. Against the prevailing discourse of freedom of religion, the groups condemned liberalism, pluralism, and minority groups. Against the growth of democratic institutions and rhetoric, HTI denounced the system as *"haram"*, while Rizieq Shihab said that adopting democracy is worse than eating pork. Similarly, against the growing anxiety about terrorism, the groups articulated suspicions of the role of the United States in fabricating a terror stigma against Muslims (Hidayatullah 2002).

This disengagement, however, limited the space for the groups to influence national politics. The distance between political Islam movements and the state was reflected in the groups' choice of tactics. FPI and FUI usually relied on mass mobilizations to increase their leverage. The groups also occasionally declared their support for certain candidates in the elections — for example, FUI supported Jusuf Kalla and Wiranto in 2009, while FPI directed support to PBB, PPP, and PKS in 2014. Although these limited involvements in electoral politics might stem from their theological positions, this minimal interaction also denotes the movements' inability to steer the direction of national politics. This lack of power was recognized by the groups. On the one hand, they declared that democracy was worse than *musyawarah*. Yet they also encouraged Muslims to elect sharia-committed leaders to avoid greater difficulty for Muslims (*Arrahmah* 2013; *Al Balagh* 2009). The movements were fully aware of this dilemma: disengagement might preserve the doctrinal purity of the movements, yet they would not be able to attain their goals.

Widodo's movement to reinforce their exclusion made the situation more difficult for political Islam. The groups confronted two major difficulties. First, there were no institutions that could be readily exploited to advance their interests. The anti-blasphemy law and MUI were useful to contest liberalization efforts, but their ability to advance the interests of political Islam was limited. The prevailing institutions imposed the logic of equality among citizens, regardless of their religion. This design made it difficult for religiously inspired — often sectarian — aspirants to access democratic institutions. Second, the dominant discursive schemas did not favour conservative political expression. In order to be recognized as a legitimate player within the political arena, it was necessary for everyone to comply with the standard rules: acknowledge democratic rules, the ideals of pluralism, and the necessity of preserving stability and national unity. The aspirations of political Islam did not fit well with this standard.

In navigating this landscape, political Islam movements made two important strategic decisions. First, the groups tried to utilize the existing democratic institutions to improve their access. Second, the groups also adjusted their ideological framework and repertoire of actions. All of these adjustments, however, were made in order to eventually realize their conservative aspirations.

Aksi Bela Islam could illustrate this shift. Aksi Bela Islam was a series of mass demonstrations at the end of 2016 and early 2017. The trigger of the protests was Basuki Tjahaja Purnama's (Jakarta's governor) statement in Kepulauan Seribu which was accused of defaming the 5:51 verse of the Koran. According to conservative interpretations, the verse forbids Muslims to elect non-Muslim leaders. The verse had been used intensively by political Islam movements in Jakarta to prevent Purnama — a Chinese Christian — from being re-elected in 2017. The protests were coalesced as a newly formed grouping, Gerakan Nasional Pengawal Fatwa MUI (National Movement to Safeguard MUI's Fatwa, GNPF-MUI). It was led by figures like Rizieq Shihab (FPI), Bachtiar Nasir (MIUMI), Muhammad al-Khaththath (FUI), and Zaitun Rasmin (Wahdah). In addition to these organizations, HTI and various Majelis Dzikir (Dzikir Groups) also joined the campaign (IPAC 2018, p. 3).

The main demand of this coalition was the imprisonment of Purnama for blaspheming against Islam. However, prior to his statement, these groups had already organized campaigns to prevent Purnama from winning the election. The argumentation to support this position was quite familiar: Purnama was a Christian, and Islam disallowed Muslims from electing non-Muslim leaders. Already in August 2016, HTI released a statement asking Muslims to "fight against candidates who are Kafir" (HTI 2016), while MIUMI began similar initiatives around June and July 2016 (ibid., p. 16). FPI even organized a demonstration in July 2014 for a similar purpose (ibid., p. 15).

This demand was strongly conservative. Religious blasphemy has long been anathema for democratic systems since it limits freedom of expression. Political Islam groups' rejection of non-Muslim candidates also did not fit into a democratic framework, where all citizens, regardless of their religion, are considered equal. The groups' hostility to non-Muslim candidates, arguably, also violated the principle of national unity and diversity. As discussed in the previous section, pro-democracy and Islamic activists voiced these criticisms of Aksi Bela Islam. Some of them went even further by arguing that the protests were infiltrated by terrorist groups and dangerous for national order (RMOL 2016). The government began largely from a similar perspective. Widodo launched the "Saya Indonesia, Saya Pancasila" (I am Indonesia, I am Pancasila) campaign (*Kompas* May 2017*a*) and formed Unit Kerja Presiden Pembinaan Ideologi Pancasila (Presidential Working Unit for the Development of Pancasila Ideology) in May 2017 (*Kompas* May 2017*b*). Saying that Pancasila was the "unifier of state and nation", Widodo tacitly assumed that Aksi Bela Islam had threatened national order and unity (*Kompas* May 2017*a*).

Political Islam movements were aware of these accusations and their potential impacts on the legitimacy and safety of the protests. In December 2016, GNPF-MUI released a statement that said that Muslims were "often accused of being nationalists, anti-Pancasila, anti-Bhinneka Tunggal Ika". However, Aksi Bela Islam was an expression of "Islamic unity that aims to strengthen Bhinneka Tunggal Ika based on the original values of the National Constitution" (GNPF-MUI December 2016*a*; CNN Indonesia December 2017). Aksi Bela Islam was regarded as an attempt to preserve *kebhinnekaan* because it encouraged people to respect the beliefs of other religions. GNPF-MUI also affirmed that the movement did not aim to topple the government (GNPF-MUI

December 2016*b*). Another remark made by Nasir also rejected the argument that GNPF-MUI contradicted democracy. For him, electing leaders based on personal beliefs did not violate the principle of democracy (*Republika* 2017).

During Aksi Bela Islam, this rhetoric enabled the movement to avoid government repression and garner support from the wider Islamic community. Framing the action as an expression of citizenship, democratic activism, and desire to preserve the unity of the nation, would make repressive measures be seen as illegitimate. At the same moment, it attracted sympathy from the Muslim community that was disengaged from political Islam movements prior to Aksi Bela Islam, particularly because of activists' and government's framing of the groups as radical, violent, and dangerous. To detach the movements from this image, FPI, HTI, and GNPF-MUI strongly condemned Sarinah and Kampung Melayu bombings in 2016 and 2017 (DPP FPI 2016; GNPF-MUI 2017). As a comparison, in 2008 Rizieq Shihab said that Amrozi was a *syahid* (martyr) when he was executed (*Eramuslim* 2008). Although this difference might be related to the affiliation of the perpetrators (ISIS in Sarinah versus Jemaah Islamiyah in Bali Bombing I), this illustration shows how FPI changed its rhetoric on violence. Wahdah also rejected terrorism and radicalism, accusing them of being threats to the unity of the nation and *umma* (Wahdah Islamiyah 2016).

Political Islam groups also no longer simply give vocal support to candidates considered to be Islamic. Nasir advocates that movements form commissions of *ulama* that will decide, on behalf of the *umma*, which candidates fulfil the criteria of being Islamic. The decision will be made based on *musyawarah*, which is to be informed by Islamic teachings (Kiblat TV 2018; *Republika* 2018). This move reflects political Islam's growing eagerness to be involved in elections. As a comparison, Nasir made a comment in 2014 that democracy was *shirik* (replaced the position of God) (TVOne 2014). Nasir's experimental strategy indicates a willingness to synthesize Islamic teachings and a democratic environment. Similarly, in recent years, Wahdah flirted with the idea of *wasathiyah* democracy as, Wahdah claimed, a middle ground between competing conceptions of democracy (Wahdah Islamiyah 2016). Despite the lack of clarity of this idea, its rise within Wahdah's narrative is interesting, for Wahdah previously denounced democracy due to its man-made character (*Al Balagh* 2009).

Political Islam's recent moves show that the groups have begun to move beyond the disengagement strategy. Aware of their relatively marginal position, the groups adopted an approach that enabled them to interact more closely with democratic infrastructure. The groups amplify the emphasis on national unity, distance themselves from violence, and experiment with strategy that balance religious orthodoxy with democratic politics. These manoeuvres are taken to counter the hostile framing of conservative Islam by pro-democracy activists and the state security apparatus and to enable the groups to move closer to the centre of national politics.

Conclusion

This chapter demonstrates that the strategy of political Islam movements in Indonesia is shifting. While the groups were previously reluctant to engage with the institutions and discourse of democracy, the groups have begun to have a closer interaction with them. This change occurs, in part, due to the changing strategic context of Indonesian politics, particularly after *reformasi*. Following the rise of democratic institutions and discourse, political Islam groups found that the opportunity to advance their interests was limited. Prevailing institutions and discourse do not benefit them and, instead, tend to have an exclusionary attitude toward conservative aspirations. In these circumstances, the movements considered that a closer engagement with democracy might increase their opportunities.

The future of these movements is nonetheless uncertain. In the last two years, the coalition of GNPF-MUI has suffered from internal frictions (IPAC 2018), the exile of Rizieq Shihab, and the disbanding of HTI. These developments have inevitably reduced the power of the movements. Additionally, the disbanding of HTI and the implementation of Perpu Ormas signal that the government will take stricter measures to limit political Islam. Within this framework, the pressure will be greater for the movements to ensure their compatibility with national ideology, not to mention that the government will have the power to interpret Pancasila. HTI's disbanding was caused by its inability to shift its approach, partly due to its ideological inflexibility. However, MIUMI, FPI, FUI, and Wahdah are able to show greater flexibility to ensure their survival. It is the groups' flexibility in navigating the complex landscape of politics that, probably, could enable them to further attain their interests.

NOTES

1. Following the rift between Soeharto and the armed forces, Soeharto started to develop a closer relationship with political Islam activists. In the mid-1980s, Soeharto began to implement policies favouring Islamists' aspirations. As observed by Liddle, for instance, *jilbab* was no longer prohibited in public schools, an Islamic court was established, Islamic family law was codified, while interfaith marriage was forbidden. Soeharto also performed the *hajj* ritual in 1990 to demonstrate his devotion to Islam. More importantly, Soeharto encouraged the establishment of ICMI to garner support from conservative Muslims. See Liddle (1996).
2. I use the term "liberal" over "progressive" because I associate "progressive Islam" with a rising stream of interpretation of Islam in Indonesia which possesses a strong sensitivity to class struggles. See Al Fayyadl (2015).
3. Quoted by Jamhari and Jahroni (2004), in Ward (2009), p. 152.
4. Ward (2009), p. 155. Yusanto, however, allowed Muslims to be involved in elections insofar as they aim to remove the democratic system. During the Jakarta gubernatorial election, HTI also released a statement that prohibited Muslims electing non-Muslim candidates (*Islamedia* 2013; HTI 2016).
5. Some MIUMI founders like Adian Husaini, Adnin Armas, and Fahmi Zarkasyi were already involved in the establishment of INSISTS (Institute for the Study of Islamic Thought and Civilizations) in Kuala Lumpur in 2003. See Makin (2017), p. 25.
6. Asas Tunggal was a regulation issued by the New Order requiring mass-based organizations to use Pancasila as their sole foundation, effectively limiting the opportunity for Islamic political parties and organizations to claim their Islamic status (Sukma 2003, p. 59).
7. The Monas incident refers to the attack organized by Islamist paramilitary groups on a peaceful protest to support the rights of Ahmadiyya minorities.
8. KISDI, for example, campaigned that the financial crisis was fabricated by the West. In support of Habibie, MUI also labelled demonstrations against Habibie as masterminded by communists (Hefner 2002, p. 759).
9. Despite his efforts to limit the military's influence, Wahid resorted to military support when his position as president was threatened. He also allowed increasing repression by the military in Aceh and Papua (Crouch 2015, pp. 31–32).

10. Aksi Bela Islam was a series of demonstrations in Jakarta to protest against Basuki Tjahaja Purnama, Jakarta's governor, for his allegedly blasphemous statements against Islam. The largest protests were organized on 4 November and 2 December 2016.

11. Although Ahmadiyya consider themselves to be Muslim, they are regarded as heretics in Indonesia; the religion is banned in several provinces. In 2008, the Ministry of Religion, Ministry of Internal Affairs, and Attorney General's Office issued a joint decree that forbade the dissemination of Ahmadiyya's teachings. See Burhani (2014), p. 143.

REFERENCES

Abuza, Zachary. *Political Islam and Violence in Indonesia.* London: Routledge, 2007.

Ahnaf, Muhammad. "Between Revolution and Reform: The Future of Hizbut Tahrir Indonesia". *Dynamics of Asymmetric Conflict: Pathways toward Terrorism and Genocide* 2, no. 2 (2009).

Al Balagh. "Kaum Muslimin di antara Inkubasi Sekularisme dan Doktrin Demokrasi", 17 April 2009.

Al Fayyadl, Muhammad. "Apa itu Islam Progresif?". *Islam Bergerak,* 10 July 2015.

Al-Waie. "Khilafah Menjadikan Kita Kuat", 2 December 2014.

Arrahmah. "Gus Hamid: Demokrasi Hilangkan Otoritas Pemimpin, Ulama, dan Intelektual", 25 March 2013*a*.

――――. "Sekjen MIUMI: Indonesia Dijajah Demokrasi", 11 March 2013*b*.

――――. "Sikap FPI Pemilu 2014: Darurat Bagi Umat Islam", 31 August 2013.

Aspinall, Edward. *Opposing Suharto: Compromise, Resistance, and Regime Change in Indonesia.* Stanford: Stanford University Press, 2005.

Ayoob, Mohammed. "Political Islam: Image and Reality". *World Policy Journal* (Fall 2004): 1.

Azca, Najib. "After Jihad: A Biographical Approach to Passionate Politics in Indonesia". Dissertation, University of Amsterdam, 2011.

Bagir, Zainal Abidin. "Defamation of Religion Law in Post-*Reformasi* Indonesia: Is Revision Possible?". *Australian Journal of Asian Law* 13, no. 2, Article 3 (2013).

――――. "Advocacy for Religious Freedom in Democratizing Indonesia". *Review of Faith and International Affairs* 12, no. 4 (2014).

Baidhawy, Zakiyuddin. "Piagam Madinah dan Pancasila: Prinsip-Prinsip Kehidupan Bersama dalam Berbangsa dan Bernegara". In *Fikih Kebhinekaan,* edited by Wawan Gunawan Abd. Wahid, Muhammad Darraz, and Ahmad Fuad Fanani. Bandung: Mizan and Maarif Institute, 2015.

Barton, Greg. *Abdurrahman Wahid: Muslim Democrat, Indonesian President.* Sydney: UNSW Press, 2002.

Bayat, Asef. "Islam and Democracy: What is the Real Question?". *ISIM Papers* 8. Amsterdam: Amsterdam University Press, 2007.

BBC Indonesia. "Front Pembela Islam: Indonesia 'bukan negara demokrasi'", 20 January 2017.

BNPT. "Strategi". <https://damailahindonesiaku.com/kebijakan/negara/strategi/>, n.d.

———. "Deradikalisasi". <https://damailahindonesiaku.com/deradikalisasi/>, n.d.

Burhani, Ahmad Najib. "Hating the Ahmadiyya: The Place of 'Heretics' in Contemporary Indonesian Muslim Society". *Contemporary Islam* 8, no. 2 (2014): 133–52.

Chaplin, Chris. "Islam and Citizenship". *Inside Indonesia* 129 (2017).

———. "Salafi Islamic Piety as Civic Activisim: Wahdah Islamiyah and Differentiated Citizenship in Indonesia". *Citizenship Studies* 22, no. 2 (2018).

CNN Indonesia. "Wiranto: Langkah Hukum Diambil untuk Bubarkan HTI", 8 May 2017.

———. "Rizieq Dorong Konsep NKRI Bersyariah di Reuni Alumni 212", 2 December 2017.

———. "Wahid Foundation: Mayoritas Muslim Antijihad Kekerasan", 30 January 2018.

Crouch, Harold. *Political Reform in Indonesia After Soeharto*. Singapore: Institute of Southeast Asian Studies, 2015.

detikNews. "Baasyir dan Habib Rizieq Desak SKB Ahmadiyah Dikeluarkan", 3 June 2008.

———. "Kisah Menag Lukman Hakim Bertemu Kelompok Minoritas", 17 July 2014.

DPP FPI. "Maklumat FPI tentang Pemilihan Presiden 2014". Press release, 4 June 2014.

———. "Pernyataan Sikap DPP FPI Terkait Bom Jakarta", 14 January 2016.

Dzuhayatin, Siti Ruhaini. "Islam, Kepemimpinan Non-Muslim dan Hak Asasi Manusia". In *Fikih Kebhinekaan*, edited by Wawan Gunawan Abd. Wahid, Muhammad Darraz, and Ahmad Fuad Fanani. Bandung: Mizan and Maarif Institute, 2015.

Eramuslim. "Habib Riziq Shihab: Amrozi cs Min Ahlil Khoir", 12 November 2008.

Fachrudin, Azis Anwar. "The Face of Islam Nusantara". *Jakarta Post*, 24 July 2015.

Fealy, Greg. "Hizbut Tahrir in Indonesia: Seeking a 'Total' Islamic Identity". In *Islam and Political Violence: Muslim Diaspora and Radicalism in the West*, edited by Shahram Akbarzadeh and Fethi Mansouri. London: IB Tauris, 2010.

Fenwick, Stewart. "Faith and Freedom in Indonesian Law: Liberal Pluralism, Religion, and the Democratic State". In *Religion, Law, and Intolerance in Indonesia*, edited by Tim Lindsey and Helen Pausacker. Oxon: Routledge, 2016.

GNPF-MUI. "Esensi Aksi Bela Islam 3". Press release, 1 December 2016*a*.

———. "Tudingan Aksi Bela Islam, Dari Anti NKRI Hingga Makar". Press release, 2 December 2016*b*.

———. "Pernyataan Resmi Ketua GNPF MUI KH Bachtiar Nasir atas Kasus Bom Bunuh Diri di Terminal Kampung Melayu". Press release, 25 May 2017.

Hadiz, Vedi. "The Organizational Vehicles of Islamic Political Dissent: Social Bases, Genealogies, and Strategies". In *Between Dissent and Power: The Transformations of Islamic Politics in the Middle East and Asia*, edited by Khoo Boo Teik and Vedi Hadiz. Basingstoke: Palgrave Macmillan, 2014.

Hassan, Noorhaidi. *Laskar Jihad: Islam, militansi, dan pencarian identitas di Indonesia pasca-Order Baru*. Jakarta: LP3ES, 2008.

Hasyim, Syafiq. "The Council of Indonesian Ulama (MUI) and 'aqida-Based Intolerance'". In *Religion, Law, and Intolerance in Indonesia*, edited by Tim Lindsey and Helen Pausacker. Oxon: Routledge, 2016.

Hefner, Robert. "Islam, State, and Civil Society: ICMI and the Struggle for the Indonesian Middle Class". *Indonesia* 56 (October 1993).

———. "Global Violence and Indonesian Muslim Politics". *American Anthropologist* 104, no. 3 (2002).

———. "The Study of Religious Freedom in Indonesia". *Review of Faith and International Affairs* 11, no. 2 (2013).

Hiariej, Eric. "The Politics of Becoming Fundamentalist in the Age of Consumer Culture". Thesis, Australia National University, 2009.

Hiariej, Eric, Frans de Jalong, Dana Hasibuan, and Ayu Rahmawati. "Post-Fundamentalist Islamism and the Politics of Citizenship in Indonesia". In *Politics of Citizenship in Indonesia*, edited by Eric Hiariej and Kristian Stokke. Jakarta: Yayasan Obor Indonesia, 2017.

Hidayatullah. "Peledakan Bom di Bali Rekayasa CIA", 14 October 2002.

———. "Habib Rizieq: Bentrok Ahmadiyah, Kutuklah Presiden", 7 February 2011.

———. "Sikap FPI tentang Bocoran Wikileaks", 8 September 2011.

———. "MIUMI Himpun Potensi Ulama Muda Lintas Mazhab Ahlus Sunnah", 22 March 2012.

———. "MIUMI Beri Dukungan Moral Pemuda Penggerak Anti Pluralisme", 17 August 2012.

———. "MIUMI Mulai Memantapkan Jaringan ke Daerah-Daerah", 9 December 2012.

———. "MIUMI Keluarkan Fatwa tentang Paham Kesetaraan Gender", 1 October 2014.

————. "MIUMI: 'Inilah Kecelakaan Terbesar dalam Berpikir'", 17 August 2015.

————. "Habib Rizieq: Tergantung Perawatnya, Pancasila Harus Dirawat Umat Islam", 11 March 2017.

————. "MIUMI Diharapkan Bisa Mempersatukan Umat", 12 March 2018.

Hizbut Tahrir. "The Khilafah (Caliphate) and Mahdi", 5 October 2017.

————. "97 Years Since the Destruction of the Khilafah", 17 April 2018.

Hizbut Tahrir Indonesia (HTI). "Hizbut Tahrir Indonesia Statement: Ahmadiyah Clashed in Cikeusik, Pandeglang". Press release, 7 February 2011.

————. "It is *Haram* to Appoint a *Kafir* as a Leader". Press release, 30 August 2016.

Hurd, Elizabeth. "Believing in Religious Freedom". In *Politics of Religious Freedom*, edited by Winnifred Sullivan, Elizabeth Hurd, Saba Mahmood, and Peter Danchin. Chicago: University of Chicago Press, 2015.

Ichwan, Moch Nur. "Towards a Puritanical Moderate Islam: The Majelis Ulama Indonesia and the Politics of Religious Orthodoxy". In *Contemporary Developments in Indonesian Islam: Explaining the 'Conservative Turn'*, edited by Martin van Bruinessen. Singapore: Institute of Southeast Asian Studies, 2013.

IPAC. "After Ahok: The Islamist Agenda in Indonesia". *IPAC Report* 44 (2018).

Islamedia. "Wawancara Ustadz Ismail Yusanto: Demokrasi, Alat Perjuangan", 19 July 2013.

Jahroni, Jajang. "Defending the Majesty of Islam: Indonesia's Front Pembela Islam (FPI) 1998–2003". *Studia Islamika* 11, no. 2 (2004).

Jawa Pos. "Pesan Kepala BNPT di Demo 2 Desember", 28 November 2016.

Kiblat TV. "Ust Bachtiar Nasir: Memilih Pemimpin dalam Pilkada 2018", 23 January 2018.

Kompas. "Rizieq: SBY Pengecut, Ahmadiyah Banci", 10 June 2008.

————. "Kepala BNPT: Ada Potensi Aksi 2 Desember Disusupi Kelompok Teroris", 28 November 2016.

————. "Jokowi: Saya Indonesia, Saya Pancasila, kalau Kamu?", 30 May 2017*a*.

————. "Jokowi bentuk Unit Kerja Pembinaan Pancasila", 31 May 2017*b*.

————. "Yenny Wahid: Pelanggaran Kemerdekaan Beragama Masih Terjadi", 4 July 2017.

Lane, Max. *Unfinished Nation: Indonesia Before and After Suharto*. London: Verso, 2008.

Liddle, R. William. "The Islamic Turn in Indonesia: A Political Explanation". *Journal of Asian Studies* 55, no. 3 (1996).

Liputan6. "FPI Menuntut Pemberlakuan Piagam Jakarta", 28 August 2001.

————. "Ratusan Anggota FPI Jakarta Merazia Tempat Hiburan", 4 October 2002.

————. "Habib Rizieq: Terdakwa Seharusnya Bukan Saya", 8 May 2003.

Makin, Al. "Homogenizing Indonesian Islam: Persecution of the Shia Group in Yogyakarta". *Studia Islamika* 24, no. 1 (2017).

Mamdani, Mahmood. *Good Muslim, Bad Muslim*. New York: Random House, 2005.

MIUMI. "MIUMI Declaration". Available at <http://miumipusat.org/tentang-kami/deklarasi/>, n.d.

Muhtadi, Burhanuddin. "The Quest for Hizbut Tahrir in Indonesia". *Asian Journal of Social Science* 37 (2009).

Munabari, Fahlesa. "Reconciling Sharia with 'Negara Kesatuan Republik Indonesia': The Ideology and Framing Strategies of the Indonesian Forum of Islamic Society (FUI)". *International Area Studies Review* 1, no. 22 (2017).

Muslim Daily. "Gus Hamid: Islam Adalah Syuro, Bukan Demokrasi!", 4 March 2013.

————. "Habib Rizieq: Ormas-Ormas FUI Sepakat Perjuangkan NKRI Bersyariah", 26 August 2013.

Nahdlatul Ulama (NU). "Sejumlah Intelektual dan Ulama Deklarasikan MIUMI", 1 March 2012.

————. "Apa yang Dimaksud dengan Islam Nusantara?", 22 April 2015.

————. "Jokowi: Alhamdulillah Kita Islam Nusantara". 14 June 2015.

Okezone. "Majelis Intelektual Muda Diresmikan", 29 February 2012.

Osman, Mohamed. "The Transnational Network of Hizbut Tahrir Indonesia". *South East Asia Research* 18, no. 4 (2010): 735–55.

Panggabean, Samsu Rizal, Ihsan Ali-Fauzi, Rudy Harisyah Alam, Titik Firawati, et al. *Pemolisian Konflik Keagamaan di Indonesia*. Jakarta: PUSAD Paramadina, 2014.

Rachman, Budhy Munawar. *Argumen Islam untuk Pluralisme*. Jakarta: Grasindo, 2010*a*.

————. *Argumen Islam untuk Liberalisme*. Jakarta: Grasindo, 2010*b*.

Republika. "Ustaz Bachtiar Nasir: Sudut Pandang HAM Satu Mata, Seperti Dajjal", 6 February 2015.

————. "Jokowi: Islam Nusantara Sudah Mengakar di Jiwa Muslim Indonesia", 14 June 2015.

————. "Gema Muktamar III Wahdah Islamiyah – WI Rekomendasikan Demokrasi Wasathiyah", 21 July 2016.

————. "Memilih Pemimpin Seiman Tak Melanggar Demokrasi", 15 January 2017.

————. "Saran Ustaz Bachtiar Nasir Agar Umat Bersatu di Tahun Pemilu", 20 January 2018.

RMOL. "Setara Institute: Aksi 4 November Arena Bangkitnya Kelompok Jihadis", 8 November 2016.

Savirani, Amalinda and Olle Tornquist. *Reclaiming the State: Overcoming Problems of Democracy in Post-Soeharto Indonesia*. Yogyakarta: Penerbit Polgov, 2015.

Siar News Service. "Struktur Organisasi Front Pembela Islam (FPI)", 24 February 2000.

Suara Islam. "Interview Al Habib M Rizieq Syihab tentang Pilpres 2014", 24 June 2014.

Subono, Nur Iman. "Deficit Democracy: Civil and Political Freedom vs Other Instruments of Democracy". In *Making Democracy Meaningful: Problems and Options in Indonesia*, edited by A. E. Priyono, Willy Purna Samadhi, and Olle Törnquist. Jakarta: PCD Press with DEMOS, 2007.

Sukma, Rizal. *Islam in Indonesian Foreign Policy*. London: RoutledgeCurzon, 2003.

Syihab, Muhammad Rizieq bin Husein. "Pengaruh Pancasila terhadap Penerapan Syariah Islam di Indonesia". Thesis, Universiti Malaya, Kuala Lumpur, 2012.

Tempo. "FPI Minta DPR/MPR Kembalikan Pancasila Sesuai Piagam Jakarta", 31 December 2003.

———. "Presiden Minta Depag Perhatikan Fanatisme Beragama", 17 May 2004.

———. "Rizieq: FPI Akan Berjuang Membubarkan Ahmadiyah", 18 February 2011.

———. "Setara Institute Kritik Latihan TNI-FPI Bentuk Milisi Sipil", 8 January 2017.

———. "Perpu Ormas: NU Mendukung, Muhammadiyah Menolak", 18 October 2017.

Tirto. "Ismail Yusanto: Soal Rencana Pembubaran, Jubir HTI: 'Kami akan Melawan'", 12 May 2017.

Tribun. "Kebebasan Beragama Terancam oleh RUU KUB", 14 November 2017.

TVOne. "Fenomena Kemusrikan". *Damai Indonesiaku* (April 2014).

US Embassy, Jakarta. "Indonesian Biographical and Political Gossip, Q4 2005/ Q1 2006". Wikileaks Cable: 06JAKARTA5851_a, dated 9 May 2006. Available at <https://wikileaks.org/plusd/cables/06JAKARTA5851_a.html>.

van Bruinessen, Martin. "Nurcholish Madjid: Indonesian Muslim Intellectual". *ISIM Review* 17 (Spring 2006).

———. "Modernism and Anti-Modernism in Indonesian Muslim Responses to Globalisation". Paper presented at the workshop "Islam and Development in Southeast Asia: Southeast Asian Muslim Responses to Globalization". JICA Research Institute, Singapore, 21–22 November 2009.

———. "Postscript: The Survival of Liberal and Progressive Muslim Thought in Indonesia". In *Contemporary Developments in Indonesian Islam: Explaining the 'Conservative Turn'*, edited by Martin van Bruinessen. Singapore: Institute of Southeast Asian Studies, 2013.

Voa Islam. "Wakil Sekjen MIUMI Pusat: Kelompok LGBT Harus Dikriminalisasi", 15 February 2016.

Wahdah Islamiyah. "10 Rekomendasi Eksternal Muktamar III Wahdah Islamiyah", 21 July 2016.

Wahid Institute. *Laporan Tahunan Kebebasan Beragama/Berkeyakinan dan Intoleransi 2014: Utang Warisan Pemerintah Baru*, 2014.

Ward, Ken. "Non-Violent Extremists? Hizbut Tahrir Indonesia". *Australian Journal of International Affairs* 63, no. 2 (2009).

Widodo, Joko and Jusuf Kalla. *Jalan Perubahan untuk Indonesia yang Berdaulat, Mandiri dan Berkepribadian: Visi Misi, dan Program Aksi*, May 2014.

Wilson, Ian. "Reconfiguring Rackets: Racket Regimes, Protection and the State in post-Reformasi Jakarta". In *The State and Illegality in Indonesia*, edited by Edward Aspinall and Gerry van Klinken. Leiden: KITLV Press, 2010.

———. "Morality Racketeering: Vigilantism and Populist Islamic Militancy in Indonesia". In *Between Dissent and Power: The Transformations of Islamic Politics in the Middle East and Asia*, edited by Khoo Boo Teik and Vedi Hadiz. Basingstoke: Palgrave Macmillan, 2014.

———. "Resisting Democracy: Front Pembela Islam and Indonesia's 2014 Elections". In *ISEAS Perspective: Watching the Indonesian Elections 2014*, edited by Ulla Fionna. Singapore: Institute of Southeast Asian Studies, 2015.

5

Creating Leadership Legitimacy in Post-Reform Indonesia

Wawan Mas'udi

Introduction

This chapter is about the process of creating political legitimacy in post-reform Indonesia (see next session for a discussion of "legitimacy"). The phenomena will be examined by analysing the emergence of Joko Widodo (Jokowi) in Solo, as mayor, later as governor of Jakarta (July 2012), and finally as president (in 2014). His political emergence has provided an alternative to the established political leadership path. Previously that path was open primarily to Jakarta-based politicians or those originating within the established political class with backgrounds as generals, members of prominent political dynasties, owners of national business conglomerates, outspoken political activists, or senior national government officials.

Jokowi is not in any of these categories. His emergence at a national political level was enabled by his popularity as a local government leader in Solo with a strong image in effective reform. The emergence of a figure like Jokowi cannot be separated from the democratic transition in Indonesia, and the introduction of direct elections for local government leaders in 2004–5, which has created a closer connection between candidates and voters. One of the main characteristics of local direct elections is the centrality of personalities or figures. Political parties are certainly central to candidate nomination, but in many places non-party figures, such as business people, bureaucrats, professionals, religious leaders, local aristocrats and community leaders, are becoming more appealing and have even become the first preference of political parties.

Figure-based politics has become a general trend in Indonesian democracy, particularly following the introduction of direct presidential elections and the open-list legislative electoral system. Under this system, candidates are elected based on the popular vote, regardless of their position in the party's list.[1] This change has shifted relations between political elites and the people or between political candidates and voters, both during and after elections. As a trend, candidates develop direct and close communication with the people, making promises to deliver concrete programmes in order to satisfy people's demands. And the public normally readjust their support for political leaders and government based on their capabilities in managing governance and delivering public goods.

In a new democracy like Indonesia's, the established political culture of patronage and client networks plays a considerable role in creating political support and legitimacy (Robison and Hadiz 2005; Hadiz 2008–9, pp. 527–36; Hadiz 2010). Nevertheless, in many election campaigns an agenda of better provision of health and education services, local economic development, and good governance emerged as successful campaign strategies (see, for example, Aspinall 2014). Many local government leaders who initiated and implemented social policies in basic services maintained popular support and were even described as exhibiting best practice decentralization. In some cases local figures, such as Jokowi in Solo (2005–12), Risma in Surabaya (2010–present), and Hasto in Kulon Progo (2012–present), combine popular policies with an inclusive and popular style of leadership in the form of direct communication with the people and participatory governance. However, whether this "new pattern of creating legitimacy" has set a new democratic mode of legitimacy or merely another form of political clientelism, is still in doubt.

This pattern is different from the centralized regime of the New Order, wherein the legitimacy of local political authorities depended on support from the central government. Because such support is now much less relevant, local political authorities need to adjust how they create legitimacy. One way of creating political legitimacy is the combined capability of political leaders and government to respond to local interests and to cope with the agenda that emerges during decentralization and democratic transition.

Political Legitimacy in Indonesia

Legitimacy and Its Creation

The creation of political legitimacy is not a singular and generic process, but is constrained by political moments and context. In non-democratic regimes, legitimacy is created through state political discipline and enforcement of sovereign rule, including the use of carrot and stick policies. People are merely positioned as objects of the process of legitimation (Brooker 2009, pp. 130–61). The legitimacy of New Order Indonesia was created in this way. Democratic legitimacy, on the other hand, can be created only with the consent of the people alongside compatibility between government action and popular needs (Stillman 1974; Lipset 1959).

The basic formal procedure to confirm people's consent is an election. Winning election is fundamental for a political leader to gain legitimacy, but electoral legitimacy will have little meaning if the elected leader and government fail to manage public authority in accordance with people's interests. Conversely, if the elected leader and government can manage authority and resources in a way that is compatible with popular expectations, political legitimacy will be created. Therefore, the actual challenge for the elected leader and government is in the post-election period, when authoritative power comes into effect (Rothstein 2009, p. 311). The creation of democratic legitimacy requires accommodation of people's interests in public policy and engagement of popular voices in the process of governance — at least to an extent acceptable to a majority. This kind of inclusion will generate a degree of compatibility between government output and people's expectations, which constitutes the condition for legitimacy.

In a post-authoritarian regime, people usually expect the new government and political leaders to resolve the impacts of socio-economic and political crises, following the fall of the old regime. In this context, compatibility is usually developed through government effectiveness in formally addressing people's expectations. The failure of a political leader to develop an effective government could jeopardize not only personal legitimacy and in turn government, but in the long run could also trigger popular distrust in democracy and pave the way for anti-democratic actors to emerge and revitalize their political power (Lipset 1959).

Dynamics of Political Legitimation

The political legitimacy of the state, regime and personal political leadership has been tested several times in recent Indonesian political life. Particularly in the period of political changes, i.e. 1998–99, the political authorities faced a declining popular acceptance of their right to rule. Challenges to the legitimacy of each of those political authorities were different. The ways in which legitimacy was created and maintained were also not alike, although frequently related. The secessionist movements of Timor-Leste, Aceh, and Papua, for example, reflected the decline of state legitimacy in those areas. Meanwhile, the collapse in the legitimacy of the regime and government had ended the Soeharto presidency.

The economic crisis and democratic movement in the 1990s had ruined the regime legitimacy of the New Order. That regime developed on the basis of political coercion, state-led economic growth, and patronage in distribution of socio-economic benefits.[2] The regime's legitimacy declined severely with the impact of the economic crisis and a growing wave of support for democratization, which led to a political leadership crisis. The desire for democratization had changed the base of legitimacy as people became more prominent in the new processes of power. The shifts changed the nature of political legitimacy from state-centred and nationally based to more people-centred and locally based.

Election becomes the main arena for winning legitimacy, and to sustain legitimacy the leader should perform effective government to answer popular expectations. This means that legitimacy is not given and fixed, but constantly changing as a result of dynamic interactions between political authorities and the people.[3] Particularly in the context of post-crisis and democratic transition, the main challenges of legitimation are associated with the vacuum of effective legitimacy in responding to public expectations.

Jokowi's Emergence

Joko Widodo's emergence signalled two things; the growing importance of a popular base of legitimacy and the importance of government effectiveness as a way to manage popular support.

Jokowi entered Solo politics in the first direct elections in 2005, in the period when democratization and decentralization as a political norm had just been established. In spite of promising the development of democratic legitimation in the form of free and fair elections, political practices that undermined democracy were dominant in the early post-New Order period. In Solo, the failures of the first post-reform mayor, Slamet Suryanto, who held office from 2000 until 2005, triggered popular discontent. Slamet failed to develop government capability in public goods provision (mainly in health, education, and city infrastructure) and was not capable of adopting a reform agenda proposed by civil society (i.e. participatory planning and budgeting). These failures caused a vacuum of political legitimacy.

In the above context, Jokowi, a successful Solo furniture business-man, won the election. He received support from the biggest party in the city, Partai Demokrasi Indonesia Perjuangan (Indonesian Democratic Party of Struggle, PDIP). The party's leader in Solo, F.X. Hadi "Rudy" Rudyatmo, ran as Jokowi's deputy mayoral candidate. The pair won the election with 36 per cent of the vote in 2005 and were re-elected in 2010 with more than 90 per cent. The re-election reflected a high degree of legitimacy created by political leadership during these five years.

As mayor, Jokowi is described as a good practitioner of decentraliza-tion and local democracy, and particularly for his profile of inclusive leadership and his achievements in governance reform (*Tempo* 2008). Rushda Majeed described him as a local leader with a true commit-ment to developing the local economy and democracy, particularly for business permits reform, participatory planning, budget transparency, and other basic service improvements (Majeed 2012; Patunru, McCulloch, and von Luebke 2012). Meanwhile, the dialogue approach he adopted to handle the problem of the informal economy (i.e. street vendors) was also popular in Solo and beyond, and was considered effective participatory governance (Pratikno 2004; Sudarmo 2009, p. 107). When he won the election in 2012 as governor and the presidential election in 2014, scholars like Marcus Mietzner described the Jokowi phenomenon as a kind of populism and even saw him as the saviour of Indonesian democracy (Mietzner 2014; Pongsudhirak 2014).

The starting point of Jokowi's political legitimacy dates back to his leadership in Solo. Over the course of his mayoralty, he not only maintained his base of legitimacy in the PDIP but also broadened this base across parties and sections of the Solo community. His strong legitimacy was a result of popular policies and a style of leadership that maintained intimate interaction with various actors. Those factors helped Jokowi to manage contested interests, which in turn helped him create a broader base of legitimacy.

Similar to other popular local leaders in post-decentralization Indonesia such as Winase in Jembrana, Hery Zudianto in Yogyakarta, and Trimawan in Purbalingga, Jokowi adopted social policies to deliver concrete benefits for the poor. Two notable social policies directly addressed the needs of the people: Surakarta health care (Pemeliharaan Kesehatan Masyarakat Surakarta–PKMS), introduced in 2007–8, and Surakarta Education Subsidy (Bantuan Pendidikan Masyarakat Kota Surakarta–BPMKS), introduced in 2010.

In spite of pre-existing national programmes, for Solo people PKMS was the first universal local healthcare insurance, since the programme was not only for the poor. All Solo residents who did not have other health insurance were eligible for membership. The BPMKS aims to guarantee access of children from poor families to basic education. The main beneficiaries were the poor sections of Solo, who were the main base of PDIP. Social policies, as for many other local governments, have been effective tools for politicians to create a popular image of reform-minded leadership (see, for example, Aspinall 2014).

Another policy that helped Jokowi build strong popular legitimacy was the deliberative relocation of street vendors from Banjarsari park, one of the main city parks, to a formal marketplace, Klithikan. While his predecessor and other city governments tended to use forceful methods, Jokowi insisted on the use of dialogue. It was reported that he held more than fifty meetings with the street vendors to discuss the relocation plan. The peaceful relocation stamped his style of dialogue and consultation (*Suara Merdeka* 2006). Apart from the deliberation on relocation, in Jokowi's view the street vendors (PKL) were a city-economic asset. The cost of relocation was a city investment that would bring benefits in the long run rather than what NGOs in Solo had imagined, a policy to empower marginalized groups.

The peaceful relocation of Banjarsari PKL to the Notoharjo Klithikan market was a critical moment for Jokowi's leadership legitimacy in Solo and beyond. National mass media, such as *The Jakarta Post* and *Kompas*, reported the events as an unprecedented peaceful relocation of street vendors, in the midst of forceful relocations that had occurred in many other cities (Poer 2008). When *Tempo* selected Jokowi as one of the best local leaders in 2008, he was described as *Wali Kaki Lima* (the guardian or mayor of street vendors) (*Tempo* 2008). Jokowi's visit to Notoharjo market, after the official announcement that he was president-elect on 26 July 2014, seemed to confirm the importance of this relocation for his political career (Kompas Cyber Media n.d.).

Furthermore, the people of Solo admired Jokowi's leadership style, typified by direct and intimate communication with all segments of the community (people and elites) and his ability to get the job done. His style is dubbed *blusukan*, a kind of leader's impromptu visit to the community. The style is effective to develop closer engagement with people as well as to ensure the effectiveness of policy implementation. In addition, to a greater extent, his leadership style was also effective for managing conflicting interests in many areas, as well as to harness the tradition of popular recalcitrance of the city.

It seemed that, for Jokowi, politics is an art to reach consensus between contradictory elements, rather than a zero-sum game or a winner takes all model. The way in which he managed different and sometimes conflicting interests reminds us how a furniture maker assembles different sizes and pieces of wood into a fine product. Jokowi appeared to apply similar logic in managing the city. Rather than focusing on one aspect and putting aside another, he tended to accommodate various and different streams of interests and actors in policy formulation and implementation.

Jokowi's experiences in Solo show that one viable path to create democratic political legitimacy is combining various rites of affirmation and accommodation to manage contested interests within the community and developing compatibility between government outputs and popular expectations. As the mayor of Solo, Jokowi showed that he was able to manage government authority and resources to produce policies that served various interests of people, rather than catering to the interests of a single group. At the same time, he managed to provide unprecedentedly effective basic public services.

His approach of combining populist leadership style and policies was extended as governor of Jakarta and further as president. As governor, Jokowi extended his style of direct communication and dialogue for managing problems of urban informality, such as the relocation of Tanah Abang street vendors. His populist image was also reflected in policies he introduced: health insurance known as Kartu Jakarta Sehat (Jakarta Health Card) and an education subsidy named Kartu Jakarta Pintar for the poor. His policy focus was also on urban infrastructure, though this was still far from complete when he decided to run for president in 2014.

After being elected president, Jokowi's populist leadership style and policies were unchanged and expanded nationwide. According to his official website (<presidenri.go.id>), by the third year of his presidency Jokowi had visited more than 280 places across the country for impromptu visits or *blusukan*. In addition to this populist style, Jokowi maintains intensive communication and dialogue with parties, political elites, and activists, including his political opponents, especially during political turmoil, such as dealing with Islamist politics and human rights issues. He also extends populist policies through cash transfers for the poor to have access to healthcare (Kartu Indonesia Sehat), education (Kartu Indonesia Pintar), and family subsidy (Program Keluarga Harapan). Infrastructure has also become a landmark of Jokowi's policies, as he boosts development of road, railways, electricity, inter-island connections, dams, and many others.

The way Jokowi created political legitimacy addresses the question of how political leaders maintain and broaden their base in transition to a democratized and decentralized Indonesia. The character of legitimacy and how it is created depend on the political system. During the centralized and authoritarian New Order, local leaders' legitimacy depended to a great extent on support from a national government that combined absolute power and the provision of public services. The wave of democratization and decentralization changed the character and process of creating legitimacy, as it requires popular support. However, there is no well-defined pattern of how political leaders create or sustain legitimacy. In fact, during the transitional period, we can identify different modes of legitimation, not only democratic representation, but also the persistence of non-democratic legitimation.

Among such uncertain ways of creating legitimacy, Jokowi emerged with new approaches that reflected the values of reform.

Jokowi's policies and leadership did not disrupt elite domination, but did resolve some of the issues in the informal economy and marginalized communities, at least on the surface. His openness and ability to accommodate various or competing aspirations and interests have also played a crucial part in legitimizing his government's policies and programmes, which then added to his leadership legitimacy. Jokowi maintains those patterns of creating legitimacy during his presidency.

Changing Nature of Legitimacy in Democratized Context

Jokowi's rise to power initially depended on the support of a political party (PDIP), as mayor, governor, and president. Subsequently, the way Jokowi conducted government by combining effective policy output and openness not only secured his legitimacy within PDIP, but also broadened it beyond. Support for his leadership expanded from the party and specific clusters of voters to cross-sections of the community, both elite and grassroots. PDIP appreciated Jokowi's leadership for two reasons: 1) many government policies provided direct benefits to people and thus were in line with the party ideology, and also benefitted the party's core supporters; and 2) Jokowi did not express any interest in contesting the party leadership, but rather put himself forward as a committed official of the party.

Although PDIP claimed that Jokowi's achievements were part of implementation of the party's three pillars strategy (the unity of the party in legislative, executive, and grassroots), Jokowi's legitimacy was significantly personal rather than identified with the PDIP or the government. When he was mayor, although his personal electoral support had skyrocketed to 90 per cent in the 2010 election, PDIP's electoral support remained at the same level as in 2005. This means that legitimacy is not transferable in many cases, as it is attached to personal leadership.

In Jokowi's case, the personalization of legitimacy occurred for two reasons. First, direct elections positioned the political candidate (mayor, head of district, governor, and president) as central to political competition. Although parties played a prominent role, the voters wanted to see how the candidates would approach the people during the campaign, and after the election the people would decide what the leader could produce for their interests. The decline of personal legitimacy of the leader would not necessarily affect support for the political party. Similarly, the emerging legitimacy of a leader does not automatically increase party support (at least to the same degree), as demonstrated by Jokowi and PDIP.

Second, many government initiatives were due to the leadership, rather than the direction of the party or the agenda of the bureaucracy. It is clear that many in the public regarded improvements in public goods provision as a result of Jokowi's work. It seems that in Indonesian democracy, political parties are short of policy platforms and figures who are capable of running for office. As a consequence, the effectiveness of government is perceived as a result of leaders' actions, not of the initiatives of political parties or the bureaucracy.

Jokowi's way of creating legitimacy appears to reflect his personal appeal, rather than stemming from non-democratic practices such as patronage and traditional power networks, common in Indonesian politics. When he was in Solo, for most sections of the community, his reform-minded policies and style of engagement with community contrasted with that of his predecessor. He received massive popular legitimacy in return. However, it is important to note that his policies and style did not disrupt the established structure of elite domination in Solo, for example by raising the city's revenue at the expense of the rich. The relocation of street vendors from the city park to a peripheral area has made the central district much more comfortable for the business of established merchants. While the policies of business deregulation and MICE (Meeting, Incentive, Conference, and Event) has triggered investment from outside Solo, especially in hotel and other hospitality business, it is at the cost of the closure of small hotels and related local businesses. At the national level, Jokowi's leadership style and policies are also not aimed for structural changes in either politics or economy. It seems that through the effective implementation of populist policies, Jokowi may even have preserved and strengthened elite interests.

Reflection: New Way of Legitimizing Politics

In a broader theoretical perspective, the emergence of Jokowi's legitimacy confirms that in a transitional context, where the procedural norms and institutional standards of political legitimation are absent or in the making, the mode of creating legitimacy is contingent and accidental, rather than planned or intended (Alagappa 1995).

The political transition in post-New Order Indonesia has changed the leadership at the top of the political pyramid. However, it did not automatically destroy established elites' structure or interests (Linz 1990). In the new political arrangement, old elites co-exist and contest with new power aspirants and interests that emerged during democratization. In Solo, for example, the electoral competition has not brought any major changes in the political and economic elite structure. The economy mostly remains in the hand of old merchants, the Chinese, Arabic, and *Laweyan* batik entrepreneurs, while cultural authority is still in the hands of royal families (Kasunanan and Mangkunegaran), though their legitimacy is declining. There is a slight change in political structure as new elites, including Jokowi, emerge, but the people of Solo in general are still trapped in precarious livelihoods.

As president, Jokowi's leadership is characterized by accommodation with various and contesting interests, as he needs to include both reformist voices and anti-reform pressure. His cabinet is a mixture of reformist aspirants, parties' self-interests, and even New Order proponents. As result, his position on reform or popular agendas is ambiguous in some areas, such as human rights investigation and economic development. Jokowi developed legitimacy by accommodating the interests of various segments, including elites, rather than by siding exclusively with popular demands.

His legitimacy in government was a result of mixed policies and leadership actions. In fact, the way Jokowi governed has preserved rather than threatened the dominance of elites. Such a mode of creating legitimacy by accommodating cross-class interests seems to address the notion of impartiality, but with a different meaning. Whereas Rothstein and Teorell defined impartiality as equal citizenship (Rothstein and Teorell 2008), here impartiality was more about leadership and short-term political strategies to accommodate conflicting interests. In the longer term, Jokowi's version of impartiality would tend to preserve, rather than eradicate, the disparity between the poor and elites.

Furthermore, leadership legitimacy is also tightly connected with the policy process, rather than simply an impact of policy output. It relates particularly with how the political leader deals with the vibrant and complex structure of community voices and interests. Therefore, the creation of legitimacy is better seen as a dynamic process rather than static. Jokowi's style of politics shows that his legitimacy is also about openness and intimate relations, embracing elements of the community and civil society. He is not only able to manage closer relations with the people as a vital source of legitimacy in a democracy, but also compiled ideas for policies from outside the formal bureaucratic process, particularly through *blusukan*. He could largely develop legitimate policies and programmes because his decisions incorporated some aspects of the people's aspirations. With *blusukan*, he also aims to ensure that public services (especially the basic ones — health and education) and infrastructure projects are working as planned. The importance of the political process adds to the established view that government output and performance are the main basis for legitimation of political authority in a post-election context, as argued by Rothstein (2009) and more specifically in a transitional context, by Lipset (1959, 1995) and Gilley (2006).

My next point concerns Jokowi's background as a commoner who was then successful in business. It lifted his socio-economic status as part of the new elite in Solo. However, it seems that he is able to build the image of a leader with non-*priyayi* (Javanese elite) attitudes, by appearing to be the guardian of interests for *wong cilik* (commoners or small people). He cultivated non-*priyayi* leadership, an attitude that seems fascinating in the eyes of Javanese commoners. Jokowi's case shows that one way for the *priyayi* elite to maintain political legitimacy is by developing associations with the culture and interests of the common people, rather than displaying the attributes and attitudes of elitism. This reveals a different mode of political legitimacy developing in the predominant Javanese political culture, outside the well-recognized argument that sees Javanese power's legitimacy as abstract and mystical (Anderson 1990). In this more familiar view, legitimacy is a given and uncontested by popular consent.

Jokowi, who entered politics within an electoral democracy framework, developed his base of political legitimacy by implementing rational and concrete calculations when dealing with policies and programmes. In part, the introduction of electoral democracy seemed to question the established conception of Javanese power. However, the humble and direct style of leadership he developed in relation to the people and his preference for "win-win" solutions still reflected a common concept in Javanese culture, namely political and social harmony. As president, he maintained good relations with Megawati (the chair of PDIP and his political mentor) through frequent consultation, while at the same time also maintaining communications and dialogue with his opponents, such as former President Susilo Bambang Yudhoyono and his rival in presidential race, Prabowo Subianto. And in many events, he utilized symbols and rites of culture as a means to legitimize government actions and programmes.

Lastly, this chapter confirms the argument of contingent and accidental legitimacy in a transitional context. In the absence of established patterns of legitimation, the search for legitimacy in an emerging democracy will always be a challenge. It is true that election procedures and standards of good government have been recognized as normative sources for legitimation of authority. But there is no generic pattern of struggle for legitimacy in real politics. Like other rational politicians, Jokowi's intent was to consolidate power. But from the trajectories of policies and actions he managed during his leadership, the broad base of his legitimacy was a result of openness and close relations with many actors and interests.

It seems that Jokowi was successful not just in exploiting opportunities brought about by decentralization and local democratization; he also managed conflicting interests in society for the purpose of political legitimacy. His leadership is one among various paths to political legitimacy available to local leaders. The broader resonance or significance of Jokowi's path is evident in his rise to power in a more complex and plural cultural and political setting in a way that old patronage politicians have not been able to match.

NOTES

1. On open-list electoral systems, see Gallagher and Mitchell (2005), pp. 5–6.
2. On the New Order political economy, see, for example, Crouch (1979); Anderson (1983); Hill (1994).
3. On the argument of legitimacy as a result of interactions between political authority and people, see for example Beetham (2013); Alagappa (1995).

REFERENCES

Alagappa, Muthiah, ed. *Political Legitimacy in Southeast Asia: The Quest for Moral Authority*. Stanford: Stanford University Press, 1995.

Anderson, Benedict. "Old State, New Society: Indonesia's New Order in Comparative Historical Perspective". *Journal of Asian Studies* 42, no. 3 (1983): 477–96.

———. "The Idea of Power in Javanese Society". In *Language and Power: Exploring Political Cultures in Indonesia*. Ithaca, London: Cornell University Press, 1990.

Aspinall, Edward. "Healthcare and Democratization in Indonesia". *Democratization* 21, no. 5 (2014): 803–23.

Beetham, David. *The Legitimation of Power*. Palgrave Macmillan, 2013.

Brooker, Paul. *Non-Democratic Regimes: Second Edition*. Palgrave Macmillan, 2009.

Crouch, Harold. "Patrimonialism and Military Rule in Indonesia". *World Politics* 31, no. 4 (1979): 571–87.

Gallagher, Michael and Paul Mitchell. *The Politics of Electoral Systems*. Oxford: Oxford University Press, 2005.

Gilley, Bruce. "The Determinants of State Legitimacy: Results for 72 Countries". *International Political Science Review* 27, no. 1 (2006): 47–71.

Hadiz, Vedi R. "Understanding Social Trajectories: Structure and Actor in the Democratization Debate". *Pacific Affairs* 81 (Winter 2008–9): 527–36.

———. *Localising Power in Post-Authoritarian Indonesia: A Southeast Asia Perspective*. Stanford: Stanford University Press, 2010.

Hill, Hal, ed. *Indonesia's New Order: The Dynamics of Socio-Economic Transformation*. Honolulu: University of Hawaii Press, 1994.

Kompas Cyber Media. "Ke Solo, Jokowi Bernostalgia di Pasar Notoharjo", n.d. Available at <http://nasional.kompas.com/read/2014/07/26/13403751/Ke.Solo.Jokowi.Bernostalgia.di.Pasar.Notoharjo>.

Linz, Juan J. "Transitions to Democracy". *Washington Quarterly* 13, no. 3 (1990): 143–64.

Lipset, Seymour Martin. "Some Social Requisites of Democracy: Economic Development and Political Legitimacy". *American Political Science Review* 53, no. 1 (1959): 69–105.

———. "The Social Requisites of Democracy Revisited". In *Einigung Und Zerfall: Deutschland Und Europa Nach Dem Ende Des Ost-West-Konflikts* (Springer 1995): 287–314.

Majeed, Rushda. "Defusing a Volatile City, Igniting Reforms: Joko Widodo and Surakarta, Indonesia, 2005–2011". Princeton, N.J.: Princeton University, 2012. Available at <https://successfulsocieties.princeton.edu/sites/successfulsocieties/files/Policy_Note_ID199.pdf> (accessed 14 April 2013).

Mietzner, Marcus. "How Jokowi Won and Democracy Survived". *Journal of Democracy* 25, no. 4 (2014): 111–25.

Patunru, Arianto A., Neil McCulloch, and Christian von Luebke. "A Tale of Two Cities: The Political Economy of Local Investment Climates in Indonesia". *Journal of Development Studies* 48, no. 7 (2012): 799–816.

Poer, Blontank. "Joko 'Jokowi' Widodo: Changing the Face of Surakarta". *Jakarta Post*, 29 October 2008.

Pongsudhirak, Thitinan. "Jokowi Saves Indonesia's Democracy (and Maybe Southeast Asia's Too)". *East Asian Forum*, 28 July 2014. Available at <http://www.eastasiaforum.org/2014/07/28/jokowi-saves-indonesias-democracy-and-maybe-southeast-asias-too/>.

Pratikno, M. "Citizen Participation in Surakarta Municipality, Indonesia". In *Citizens in Charge: Managing Local Budgets in East Asia and Latin America*, edited by Isabel Licha. Washington, D.C.: Inter-American Development Bank, 2004.

Robison, Richard and Vedi R. Hadiz. "Reorganising Power in Indonesia: The Politics of Oligarchy in an Age of Markets". *BIES* 41, no. 1 (2005). <http://www.tandfonline.com/doi/full/10.1080/00074910500306619>.

Rothstein, Bo. "Creating Political Legitimacy: Electoral Democracy Versus Quality of Government". *American Behavioral Scientist* (2009).

Rothstein, Bo and Jan Teorell. "What is Quality of Government? A Theory of Impartial Government Institutions". *Governance* 21, no. 2 (2008): 165–90.

Stillman, Peter G. "The Concept of Legitimacy". *Polity* 7, no. 1 (1974): 32–56.

Suara Merdeka. "Menangani PKL Ala Solo". 27 July 2006, sec. Wacana.

Sudarmo. "Participation Efforts of Solo's Street Vendors in Policy Formulation during the Reform Era but without Results". *ALAR: Action Learning and Action Research Journal* 15, no. 1 (2009): 107–40.

Tempo. "10 Tokoh 2008: Mereka Bekerja Dengan Hati Menggerakkan Daerah", 28 December 2008.

6

The Political Middle Class in Post-Soeharto Era Indonesia

Amalinda Savirani[1]

This chapter explores the politics of the middle class in Indonesia after *reformasi*. It argues that different sections of the middle class have expanded their political roles into more and varied arenas than in the previous era. They are also increasingly ideologically fragmented, and this pattern relates to the type of resources they base themselves upon: either state resources or those from the market.

Generally, the social entity located in the "middle" — between a wealthy elite and a mass of the poor — economically, socially and politically is regarded as the "middle class". One point of view regards the middle class as inherently having progressive or at least liberal political views and as being independent from dominant political and economic power. Socially, they are seen as distinct too: they have a stronger educational background (compared to the rest of the population), and this allows them access to social and economic resources. They may not be rich, but with their social network, they can access significantly greater resources than the poor majority. However, in the context of Indonesia, it is not clear that all of the middle class can be described as having such liberal political views. If we use that as a defining feature, we will focus only on groups outside the state, ignoring those inside.

Taking into account the above factors, this chapter explores the Indonesian middle class in two areas: the middle class in the political society arena (parties and legislature), and the middle class in the civil society arena. The first group are members of the middle class who have careers in national and local politics. They make a living (in addition to any other income) from their participation in electoral institutions. The second group are activists, both professional (working for non-governmental organizations or NGOs), and non-professional (who voluntarily contribute on issues they think important). While the first group is very political, in the sense of being directly oriented to power, there are varieties in the second. They can be grouped relating to their view on democratic politics: pro-politics or anti-politics. Sociologically, those active in these two arenas belong to the middle class. If they did not have access to middle class resources, they would not be able to become a member of parliament, or even a candidate. The same applies to activists in civil society. These two types of middle class between them represent the political outlook of the majority of this class. This chapter has insufficient space to explore other members of the middle class such as academics, who are also regarded as middle class.

This chapter will analyse the dynamics of political activity of these sections of the middle class in post-Soeharto Indonesia in four main sections. The first explores the structure of political economy in which the Indonesian middle class is situated. The second and third sections explore the two cases of political middle class: members of parliament, and the activists; the last section is conclusion.

Indonesian Economic Structure as a Setting for the Middle Class

Indonesian economic growth has been 5–6 per cent over the last period. Growth has been dependent on domestic consumption as the population has steadily grown, while investment has been ups and down. In the fourth quarter of 2014, foreign direct investment (FDI) in Indonesia was Rp 78.7 trillion, while in 2018 (first quarter), it was valued at Rp 108.9 trillion. The peak was in 2017 (fourth quarter), which was Rp 112 trillion (Indonesian Investment Board 2018).

If we look at data on the Indonesian state budget over the past years, national income has steadily increased. In 2015, state income was Rp 1,793.60 trillion, and in 2018 it was Rp 1,894.70 trillion, an increase of 5.6 per cent. This increase is coupled with an increase in expenditure too. In 2015, the expenditure was Rp 2,039.5 trillion, and in 2018 it was Rp 2,220.70 trillion, an increase of also around 8.8 per cent (see Table 6.1). This deficit has been covered by foreign debt, which has soared over the past years. In August 2018, for instance, Indonesian economy's deficit is 1.02 times of Indonesia gross domestic product (Putera 2018).

TABLE 6.1
Indonesian State Budget, 2015–18

Year	National Budget (in IDR Trillion)	
	Incomes	Expenditure
2015	1,793.60	2,039.50
2016	1,822.50	2,095.70
2017	1,750.30	2,080.50
2018	1,894.70	2,220.70

Source: Indonesian Ministry of Finance.

While the national budget has steadily increased, foreign debt has increased as well. Between 2014 and 2018, debt has increased 35.9 per cent (from Rp 255.7 trillion to Rp 399.2 trillion). This is why economists argue that the Indonesian economy depends on foreign source. If state budget shows a dependency on foreign loan, another statistics on international trade do not show good signs either. Between 2009 and 2013, import of goods increased, surpassing goods export (see Table 6.2). In addition, imports of goods have increased by US$97,405 million, while exports have increased by US$63,902 million. This shows that the proportion of import of goods is higher than export of goods. Similar trend also happens in import of services. This again shows the Indonesian economy's dependency on external force.

TABLE 6.2
Indonesian Profiles on International Trade, 2009–13

Foreign Trade Indicators	2009	2010	2011	2012	2013
Imports of Goods (million USD)	89,964	135,323	176,201	190,383	187,369
Exports of Goods (million USD)	119,646	158,074	200,788	188,496	183,548
Imports of Services (million USD)	27,625	25,599	30,788	33,302	33,842
Exports of Services (million USD)	13,238	16,211	20,118	22,523	21,948

Source: <http://fita.org/countries/indonesia.html>.

Indonesia's growing population and their consumption save the economy. McKinsey shows that, in consumption, Indonesia is the 16th largest economy in the world, with 45 million members of the consuming class, twice Australia's population in 2016 (McKinsey 2012).

High consumption seems related to the strength of the informal sector. In 2017, this sector employed 72.2 million people, or 58.3 per cent of the labour force. The top three sectors with a high population

TABLE 6.3
General Characterization of Indonesian MSMEs, 2009–10

Business Scale	2009		2010		Growth	
	Total	Share (%)	Total	Share (%)	Total	Share (%)
Micro, small, and medium scale business	52,764,603	99.99	53,823,732	2.01	1,059,129	2.01
a. Micro	52,176,795	98.88	53,207,500	98.85	1,030,705	1.98
b. Small	546,675	1.04	573,601	1.07	26,926	4.93
c. Medium	41,133	0.08	42,631	0.08	1,498	3.64
Big Scale business	467	0.01	4,838	0.01	161	3.43

Source: Bellefleur, Murad and Tangkau (2012).

of Micro and Small Medium Enterprises (MSMEs) are agriculture, livestock, forestry and fisheries; trade, hotels and restaurants; and transportation and communication. The informal sector absorbs employment. Rate of unemployment in the formal sector has risen from Rp 7.03 million in 2016 to Rp 7.04 million in 2017. Open unemployment also increased, from 5.5 per cent in 2016 to 5.56 per cent in 2017 (*Jakarta Post* 2017).

Stable growth is coupled with inequality. Credit Suisse Research Institute in its seventh Global Wealth Report found that the richest 1 per cent of Indonesia's adult population of 164 million owned 49.3 per cent of the country's $1.8 trillion wealth in June 2017. The four richest men in Indonesia have more wealth than the poorest 100 million (Diela 2016). This is, in fact, a global trend: in 2016, 1 per cent of the world population owned 49 per cent of total wealth (Oxfam 2017).

In short, the Indonesian economy, despite its stable increase of GDP, is weak in economic fundamentals. Inequality is rising persistently. Although the consuming class has grown over the past decade, it has not yet contributed to a stronger foundation of the country's economy, which would allow it to sustain its development. Within this context of weak economy and increased inequality, the resources for the political middle class, especially the legislatures seem to come from the state or from corporations.

Political Middle Class in Political Society

This section and the next explore two cases of members of the middle class in the political arena. The first looks at candidates running and winning national, provincial and district legislative elections. The second is the middle class "voluntary group" in civil society.

In 2014, there were almost 200,000 candidates (Aspinall and Sukmajati 2016), who vied for a total of 20,389 legislative positions in the senate (132 seats), national parliament (560 seats), provincials parliaments (2,137 seats), and district/city parliaments (17,560 seats), spread in 34 provinces and 497 districts/cities in the 2014 election. For the national parliament, there were more than 6,000 candidates from nine parties (see Table 6.4). They can be regarded as having sufficient funds to finance their campaign, or at least possess social capital networks through which to access resources.

TABLE 6.4
Number of Seats and Candidates for DPR RI Election in 2014

No	Parties	Number of Seats Garnered	Number of Candidates (*Daftar Calon Tetap*)
1.	PDI Perjuangan	109	560
2.	Golkar	91	560
3.	Gerindra	73	557
4.	Demokrat	61	560
5.	PAN	49	560
6.	PKS	40	490
7.	PPP	39	548
8.	Nasdem	35	559
9,	Hanura	16	558
	Total	**560**	**6,608**

Source: <https://nasional.sindonews.com/read/727138/12/kpu-sediakan-20257-kursi-di-pemilu-2014-1363241101>.

More than 40 per cent of members of parliament are 41–50 years old, almost 30 per cent are 51– 60 years old, and 14.5 per cent are aged 31–40. Members below 30 years old only constitute 2.7 per cent, and above 60 years make up 12.3 per cent. Thus, members aged 41–60 are around 70 per cent (FORMAPPI 2014).

In terms of education, 44.8 per cent of parliament members are bachelor degree graduates. Significant members have master degrees (38 per cent) and PhDs (7.7 per cent). Graduates with high school and diploma qualifications constitute 8.3 per cent. Therefore, majority of national parliament members have a middle class educational background. The largest number were businesspeople (41.27 per cent) before they become politicians. A significant percentage were already politicians before becoming members of the national parliament (24.3 per cent). High-ranking administrators constitute 12.9 per cent, civil servants and retirees make up 4.05 per cent, and other professions (such as housewife) amount to 13.7 per cent (FORMAPPI 2014). In essence, members of national parliament have a business background, they are educated, and are aged 41– 60 years. They can all be classified as middle class.

There are no comprehensive data for members of provincial and district/city legislatures. However, there are ten provinces for which data can be accessed online: Jambi, Riau, West Sumatra, Banten, East Java, Central Java, Bali, West Nusa Tenggara, Gorontalo and West Kalimantan. Figure 6.1 shows the education profile of members of the local legislatures.

FIGURE 6.1
The Education Profile of Members of Local Legislatures

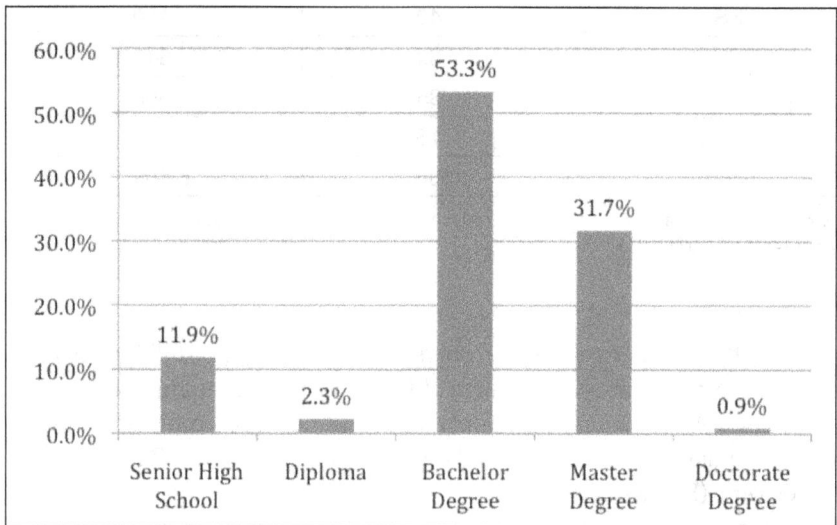

Source: Compilation from the Local Election Commission in ten provinces.

Figure 6.1 shows that a majority (55.6 per cent) of members of parliament in ten provinces hold diploma or bachelor degrees. More than 32 per cent have master or doctoral degrees, and almost 12 per cent are high school graduates.

From Table 6.5, we understand that a majority of members of local parliament in ten provinces were born in the 1960s and 1970s (74.2 per cent), and 18.8 per cent were born in 1950s, 1940s, and 1930s. Members in their thirties and late twenties contributed 7 per cent of total members of legislatures in ten provinces.

TABLE 6.5
Year of Birth of Members of Local Parliaments in Ten Provinces

Year of Birth	Percentage
1930s	0.3
1940s	2.9
1950s	15.6
1960s	42.1
1970s	32.1
1980s	6.6
1990s	0.4

Source: Compilation from the Local Election Commission in ten provinces.

The total number of parliament members in these ten provinces is 698. This is more than 32 per cent of the total number of 34 provincial parliament members (2,137 people). We can assume that the above age distribution and educational background are the main pattern of provincial parliament members. This local social profile is quite similar to the national one.

Political Middle Class and State Resource Dependency

These members of parliament spend a lot of money to finance their campaigns. According to research results from Economic and Development Research Unit (LPEM) at Universitas Indonesia,, the average cost per candidate of running for the national legislature is Rp 1.18 billion (see chapter 8 of this book). This sum is almost four times higher than in the 2009 election. For a provincial legislative candidacy, the cost is Rp 320–481 million, and perhaps half that for district/city legislatures (Ramadhan 2014).

The total funds circulated and distributed in 2014 legislative elections was Rp 115 trillion, or three times more than in 2009 (Prabowo 2014). Since Indonesia adopted an open proportional election system in 2009, the political cost has increased (Mietzner 2013). In this system, competition among candidates takes place within and between parties. Parties receive a subsidy from the state of Rp 1,000 per vote. In 2014, the parties that received the largest subsidy were PDI Perjuangan (18.95 per cent), Golkar (14.75 per cent), and Gerindra (11.81 per cent). This money is considered small (Mietzner 2013, p. 125) and is only enough for routine expenses of provincial secretariats and branches.

Where do candidates get money for their political costs? By law (8/2012, Article 130), candidates are allowed to receive funds from only three sources: individuals or groups, corporations, and non-government enterprises. In reality, most funds are sourced from unofficial channels, namely from businesspeople (Mietzner 2013, p. 124). At the local level, they are mostly from contractors.

Close observations during the 2009 legislative election in Pekalongan City, Central Java, where the author conducted ethnographic fieldwork on business and politics, revealed how contractors gained political access by financing candidates' campaign costs (Savirani 2014). The connection between contractors and local politicians is also found in other areas such as Aceh (Klinken and Aspinall 2011), Bogor and Surabaya (Mustofa 2017). Middle class politicians are integrated with economic power via local businesses.

To give an example, in Pekalongan, Central Java, the estimated cost per candidate in 2009 was Rp 300–400 million to reach the minimum number of BPP (*Bilangan pembagi pemilih*), a proportion between the number of voters and the number of seats allocation in each electorate area (Savirani 2014). Contractors selected candidates whom they thought would win. They came from the big parties in Pekalongan. The candidates were incumbents and were likely to be re-elected. Contractors allocated Rp 100 million among four candidates. This is part of their political investment, which would be returned once the candidates are elected.

Conservatism of the Political Middle Class

If state resources and social networks are the key resource for electoral politicians, they tend to be pro status quo, conservative. This can be seen from their policy stances. A recent issue in the national parliament was the bill on the Supreme Court, national parliament, provincial parliaments, district parliaments, and Senate, popularly known as the bill on "MD3" ("M" is for *Mahkamah Agung* or Supreme Court, and "D" is for DPR, legislative body). The bill on MD3 contradicts the spirit of democracy in Article 122, point (k), on defamation of legislators. In this article, criticism of members of parliament is restricted. This may threaten activists, society, and the press. Article 245 grants immunity for members of parliament by setting a complex process for members of parliament involved in a criminal case (Prastiwi 2018).

Strong conservatism among members of parliament regarding minority rights is shown in a civil law bill, especially in articles regulating adultery. Its definition is extended, which harms LGBT (lesbian, gay, bisexual, and transgender) people. The bill endorses citizens-led prosecution, which has been rampant in Indonesia recently. Failure to protect religious minority groups has often occurred. One example concerns church construction in Tolikara district in Papua. The local parliament allowed only a church belonging to the "Gereja Injil" (Bible of Church) denomination to be built in the district, because "Gereja Injil" has existed in the area for a long time. Newcomers are forbidden. Similar conservatism of parliament members can be found in many other districts and provinces. Local by-laws are filled with such sentiments. Between 1999 and 2009, there was a total of 19 shariah-based by-laws at provincial level and 150 at district level (Buehler 2013). In Sampang, Madura Island, members of parliament are silent concerning minority rights, such as issues of the Muslim sect, Shiite group.

Another conservatism of members of local parliament is in the city of Batu, Malang, where they ignore environmental impacts of local development and promote a strategy to increase local income. WALHI published a report in 2017 showing natural degradation due to aggressive strategies to get more money from tourism (Firman 2017). Similar silence concerning public interest among members of local parliament also took place in the city of Yogyakarta. Expansive tourism development by hotels has caused water scarcity during dry season that has caused the local population around the hotel area to suffer. This is because there is no clear regulation on ground water extraction for commercial purpose.

The self-interested attitude of members of local parliaments is obvious too in the way they allocate funds for themselves. This happened in Jakarta's parliament in early 2018. Nationwide, the national government allocates wages for members of local parliaments of Rp 8.2 trillion (US$630,769,230). The cost of field visits by Jakarta's parliament increased from Rp 8.8 billion to Rp 107.7 billion (from

US\$676,923 to US\$8,284,615), or more than 12 times, between the era of Basuki Tjahaja Purnama (2013–17) and the era of Anies Baswedan governorship (2017–present). Other expenses also increased, but the field visit allocation was the most significant (Sianipar 2017). Apart from Basuki Tjahaja Purnama, who minimized budget allocation for local parliament members due to efficiency, they pressure the governor to increase budget allocation to what they have invested during their election campaign, especially their connection to local businesspeople. Once elected, they need to facilitate access for businesspeople to state resources through procurement, which in most areas involves a significant amount.

From the exploration above of the political middle class in parliament, we can detect three points. *First,* the middle class in the parliament spends a huge amount to be elected, which is often sourced from local businesspeople. Sometimes social capital can help to win (sons of local or religious leaders), but most of the time middle class members have to survive by themselves, by forging alliances with anyone who can finance them. *Second,* this eventually influences their performance during their five-year tenure. During their terms, they must prioritize development oriented towards increasing revenue, to which they facilitate access for their financiers. This makes them very conservative and pro status quo. *Third,* due to expensive cost of running for elections, their political attitudes are generally self-interest and pragmatics, with no clear ideology.

Partai Solidaritas Indonesia (PSI): Middle Class Members in a New Political Party

There is another group of politicians, who are not part of existing political power. A new party is the Partai Solidaritas Indonesia (PSI), which successfully registered in October 2016. It will field candidates in the 2019 legislative election. The party was established in 2014, and is seen by many as countering the common perception of political parties, namely that they are populated by an older generation and are associated with old power holders, such as conservative parties and former administrators. The PSI claims to be a party of young people, who mostly live in urban areas and are educated. It requires its political candidates be under 45 years old and never to have joined any political party. These two requirements are to ensure that PSI is genuinely a "young people's party" and not part of the status quo. During the first round of selecting its legislative candidates, 60 per cent were born between 1981 and 1994.

If the party aims to be anti-status quo, it has a weak foundation, judging from its financiers. Jeffrie Geovani, a former politician from PAN, is one of them. Geovani is known as a politician who jumps around many parties: after PAN, he moved to Golkar, then Nasional Demokrat, then to Perindo, and his last post is as a member of DPD (regional senator) from West Sumatra province. He is now head of the advisory board of PSI. Saiful Mujani (a political scientist who is also director of a political consultant of SMRC) is also a member of the advisory board. There are other public figures, such as Giring Ganesha (popular singer), Grace Natalie, Isyana Bagus Oka, and Ni Luh Djelantik, who join the party. Raja Juli Antoni (Muhammadiyah cadre), who has a PhD from an Australian university, is a member of PSI daily board, and he runs for the 2019 election. Later, another young millennial, who is also a popular public figure, Tsamara Amany, joined PSI.

As a "millennial" party with young voters as its main target, PSI operates accordingly, which shows its strategies as different from other political parties. *First*, the party uses many terms familiar to young people. For example *kopi darat* or "offline meeting" replaces "national meeting", which sounds old and very formal. *Second*, it heavily uses social media such as Twitter, Facebook, and Youtube. PSI's Facebook account has 1.8 million followers. These strategies are foreign to older parties. *Third*, PSI tries to be inclusive and participative in governing the party. For example, they exercised an open and transparent selection of candidates to run in the 2019 election. There were more than 1,100 participants in the first round of selection in 2017. The party uses fundraising activities to collect resources for campaigns, and open donations for transparency in its financial activities, although so far they have not published the names of donors. PSI aims to collect public contributions of Rp 1 trillion to finance its 2019 campaign. It is not too clear how the money will be spent: whether as a party contribution to the candidate or for other expenses.

"Solidarity" in the PSI name relates to its belief in pluralism and advocating women's and young people's rights. Its tagline is "to spread good deed, to assure plurality, and to strengthen solidarity" (*menebar kebajikan, merawat keragaman, mengukuhkan solidaritas*). Many members of PSI were active in voluntary movements (*relawan*) during the 2014 presidential election and the 2017 Jakarta gubernatorial election. They supported Basuki Tjahaja Purnama (Ahok). The general secretary of the PSI, Raja Juli Antoni, was the spokesman for Basuki–Djarot.

Unlike members of the middle class who are already members of parliament, PSI seems to base its future prospects on the values of pluralism, accountability and transparency. We still need to observe it after the 2019 election. While their vision promotes progressive values, their funds come from political adventurers, so we can suspect that, once PSI cadres are elected, their attitude may follow that of their seniors from older parties.

Political Middle Class in Civil Society Arena

The second group is the middle class in the arena of civil society organizations. This is another social group who can be considered members of the middle class because of their knowledge, education, and social networks. They are not rich materially, but they have ample opportunities to influence policies. Generally, there are varieties of them. *First*, NGOs activists who are professionals in this field. They usually have a long career and training, or graduate from abroad on development issues; *second*, ordinary citizens who are not part of the professional NGOs but, due to their alienation from political events such as elections, set up voluntary groups in many sectors.

With regards to the middle class in civil society arena, they are the professionals, who have careers at NGOs. The population of NGOs blossomed after the fall of Soeharto, and they have played roles as watchdog of the government (Antlöv et al. 2012). If during the Soeharto era, the government effectively controlled NGOs activities, after Soeharto NGOs have been part of democratization. Sociologically, NGO activists are universities graduates and faculty members of prominent Indonesian universities (Sidel 2004). They are the middle class. According to data from SMERU Research Institute (n.d.), there are around 3,000 NGOs in Indonesia. These NGOs depend on foreign donors. Millions of dollars have been poured to Indonesia after *reformasi* (Loulena 2002).

Despite high dependency on foreign donors, NGOs in Indonesia play politics as well, although they claim to be neutral. I suggest they are involved indirectly in politics. They have become interest groups and their discourses and policy influences on the issue of human rights have coloured Indonesian politics post-Soeharto. During the 2014 presidential election and 2017 Jakarta gubernatorial election, NGOs activists took political side with two running candidates, showing their political roles and orientations in politics. If during the 2014 presidential election, most of the NGO activists defended Joko Widodo (Jokowi) as a candidate with no record of human rights abuses, during the 2017 gubernatorial election, human rights defenders split between those who supported Basuki Tjahaja Purnama for his anti-corruption campaign, and those who took side with Anies Baswedan, with his policy agenda of housing security for the urban poor. Either or, they have played roles in politics. When Jokowi became president, many activists became part of the regime. They were supposed to bridge the voices from civil society to the government. In many cases, this is not happening, although in many other cases, it works.

With regards to the second group of middle class in civil society, Indonesia has witnessed an increase of voluntary group activities, starting from the Jakarta gubernatorial election in 2012, when Joko Widodo and Basuki Tjahaja Purnama were candidates. It continued in the 2014 presidential election, when voluntary groups boomed. They mostly supported the Joko Widodo– Jusuf Kalla candidacy. Sociologically and politically, volunteer groups consists of two main groups: former activists who were involved in the 1990s pro-democracy movement; and professionals who first got involved in the 2014 election (Savirani 2015). The latter have less experience in politics, but their contribution during the 2014 election was significant.

Citizens' voluntary activities in social and political life are not new in Indonesia. In fact, it is argued to be part of organizing citizens in daily social life. Communal works (*gotong royong*) are one form. In political life, voluntary activities have been known for a long time. The largest political party, Partai Demokrasi Indonesia Perjuangan, is known to be run by many voluntary activities, for example *Posko Gotong Royong* (a small hut usually constructed by cadres in a neighbourhood, used for gathering cadres), or the community-based party financing scheme, *Pembiayaan Gotong Royong* (Dwipayana 2013). The posko was popular during the 1999 election. During the Soeharto era, many voluntary political events were organized collectively to protest against the authoritarian regime, such as *Peristiwa Yogya* 1992 (Yogya 1992 events) (Susanto 1993), in which white flags were raised all over the city as a protest against Golkar banning campaign activities using motorcycles. Another voluntary political event was the citizens' movement supporting Megawati Sukarnoputri and Sri Bintang Pamungkas during the 1997 election. In short, voluntary citizens-driven activities are not new in Indonesian politics.

In the post-Soeharto era, there have been increased voluntary activities among citizens on various issues. There are high profile cases, such as political support for the Corruption Eradication Institution (KPK) during its political fight with the police, popularly known as "Lizard versus Alligator". "Lizard" is a metaphor for a politically weak but smart party (*detikNews* 2009).

"Justice Coin for Prita" is another voluntary citizens-based event to collect money to support Prita Mulyasari. She was a patient in a private hospital who expressed her dissatisfaction with the hospital by sending a "letter from a reader" to a national newspaper. After the letter was published, the hospital sued her for defamation. The public was furious with the hospital. "Justice Coin for Prita" was organized to support her legal and other expenses (*Tempo* 2009).

A main difference between voluntary activities before and after Soeharto is the use of social media and information technology. Voluntary activities before Soeharto were more physical mobilizations, in which the people were usually present physically. After Soeharto, many of the activities were conducted virtually, or as a mixture of online and offline.

There are volunteer groups with a political agenda, *relawan* as an instrument to win elections. After Jokowi won, many figures who had been active in *relawan* activities gained political positions. Many activists became commissioners of state-owned enterprise or secured positions close to the president, such as Special Office for the President (KSP). In the 2017 Jakarta election, there were well-designed voluntary activities to support Ahok–Djarot, including Teman Ahok, a youth organization which claimed to be voluntary. In fact, it was set up by Cirus, a political consultant of Basuki Tjahaja Purnama (*Tempo* 2016).

However, other volunteer groups have nothing to do with real politics. They are commonly citizens who seem to be genuinely taking part in solving problems that the country faces. They are generally foreign to political games and seem to be "anti-politics", meaning they dislike politics and think politicians should not be part of Indonesian democracy. Technocrats (generally themselves) are regarded as heroes who can solve problems based on their expertise. This shows how diverse is the political outlook of the middle class in civil society. Those who support politics have a political agenda when the candidate they support wins election. Not all of them gain positions, but at least their political networks expand. Voluntary groups, which are idealists with no direct interest in positions, return to their daily life as professionals after the election.

Conclusion and Reflection

I began this chapter by asking how the middle class has fared after two decades of *reformasi*. Political middle class is a plural entity in Indonesia. They are politicians in political society (in parliament and political parties), as well as activists and voluntary groups in civil society arenas. The politicians in the political society have a strong power orientation. They are the huge number of people, from an overwhelmingly middle class background, who have stood for national or local parliaments. As the exploration above has shown, many of them are integrated with the local business middle class, and depend their lives on the state's resources. Activists and voluntary groups claim to have less orientation towards power, although over the past years they, too, join electoral politics as supporters of candidates. Activists have professional careers in NGOs with high dependency on foreign donors, while the voluntary groups are more plural with background ranging from professionals to ordinary citizens who want to do something for the country's political betterment.

Having said that, the two groups play politics in a different manner. They are different in terms of the degree and form of involvement (direct or indirect). Another difference is that members of parliament, who have secure seats tend to be inward looking, pro-status quo regarding democratic values, and with a self-serving attitude; while the second group is generally outward looking and progressive. Volunteer groups have coloured public discourse in their initiative to defend victims in social and political occurrences, such as the case of "Justice Coin for Prita" and "Lizard versus Gladiator". Their form of mobilizations is based on spontaneity and voluntary. This is why they tend to be short-life, with no systematic long-term consolidation.

One explanation of the different orientation is rooted in the type of resources the groups depend on. Members of parliament and voluntary political groups depend on state resources. The antipolitical volunteers are professionals, whose lives depend on their professional careers, and the activists who depend on foreign donors. The degree of dependency on state influences the way the two groups perceive politics. For the first group, politics is a resource for living, while for the second politics is an opportunity to improve society.

As long as Indonesia adopts representative democracy, political middle in political society will play substantial roles in the future of Indonesian democracy, despite being inward looking. Civil society with strong citizens' initiative will play roles too.

NOTE

1. The author would like to thank Jodi Hafidz Pratama for his assistance in exploring secondary data.

REFERENCES

Antlöv, Hans, Rustam Ibrahim, and Peter van Tuijl. "NGO Governance and Accountability in Indonesia: Challenges in a Newly Democratizing Country". In *NGO Accountability: Politics, Principles and Innovation*, edited by Jordan Lisa and Peter van Tuijl. London: Routledge, 2012.

Aspinall, Edward and Mada Sukmajati, eds. *Electoral Dynamics in Indonesia: Money Politics, Patronage and Clientelism at the Grassroots*. Singapore: NUS Press, 2016.

Bellefleur, Daniel, Zahra Murad and Patrick Tangkau. "A Snapshot of Indonesian Entrepreneurship and Micro, Small, and Medium Sized Enterprise Development". SMERU-USAID, 2012.

Buehler, Micheal. "Subnational Islamization through Secular Parties: Comparing Shari'a Politics in Two Indonesian Provinces". *Comparative Politics* 46, no. 1 (October 2013): 63–82.

detikNews. "Gerakan Cicak Vs Buaya Ramai di Facebook", 10 July 2009. Available at <https://news.detik.com/berita/d-1162738/gerakan-cicak-vs-buaya-ramai-di-facebook>.

Diela, Tabita. "Indonesia's Richest One Percent Controls Nearly Half of Nation's Wealth: Report". *Jakarta Globe*, 1 December 2016. Available at <http://jakartaglobe.id/business/indonesias-richest-one-percent-controls-nearly-half-nationswealth-report/>.

Dwipayana, AAG Ngurah Ari. "Pembiayaan Gotong Royong: Studi tentang Dinamika Pembiayaan Partai Demokrasi Indonesia Perjuangan pada Periode 1993–1999". Unpublished PhD thesis, Universitas Gadjah Mada, 2013.

Firman, Tony. "Warga Sumber Mata Air Kota Batu Melawan Pembangunan Hotel". *Tirto.id*, 3 July 2017. <https://tirto.id/warga-sumber-mata-air-kota-batu-melawan-pembangunan-hotelcrSi>.

FORMAPPI. "Anatomi Caleg DPR RI Terpilih Pada Pemilu 2014", 5 June 2014. Available at <http://parlemenindonesia.org/wp-content/uploads/2014/07/ANATOMI-CALEG-TERPILIHPEMILU- 2014_FORMAPPI.pdf> (accessed 28 February 2018).

Indonesia Investment Board. "Foreign Direct Investment in Indonesia Hit Record High in 2014", 2014. Available at <https://www.indonesia-investments.com/news/news-columns/foreign-direct-investment-in-indonesia-hit-record-high-in-2014/item5262>.

Jakarta Post. "Number of Unemployed Rises to 7.04 Million", 6 November 2017. Available at <http://www.thejakartapost.com/news/2017/11/06/number-of-unemployed-rises-to-7-04- million.html>.

Kurniawan, Haris. "KPU sediakan 20.257 kursi di Pemilu 2014". *Sindonews.com*, 14 March 2013. Available at <https://nasional.sindonews.com/read/727138/12/kpu-sediakan-20257-kursi-dipemilu- 2014-1363241101>.

Loulena, Anu. "Take the Money or Die". *Inside Indonesia*, Edition 69, January–March 2002. Available at <https://www.insideindonesia.org/take-the-money-or-die>.

Malang Post. "Sidang Paripurna, Target PAD Rp 135 M", 15 November 2017. Available at <https://malang-post.com/berita/kota-batu/sidang-paripurna-target-pad-rp-135-m>.

McKinsey Global Institute. "The Archipelago Economy: Unleashing Indonesia's Potential", 2012. Available at <https://www.mckinsey.com/~/media/McKinsey/Global%20Themes/Asia%20Pacific/The%20a rchipelago%20economy/MGI_Unleashing_Indonesia_potential_Executive_Summary.ashx>.

Mietzner, Marcus. *Money, Power, and Ideology: Political Parties in Post-Authoritarian Indonesia*. Singapore: NUS Press, 2013.

Mustafa, Mochamad. "Democratic Decentralization and Good Governance: The Political Economy of Procurement Reform in Decentralized Indonesia". Unpublished PhD theses, The University of Adelaide, South Australia, 2017.

Oxfam. "Towards a More Equal Indonesia: How the Government Can Take Action to Close the Gap between the Richest and the Rest". Oxfam Briefing Paper, February 2017. Available at <https://www.oxfam.org/sites/www.oxfam.org/files/bp-towards-more-equal-indonesia- 230217-en_0.pdf> (accessed 21 March 2018).

Prabowo, Dani. "Dana Bergulir Saat Pemilu Rp 115,3 Triliun, tetapi Tak Berdampak Signifikan". *Kompas*, 3 April 2014. Available at <https://nasional.kompas.

com/read/2014/04/03/1956204/Dana.Bergulir.Saat.Pemilu.Rp.115. 3.Triliun. tetapi.Tak.Berdampak.Signifikan>.

Prastiwi, Devira. "Alasan DPR Tetap Sahkan Revisi UU MD3". *Liputan6*, 13 February 2018. Available at <http://news.liputan6.com/read/3282090/alasan-dpr-tetap-sahkan-revisi-uu-md3>.

Putera, Andri Donnal. "Per 31 Agustus, Defisit APBN Sentuh Rp 150,7 Triliun". *Kompas*, 21 September 2018. Available at <https://ekonomi.kompas.com/read/2018/09/21/181034826/per-31-agustus-defisit-apbnsentuh-rp-1507-triliun>.

Ramadhan, Bilal. "Hasil Riset, Ini Jumlah Rata-Rata Dana Kampanye Caleg DPR". *Republika*, 19 March 2014. Available at <http://www.republika.co.id/berita/nasional/politik/14/03/19/n2o11c-hasil-riset-ini-jumlahratarata- dana-kampanye-caleg-dpr>.

Savirani, Amalinda. "The Persistence of Neopatrimonialism in Pekalongan, Central Java, Indonesia". In *In Search of Middle Indonesia: Middle Classes in Provincial Town*, edited by Gerry Van Klinken and Ward Berenschot. Leiden-Boston: Brill, 2014. Available at <www.brill.com/printpdf/26811>.

―――. "Jokowi's Supporters are Starting to Doubt the 'Indonesian Obama'". *The Conversation*, 24 February 2015. Available at <https://theconversation.com/jokowis-supporters-are-starting-to-doubt-the-indonesian-obama-37843>.

Sianipar, Tito. "Anggaran Jakarta melonjak: 'Semuanya lapar dan haus', kata seorang anggota DPRD". BBC Indonesia, 21 December 2017. Available at <http://www.bbc.com/indonesia/indonesia-42098725>.

Sidel, John. "Watering the Flowers, Killing the Weeds: The Promotion of Local Democratization and Good Governance in Indonesia". Unpublished report to the Ford Foundation, Jakarta, September 2004.

SMERU Research Institute. "NGO Database", n.d. Available at <http://www.smeru.or.id/en/content/ngo-database>.

Susanto, Budi. *Peristiwa Yogya 1992: Siasat Politik Massa Rakyat Kota*. Yogyakarta: Kanisius, 1993.

Tempo. "Info Lokasi Pengumpulan Koin Peduli Prita", 11 December 2009. Available at <https://metro.tempo.co/read/213348/info-lokasi-pengumpulan-koin-peduli-prita>.

―――. "EKSKLUSIF: Perjalanan Duit Rp 30 Miliar ke Teman-teman Ahok", 20 June 2016. Available at <https://metro.tempo.co/read/781506/eksklusif-perjalanan-duit-rp-30-miliar-ke-temanteman- ahok>.

Van Klinken, Gerry and Edward Aspinall. "Building Relations: Corruption, Competition and Cooperation in the Construction Industry". In *The State and Illegality in Indonesia*, edited by Edward Aspinall and Gerry van Klinken. Leiden: KITLV Press, 2011.

7

The Politics of Centre–Local Relations in Contemporary Indonesia

Cornelis Lay

Background

One of the earliest and most significant transformations implemented as part of reform in Indonesia since 1998 has been the restructuring of relations between the national government in Jakarta and local governments. In the early years of independence, demands for representation and access to resources and economic activities led to what were widely termed "regional rebellions" in several parts of Indonesia: Aceh, West Sumatra, and North and South Sulawesi. Incidents between 1950 and the early 1960s, which Harvey (1977) labelled "half-hearted rebellions",[1] led to the creation of new autonomous regions (provinces, regencies, cities) as well as the granting of special autonomy to Aceh.[2] At the same time, as late over the course of the New Order, the government promoted the migration of local capitalists to Jakarta, where they either entered new activity spaces or lost their local living spaces. Examples are the migration of local entrepreneurial families — such as Kalla, Hasyim Ning, Bakrie, etc. — and the end of local economic dynasties, such as the Pardede in North Sumatra. As will be discussed in further detail, the demand to restructure centre–local relations after

1998 marked a reversal of this trend, as local entrepreneurial forces became stronger and offered an alternative means of recruiting local political elites.

Under the authoritarian New Order regime, such demands were never openly voiced. However, haunted by the spectre of previous regional rebellions, Jakarta took a number of preventive measures aggressively to consolidate its power through its increasingly strict regional penetration and control. This meant rampant centralization, which occurred together with widespread standardization. Over time, this created highly unbalanced power relations, "Jakarta" seemingly becoming synonymous with Indonesia as a whole (Lay 2001).

The central government's preventive measures were comprehensive. *First*, they included the creation of a military structure parallel to the civil one, from the (inter-)provincial level — represented by the Regional Military Command (Komando Daerah Militer) — to the village level — the Village Guidance Unit (Bintara Pembina Desa, Babinsa). Military commanders at each level became part of the local strategic decision-making institution known as a "council of leadership" (*musyawarah pimpinan*) at the regional (provincial/regency/city) and district levels. Today, this military structure remains, though it is no longer involved in decision making and has thus lost its effectiveness as a means of central control over regional governments. A *second* measure was the "karya"ization or civilian tasking of military officers, either as members of legislatures or as executive officials (governors, regents, mayors) in areas considered "strategic" for their economic value or political vulnerability (Anderson 1983, p. 490). Data from 1999 indicate that some 6,800 active members of the military were occupying non-military positions (Bhakti, Tyas, and Cahyono 1999, p. 143). In parliament, members of the military held 75 of 500 seats, as well as 2,800 seats in local parliaments (Crouch 2010, pp. 133–34; Robinson 2001, pp. 234–35). Since 2004, the military has not been allocated any parliamentary seats or received any special rights to executive office; when members of the military seek such positions, they must contest elections and leave the military.

Third, a monolithic loyalty was created within the bureaucracy through the Corps of Ministry of the Interior (Korps Karyawan Kementerian Dalam Negeri), which was controlled strictly by Jakarta (Beittinger-Lee 2009, p. 61). After 1998, even as staff continued to draw their wages from the national budget, centre control began eroding.

A number of cases indicate that civil servants were under the control of regional leaders and used as political tools in electoral contests (Agustinus 2014; Hamid 2011). Finally, professionals were controlled through state corporatism (Eldridge 1989; Eldridge 1995; Hadiz 2005). This corporatism, however, has eroded as groups have received greater freedom of association and expression.

Demands, both open and covert, for greater regional authority in the lead-up to reform in 1998, followed similar patterns: they were motored by local economic, political, and military elites who jointly demanded regional "economic justice". In the reform era, a different demand was voiced by a group of a different character: educated youths on (predominantly Javan) campuses sought "democracy" as their ultimate goal. They relied on extra-parliamentary means such as demonstrations, and from the beginning "the broadest autonomy and decentralization" was one of their six key political demands.[3]

This chapter focuses on recent developments, exploring the transformations and stagnations in the structuring of centre–local relations between 1999 and 2013, and in particular the most recent developments (2014–18). Unlike most studies of local and national politics in Indonesia (for example, Riwu 2002; Riwu 2012; Aspinall and Fealy 2015; Gerritsen and Situmorang 1999), this chapter will simultaneously explore state and non-state spheres. This recognizes that intra-bureaucratic or state-centric analyses have long viewed non-political dynamics as irrelevant and thus have produced only narrow understandings.

The Legacy of 1999–2013

The most fundamental response to demands for restructured centre–local relations in the reform era was the establishment of new political institutions. As such, 1999–2013 is important because it laid the foundation for new institutions. This period marked the passing of various laws and government regulations. The new laws (see Table 7.1) covered almost all aspects of civilian governmental structure, including electoral processes and aspects of the structuring of the military and police.

The combined effect of the reforms was extraordinary: the transformation of centre–local power relations in an unprecedented and unforeseen form. This involved, first, the establishment of formal institutional channels to provide regional governments with a voice in

TABLE 7.1
Laws, 1999–2013

No.	Number	Regarding
1	Law No. 2/1999, revised through Law No. 31/2002, Law No. 2/2008, and Law No. 2/2011	Political Parties
2	Law No. 3/1999	General Elections
3	Law No. 4/1999, then replaced by Law No. 22/2003, replaced by Law No. 8/2008, and then Law No. 8/2012	Composition and Position of the People's Consultative Assembly, Regional Representatives Council, and Local Parliament
4	Law No. 2/2002	Indonesian National Police
5	Law No. 33/2004	Financing of Central and Regional Governments
6	Law No. 34/2004	Indonesian Military
7	Law No. 42/2008	Presidential Election
8	Law No. 15/2011	Election Organizer
9	Law No. 8/2012, replaced by Law No. 7/2017 on General Elections	Election of People's Consultative Assembly, Regional Representatives Council, and Local Parliament
10	Law No. 17/2013, replaced by Law No. 2/2017	Civil Society Organizations

national decision making. This was fundamental, as it involved constitutional amendments to provide space for the Regional Representatives
Council. Furthermore, this institution was created through electoral
competition that differed in form from previous competitions. Previously, regional governments received only symbolic and ad hoc
representation through "regional delegates" to the People's Consultative
Assembly — before constitutional amendments, the highest decision-
making body in Indonesia. Pursuant to Law No. 8/2012, every province
received four representatives. Although the new Regional Representatives Council had limited authority, it offered a means to involve

regional governments in national politics, one for future consolidation, with the added legitimacy of being elected.

Second, formal government authority, including in the hiring of staff, was transferred to local governments. For the first time, Jakarta's authority was limited to five strategic fields: security, economy, international relations, justice, and religion. Furthermore, asymmetrical decentralization, a form of political regulation that emphasizes the asymmetrical distribution and setting of power between two regions, or between a region and the national government (Haryanto, Lay and Purwoko 2018, p. 367), was implemented, ending the dominance of "standardization" in regional management models.

Third, during this period, local power was distributed through administrative division. This boom in new administrative districts — far surpassing that of the 1950s — fundamentally transformed the position of local government relative to Jakarta. For the first time, local governments could challenge the administrative boundaries unilaterally imposed by the central government. They gained the right to propose new administrative divisions. Although regulations set complicated and difficult criteria,[4] the practice of showing "regional aspirations", combined with the mechanism of bribery within the national parliament and Ministry of the Interior, became nearly the sole rationale for establishing new administrative districts.[5] It is not surprising that the number of administrative districts increased from 298 regencies/cities and 27 provinces in 1999 to 493 regencies/cities and 33 provinces in 2011 and 508 regencies/cities and 34 provinces in 2014.

The uncontrolled growth of new administrative districts forced the central government to take action, revising Government Regulation No. 78/2007 regarding the Creation, Elimination, and Combination of Administrative Districts. This revision permitted the creation of new administrative districts only within areas of sufficient age, ten years for provinces and seven years for regencies/cities; previous regulations had permitted immediate administrative division. Another change came to the minimum number of regencies/cities for new provinces; Government Regulation No. 129/2000 required a minimum of five regencies/cities for new provinces, one more than previously. The minimum number of districts required for the creation of new regencies/cities was increased from three to four. This government regulation also offered a legal means for the central government to liquidate regional governments incapable of properly implementing their autonomy. Further-more, the government and parliament implemented a moratorium on the creation of new administrative districts (*Beraunews.com* 2017). However, these steps were incapable of stemming the demand for new administrative divisions. In February 2017, the Ministry of the Interior had 237 proposals for new administrative divisions, a number that had increased to 314 in February 2018 (*Beritasatu* 2018). Presently, the Ministry of the Interior is preparing two laws — on Regional Planning and on the Basic Design of Regional Planning — to provide a legal basis for the establishment and adaptation of administrative districts (*Tempo* 2016).

Fourth, regulations facilitated the process of political liberalization, which resulted in power migrating from the state to society. This included, among other things, direct elections of regional leaders (Law No. 32/2004). This offered considerable penetration to local communities, and could better influence regional policy (Lay 2007). During the New Order, the local parliaments had functioned only to offer a maximum of two alternative candidates to be appointed by the president through the Ministry of the Interior. Candidacies became monopolized by the bureaucracy and parties, a situation seriously disrupted by the inclusion of non-party and individual candidates — i.e. "independent candidates" — through Constitutional Court Decision No. 5/PUU-V/2007. Even though few independent candidates were elected,[6] and the criteria for such candidacies were difficult,[7] their presence broadened citizens' rights and access to public office. The presence of independent candidates transformed local governments into important political loci that, in electoral logics, gave local issues and voices new relevance. In the future, this will become increasingly important as direct elections are held simultaneously.[8]

Fifth, the restructuring of centre–local relations offered increased security and increased fiscal capacity through the granting of funds as a fixed percentage of the national budget. Thus the sources of regional income became stabilized and received more space for planning and budgeting. Where areas rich in natural resources had previously failed to enjoy the fruits of their exploitation, "profit sharing" has offered regional governments a greater fiscal capacity and distribu-tive justice.[9]

Decentralization

Over the past four years, centre–local relations have continued to be restructured. Indonesia is presently experiencing a period of expanding decentralization. However, the consequences of this are difficult to predict.

A. Decentralization Down to the Village

Since the passing of Law No. 6/2014, transformations in centre–local relations have taken deeper root, reaching the lowest administrative structures. Villages have transformed into important loci for politics and development because of legislation that has given legal recognition to the diversity of villages and their centrality in empowering members of society as subjects of development. Recognition of villages is also evidenced in the significant amount of money being granted to them.[10]

However, processes that were hypothesized to empower villages — and the regions around them — economically, culturally, and politically have faced serious questions due to overemphasis on "village funds". In 2015, the national government implemented a programme to divide Rp 20.77 trillion among Indonesia's 74,958 villages. This increased to Rp 46.98 trillion in 2016, Rp 58.2 trillion in 2017, and Rp 60 trillion in 2018 (Purnamasari 2018).

Due to this significant funding, various supra-village forces have entered villages with their own interests, agendas, and methods. Available observations and data indicate that the funding is treated as a project of the Jakarta-based government and thus subject to multilayer surveillance. The Ministry of Finance emphasized that 82.2 per cent of village funds have been used for infrastructure development: roads, irrigation, etc. Only 7.7 per cent have been used for social empowerment (Purnamasari 2018). Furthermore, in the name of transparency and accountability — key jargon promoted by the World Bank — the national government has been involved in greater interventions and monitoring in villages (communities). This can be seen, *first*, from the establishment of Village Fund Units in mid-2017 to accelerate the distribution, management, and supervision of projects. These units were under the coordination of Bibit Samad Rianto, the former leader of the Corruption Eradication Commission (Komisi Pemberantasan Korupsi, KPK) (Julianto 2017). *Second*, this was followed by the expansion of institutions representing the central government, particularly for monitoring. This began with the signing of a memorandum of understanding[11] regarding the prevention, monitoring, and handling of village funds, to be handled by the regional police and as well as the Financial Auditing Agency (Badan Pemeriksa Keuangan, BPK) (Zuhriyah 2017). Meanwhile, the KPK kept monitoring the programme, and recently detained several village chiefs (Gabrillin 2017).

Villages have not only witnessed the expansion of contestation between national political authorities, as shown above. They have also witnessed the activities of various national and international civil society organizations. Villages, through their collaboration with Jakarta, have also begun working with international donor institutions such as the World Bank,[12] which represents market interests. The process of decentralization through villages, thus, has also promoted a free market ideology, one that — historically speaking — was not unprecedented, as similar phenomena had followed the introduction of a "money" system through the land taxes introduced by Daendels (1808–11) in the colonial era. Although more detailed research is necessary, it is clear that the widespread infiltration of supra-village forces has brought high levels of politicization and control. This carries the long-term risk of eroding village autonomy, even as the decentralization policy promotes it.

All of the developments discussed above indicate contestation between two opposed local processes: a deepening of decentralization simultaneously with an erosion of decentralization.

B. Central Intervention via National Prioritization of Projects

The structuring of centre–local relations has involved not only various political instruments but also technocratic ones directly related to economic development activities. This has involved a shift in the approaches to and locus of development. Previous top-down development mechanisms, which centred on Java, have over the past four years shifted dramatically. What is known as "development from the margins" represents this fundamental shift.[13] Border regions, for example, which were previously "protected" by military force, are now protected by infrastructure development and local economic activities. Miangas Island, which borders the Philippines, now has an airport to promote the distribution of foodstuffs/goods and mobility, as well as to improve security and defence. Since independence, Miangas was practically isolated, relying solely on sea shipments from Bintuni, Papua, a journey that took more than twenty-four hours (Ika 2016). Likewise, long underdeveloped border regions — Entikong, Badau, and Aruk in West Kalimantan; Motaain, Matamasin, and Wini in East Nusa Tenggara, and Skouw in Papua — have experienced rapid infrastructure development and economic investment (Candra 2018). Similar plans will be implemented in other border areas (Bere 2018).[14]

The change in development strategies and locus has been supported by planning agendas that have positioned infrastructure as their greatest priority. Since 2016, national spending for infrastructure has increased dramatically, from Rp 317.1 trillion (15.2 per cent of the national budget) to Rp 387.3 trillion (18.6 per cent) in 2017 (*Katadata* 2016). This increased to Rp 410.7 trillion in the 2018 budget (Prabowo 2017). Furthermore, the distribution of infrastructure prospects has changed dramatically, reaching areas that had previously been unaffected by the National Strategic Projects.[15] Map 7.1 also indicates a

MAP 7.1
Distribution of National Strategic Projects

Source: National Strategic Projects, Committee for the Acceleration of the Provision of National Infrastructure, available at <https://kppip.go.id/proyek-strategis-nasional/>.

transformation in development perspectives, from the Java-centrism of the past to Indonesia-centrism. Indonesia's strength as a nation is no longer measured by its strongest chain, but by its weakest link.

This provision of infrastructure is intended to make manifest the ideological goal of social welfare for all of Indonesia's people, as repeatedly asserted by President Joko Widodo (Jokowi).[16] Early steps in this direction appear promising. Over time, this may better balance the capacities of different regions, which in turn will promote massive economic growth.

Jokowi has received some harsh criticism for his prioritization of infrastructure development (Warburton 2016). However, in the long term, this will have significant consequences for centre–local relations. This must, of course, be considered carefully. The shift in development locus and priority — as with that of decentralization — has dual implications. On the one hand, it could strengthen the national presence through the impact of nationally decided projects, increasing the potential for re-centralization. On the other hand, it could empower the local. However, I expect that dialogue between these processes to slowly transform the New Order logic of power that demanded central control over the local. This will offer a new perspective for understanding centre–local relations and consolidating Indonesia into a single sociocultural, economic, and political unit. Strong local governments need not be compensated by weakening the centre, and vice versa.

The above situation has been made possible by the shift in the priorities and locus of development. *First*, it has reduced isolation by improving interconnectedness, something that has been supported by the creation of a transportation system (or "sea toll lane") connecting the outer islands (Wicaksana 2017). *Second*, it has offered a means for solving underdevelopment by improving regional economies and improving access to basic public services (*Katadata* 2017). Proper infrastructure, thus, enables communities to access basic services quickly and cheaply. *Third*, it has offered a potential answer to the "interregional gap" that has plagued Indonesia since independence. Tensions between the centre and local — including, most recently, in Aceh and Papua — have underscored the importance of identity politics. Without ignoring this factor, it is clear that addressing the three issues discussed above — isolation, underdevelopment, and welfare disparity — will prove an important step towards consolidating the Indonesian nation.

Effects

A. Rise of Local Entrepreneurs

The transformations in centre–local relations discussed above have broadly affected politics. First, they have led to the creation of local bourgeoisie on a massive scale, even as this bourgeoisie may not serve as the foundation for a national capitalist class (Lane 2014). The shift of power to the local has offered greater space for the rise of local capitalism. This has had two major effects: the creation of political contestation at a much more local level — be it between older generations of local capitalists or between members of their group[17] — as well as the dependency of local politics on this class.

During the New Order, local politics in Indonesia was dominated by bureaucrats and the military, as shown by van Klinken in East Nusa Tenggara (van Klinken 2007; van Klinken 2014; van Klinken and Berenschot 2014); local nobility, as shown by Haryanto with his study of the Qahhar Mudzakkar clan in South Sulawesi (Haryanto 2014); and commercial and landed aristocracy in former harbour principalities and kingdoms, as shown by Burhan Magenda in West Nusa Tenggara (Lombok and Sumbawa), East Kalimantan, and South Sulawesi (Magenda 1989); and Dwipayana Bali (Dwipayana 2001). Following reform, new local politics emerged, produced through completely different political processes. In the years following reform, no formal recruitment mechanisms existed; this is verified by the presence of new members of parliament and executive leaders in the 1999 elections. The social basis of these local politicians cannot be clearly identified, except that they gained their political support through party backing in electoral contests. It is thus unsurprising that the 1999 elections produced diverse members of parliament and executives. They included bread-sellers (Fahriyanto, mayor of Magelang 2000–5 and 2005–10), used car salesmen (Freddy Harry Sualang, deputy governor of North Sulawesi 2000–5 and 2005–10), work unit leaders (Sunarna, regent of Klaten), and religious leaders (Kyai Haji Robbach Maksum, regent of Gresik 2000–5 and 2005–10), professors (I Gede Winasa, regent of Jembrana 2000–5, 2005–10), entrepreneurs (Untung Wiyono, regent of Sragen 2001–6, 2006–11), and activists (Frans Lebu Raya, deputy governor of East Nusa Tenggara 2003–8 and governor 2008–18). As regional election bodies became increasingly institutionalized, local political figures' bases became increasingly consolidated. Election data since 2004, particularly on the 2014 general election and 2015 and 2017 simultaneous regional elections, indicate a dramatic shift. The unclear bases of local politicians in the 1999 election were rapidly consolidated, while former sources — i.e. the bureaucracy and military — were unable to return to their previous glory. It has become evident that the bases of local politicians became consolidated primarily among the new local bourgeoisie, particularly those involved in infrastructure development and natural resources, as shown in the following cases.

In the 2017 mayoral contest in Jayapura, though it ultimately produced only one candidate, four of the six potential candidates were career contractors. Benhur Tomi Mano ran with Rustan Saru, a contractor and head of the National Mandate Party (Partai Amanat Nasional, PAN) in Papua. Boy Markus Dawir ran with Nuralam, a Working Groups Party (Partai Golongan Karya, Golkar) member who became a Democrat (Demokrat) and occupied strategic positions in three organizations active in construction: Indonesian Contractors Association (Ahli Pemborong Indonesia, Atapi), Association of Construction Workers in Indonesia (Asosiasi Konstruksi Pemborong Indonesia, Askopindo Papua), and Association of Goods Providers and Distributors (Asosiasi Rekanan Pengadaan Barang dan Distributor, Ardindo). Abisai Rollo was a Golkar politician who owned the real estate developer Rollo Green Diamond and headed the National Union of Construction Providers (Gabungan Pelaksana Konstruksi Nasional Indonesia, Gapensi). His deputy, Dipo Wibowo, was also a contractor (Lay et al. 2017, pp. 439–40). In the 2017 regional head election, 50 per cent of 310 candidates were from private or business entities, the rest were incumbent members of national/local parliament, TNI/Polri, and village heads, while in 2018, the number of candidates with private or business background reached 44.89 per cent of 569 candidates (The Indonesian Institute – Center for Public Policy Research 2018).

Over the long term, this new class has had fundamental effects. Positively, it has the potential to thaw the ascriptive identities and ordinal parameters that have long dictated local social, economic, and political relations. The experiences in Papua described above may represent an early step in this process. However, reflecting on the current situation that has emphasized identity politics, this optimism must be tempered. As shown by Fox (2018), the elections system in Indonesia's shift from the "party-centric rules" of 1997–2004 to "candidate-centric rules" of 2009–14 occurred simultaneously with increased ethnic politicization. This situation is particularly important given Indonesia's increased digitization, as well as the rise of post-truth society in which information has a minimal role in shaping perceptions (Tapsell 2017). This emphasis on ethnicity may not only negatively affect (local) democracy in Indonesia, but also centre–local relations.

Furthermore, the rise of state-led or state-dependent classes because of various economic activities (involving both resources and infrastructure) has brought with it questions of democracy. Even though they come from an entirely new class, new political actors still have difficulty freeing themselves of their dependence on the local state. This has the potential to reinforce the inward-looking mentality of entrepreneurs that took shape during the New Order as a result of Indonesia's difficulty consolidating its bourgeoisie to compete globally. In the past, the (national) entrepreneurs of Indonesia were considered "cage jockeys" (*jago kandang*). Over time, this stigma was not eliminated through the localization process, but rather exacerbated. There is some optimism that the development of digital technology can free them from their increasingly smaller "spatial prison", but this requires hard work, sufficient infrastructure (such as electricity), and — most importantly — cultural transformation.

Another issue involves the pathological class issues that have spread from the national to the local. Practices such as rent-seeking, patronage, and brokerage (Berenschot 2018; Aspinall and Sukmajati 2015; Stokes et al. 2013) may only be reinforced by the emergence of this new entrepreneurial class through decentralization. Research has confirmed such tendencies, which have resulted in local power overlaps. However, at the same time, electoral democracy has facilitated their access to and control over power, to the exclusion of others. Their attention has been focused on decentralization — the transfer of authority from the centre to the local — without concern for democracy. The distribution of power involves them greatly, as they have the potential to hijack local democracy, unlike in the early years of reform, when the democratic process was hijacked by those who had previously enjoyed power (Erb and Sulistiyanto 2009; Robinson and Hadiz 2004; Hadiz 2010).

B. More Actual Political Space for Initiatives

Another effect of restructuring centre–local relations is the rise of new local policy and governance initiatives. Jakarta, thus, no longer determines political agendas.

A number of regencies and cities have become "schools" for other administrative districts, such as Jembrana (Eko 2015) in healthcare and education and Blitar for basic social services such as home rehabilitation and citizen charter, a written declaration between government as service provider and citizens that highlights the standard of service delivery. Early regional initiatives found their momentum as direct regional elections were implemented and candidates were expected to come up with fresh ideas to promote their electoral goals. This has offered space for horizontal learning through which particular initiatives and practices are spread from region to region.[18] This horizontal learning process is not sporadic, but institutionalized through cooperative initiatives, such as the transportation and garbage management programmes involving Yogyakarta, Sleman, and Bantul; the tourism initiative Java Promo involving thirteen regencies throughout Central Java and Yogyakarta province; the economic infrastructure development programme of Banjarnegara, Purbalingga, Banyumas, Cilacap, and Kebumen regencies; the joint secretariat of Pacitan, Wonogiri, and Gunung Kidul regencies intended to accelerate coastal development; and the collaboration between Surakarta city, and Boyolali, Sukoharjo, Karanganyar, Wonogiri, Sragen, and Klaten regencies to improve public service (PLOD 2007). Different regions have also functionally organized themselves into interregional institutions such as the All-Indonesia Association of City Governments (Asosiasi Pemerintah Kota Seluruh Indonesia, APEKSI), All-Indonesia Association of Regency Governments (Asosiasi Pemerintah Kabupaten Seluruh Indonesia, APKASI), and the All-Indonesia Association of Provincial Governments (Asosiasi Pemerintah Provinsi Seluruh Indonesia, APPSI). Such initiatives, previously unimaginable, have become increasingly diverse, with equally diverse levels of success and failure. Some have attracted the national government's interest in formulating similar programmes, such as the Kartu Indonesia Pintar and Kartu Indonesia Sehat programmes,[19] which expanded upon local initiatives (Mas'udi and Lay 2018).

The reinforcement of the local and the creation of new leadership standards, with increased emphasis on capacity to deliver promised programmes, have become important in the evaluation of leaders' success. This is demonstrated by several cases, including that of Jokowi in Solo and Jakarta (Mietzner 2015; Pratikno and Lay 2013;

Mas'udi 2017), Tri Rismaharini in Surabaya, Djarot Saiful Hidayat in Blitar, Hasto Wardoyo in Kulonprogo (Mas'udi and Kurniawan 2017), Nurdin Abdullah in Bantaeng, Abdullah Azwar Anas in Banyuwangi, Suyoto in Bojonegoro, Yoyok Riyo Sudibyo in Batang, Ridwan Kamil in Bandung city, Aripin Arpan in Tapin, Yansen Tiba Pandan in Malinau, and Mohammad Ramdhan Pomanto in Makassar (Firmanto 2017).

Conclusion

Discussion has shown that, since *reformasi* began in 1998, the transformation of the power relations between the national government in Jakarta and the regional governments has been dynamic. Changing regimes, political actors, and institutions have transformed the political system through various regulations and simultaneously dictated the transformations of the dynamics of power relations.

Between 1998 and 2014, the pendulum swung towards decentralization through dual processes of broadening and deepening. This second process has intensified since 2014, when decentralization began to reach the lowest political structures, i.e. villages. However, in this era decentralization has become simultaneously increasingly deep and shallow, as the political space of the village has served as an arena for outside contestations. This phenomenon of recentralization occurring together with decentralization has continued until the present day. Although the ultimate resolution of this situation remains unknown, general tendencies indicate that it will end with the creation of a new balance, in which the definition of "Indonesia" is no longer dictated by the central government in Jakarta. In this era, no longer will Jakarta be able to pompously proclaim, "I am Indonesia".

NOTES

1. As with the "rebellion" of the Revolutionary Government of the Republic of Indonesia (Pemerintahan Revolusioner Republik Indonesia, PRRI), which was declared in 1958 and supported by the Permesta movement in North and Central Sulawesi in response to the central government's new autonomous region policies.

2. A list of the provinces established during this period follows:

1950: Sumatra was divided into North, Central, and South Sumatra; Yogyakarta received regional autonomy.

1956: Kalimantan was divided into West, South, and East Kalimantan; Aceh was created from North Sumatra.

1957: Jakarta was given special capital status.

1958: Central Sumatra was divided into Jambi, Riau, and West Sumatra; Lesser Sundas was divided into Bali, West Nusa Tenggara, and East Nusa Tenggara; Central Kalimantan was created from South Kalimantan.

1960: Sulawesi was divided into North and South Sulawesi.

1963: West Irian was created.

1964: Lampung was created from South Sumatra; Central Sulawesi was created from North Sulawesi; Southeast Sulawesi was created from South Sulawesi.

See "Pemekaran Daerah di Indonesia" [Regional Administrative Division in Indonesia], Wikipedia, available at <https://id.wikipedia.org/wiki/Pemekaran_daerah_di_Indonesia> (accessed 17 January 2018).

3. The six demands were: Amendments to the 1945 Constitution; trial of former President Soeharto and his cronies; eradication of corruption, collusion, and nepotism; rescinding the packet of five political laws; rescinding of dual function of the military; and granting of the broadest regional autonomy. Litbang Kompas, "Indonesia Selama 20 Tahun Era Reformasi", *Kompas*, 21 May 2018, p. 2.

4. Government Regulation No. 78/2007 set administrative, technical, and physical criteria for the establishment of new autonomous regions. Administrative criteria included: approval of regional parliament; approval of governor/regent/mayor; and ministerial recommendation. Technical criteria included: economic capacity, regional potential, socio-cultural situation, socio-political situation, population, security, welfare, and government control. Physical criteria included: location of potential capital, infrastructure, and facilities.

5. Together with a UGM team, the author was included in the examination of several regions for administrative division. In the author's experience, rumours spread widely, and various inappropriate means were used to fulfil the criteria through population growth (Padmasari 2017).

6. The Association for Elections and Democracy (Perkumpulan Untuk Pemilu dan Demokrasi, Perludem) records 135 independent candidates and 13 elected candidates (Tomohon, Tanjungbalai, Bukittinggi, Bontang, Banjarbaru, Supiori, Sabu Raijua, Rembang, Rejanglebong, Kutai

Kertanegara, Ketapang, Gowa, and Bandung) in the 2015 regional elections. In 2017, only eight independent candidates were chosen, with three victors: Pidie, Boalemo, and Sarmi (*Republika* 2017).

7. Article 41 of Law No. 10/2016 regulates the support necessary (in terms of percentage of registered voters) for independent candidates. At the provincial level, where there are 2 million or fewer registered voters, independent candidates must have the support of no fewer than 10 per cent of registered voters; 2–6 million, 8.5 per cent; 6–12 million, 7.5 per cent; more than 12 million, 6.5 per cent. This support must be distributed among at least 50 per cent of the regencies/cities in the province. Independent regent/mayoral candidates in areas with 250,000 registered voters or fewer than 10 per cent of voters; 250,000–500,000, 8.5 per cent; 500,000–1 million, 7.5 per cent; and more than 1 million, 6.5 per cent. This support must be distributed among at least 50 per cent of the districts in the regency/city — an increase from the requirement of 3–6.5 per cent set by Laws No. 2/2008 and No. 1/2015.

8. In the first simultaneous regional election, on 9 December 2015, 269 regional leaders — 9 governors, 30 mayors, and 224 regents — were elected. The 2017 regional election involved 101 administrative districts: 7 provinces, 18 cities, and 76 regencies. The June 2018 election will be held in 171 administrative districts: 17 provinces, 39 cities, and 115 regencies.

9. The profit-sharing results are cash transfers for five types of resources: forests; oil and gas; minerals and coal; geothermal energy; and fisheries.

10. Article 3 of the Village Law emphasizes that village governance is based on recognition, subsidiarity, diversity, unity, mutual assistance, discussion, democracy, independence, participation, equality, empowerment, and sustainability.

11. The signing of the accord involved the Minister of Villages, Regional Development, and Transmigration Eko Sandjojo as well as the Minister of Interior Affairs Tjahjo Kumolo and Police Chief General Tito Karnavian on 20 October 2017.

12. The World Bank is presently funding the village innovation programme (Program Inovasi Desa, PID), which is under the umbrella of the Decree of the Minister of Villages No. 83/2017 regarding the Guidelines for the Village Innovation Programme. PID is funded through a loan from the International Bank for Reconstruction and Development. This programme is a cross-ministerial one, involving the Coordinating Minister for Human Development, the Minister of Interior Affairs, and the Minister of National Development Planning. PID is intended to increase the quality of village fund usage through various development and social empowerment

activities. It has been implemented in 434 regencies/cities in 33 provinces (except the Jakarta Capital Region) (*PIDmorut* 2018).

13. This represents the third of nine Jokowi–JK priorities, known jointly as Nawa Cita.

14. These nine border crossings are in Rupat, Bengkalis Regency (Riau), Serasan, Natuna Regency (Riau Archipelago), Jagoi Babang, Bengkayang Regency (West Kalimantan), Jasa, Sintang Regency (West Kalimantan), Sei Pancang, Nunukan Regency (North Kalimantan), Napan, in Northern Central Timor Regency (East Nusa Tenggara), Maritaeng, Alor Regency (East Nusa Tenggara), Oepuli, Kupang Regency (East Nusa Tenggara), and Waris, Kherom Regency (Papua) (Simorangkir 2017).

15. On 19 April 2017, the government, through the Committee for Accelerating the Provision of Infrastructure (Komite Percepatan Penyedian Infrastruktur) announced the removal of fourteen projects from the National Strategic Project (Putsanra 2018).

16. On the reading of the 2018 budget planning note, 16 August 2017, President Jokowi stated that infrastructure development would remain a priority in the promotion of social justice, equality, and welfare. This was repeated during his address to the Islamic Students' Association (Himpunan Mahasiswa Islam, HMI) at Pattimura University, Ambon, on 14 February 2018 (*Beritasatu* 2017; *Antara* 2018).

17. As with Sihar Sitorus, the deputy gubernatorial candidate for North Sumatra, whose wealth was appraised at Rp 359,887,340,551 by the KPK. A second-generation entrepreneur, the son of the late "oil palm king" D.L. Sitorus owns 47,000 hectares of oil palm plantations in South Tapanuli, North Sumatra. He also inherited an education foundation, hospital, showroom, hotel, and bank (Sitompul 2018; Leandha 2017).

18. Jembrana and Sragen regencies were most frequently visited in the early and mid-2000s to investigate the policy of combining social welfare — health and education — with good governance through integrated service.

19. The Indonesia Sehat Program, first, guarantees poor residents healthcare services through the BPJS Kesehatan National Health Insurance Programme; second, expands the scope of financial assistance programmes to persons suffering from social prosperity issues and the children of financial aid recipients; and, third, gives the extra benefits of preventive treatment and early detection. The Indonesia Pintar Program is intended to increase citizens' participation in primary and secondary education, increase the rate of continued education (as marked by a decrease in dropout rates), reduce the education gap between poor and rich citizens as well as men and women, and increase secondary students' preparedness to enter the workforce or continue their studies.

REFERENCES

Agustinus, Leo. "Patronase Politik Era Reformasi: Analisis Pilkada di Kabupaten Takalar dan Provinsi Jambi". *Jurnal Administrasi Publik* 11, no. 2 (2014): 69–85.

Anderson, Benedict R. O'G. "Old State, New Society: Indonesia's New Order in Comparative Historical Perspective". *Journal of Asian Studies* 42, no. 3 (1983): 477–96.

Antara. "Presiden: Infrastruktur untuk Ekonomi dan Keadilan Sosial", 14 February 2018. Available at <https://www.antaranews.com/berita/685730/presiden-infrastruktur-untuk-ekonomi-dan-keadilan-sosial> (accessed 8 January 2018).

Aspinall, Edward and Greg Fealy. *Local Power and Politics in Indonesia: Decentralisation and Democratisation*. Singapore: ISEAS – Yusof Ishak Institute, 2015.

Aspinall, Edward and Mada Sukmajati. *Politik Uang di Indonesia: Patronase dan Klientelism pada Pemilu Legislatif 2014*. Yogyakarta: PolGov, 2015.

Beittinger-Lee, Verena. *(Un)Civil Society and Political Change in Indonesia: A Contested Arena*. New York: Routledge, 2009.

Beraunews.com. "Mendagri: Tidak Ada Pembentukan DOB Hingga 2018", 20 June 2017. Available at <http://www.beraunews.com/serba-serbi/4007-mendagri-tidak-ada-pembentukan-dob-hingga-2018> (*accessed* 17 January 2018).

Berenschot, Ward. "The Political Economy of Clientelism: A Comparative Study of Indonesia's Patronage Democracy". *Comparative Political Studies* 51, no. 12 (2018): 1563–93.

Bere, Sigiranus Marutho. "Jokowi Resmikan Pos Lintas Batas Negara Motamasin dan Wini di NTT". *Kompas*, 9 January 2018. Available at <http://regional.kompas.com/read/2018/01/09/20180171/jokowi-resmikan-pos-lintas-batas-negara-motamasin-dan-wini-di-ntt> (accessed 14 January 2018).

Beritasatu. "Infrastruktur Tetap Prioritas Jokowi Wujudkan Keadilan Sosial", 16 August 2017. Available at <http://www.beritasatu.com/bisnis/447623-infrastruktur-tetap-prioritas-jokowi-wujudkan-keadilan-sosial.html> (accessed 10 January 2018).

———. "Mendagri: Ada 314 Usulan Pemekaran Daerah", 19 February 2018. Available at <http://id.beritasatu.com/home/mendagri-ada-314-usulan-pemekaran-daerah/172172> (accessed 22 February 2018).

Bhakti, Ikrar Nusa, Harganing Tyas, and Heru Cahyono. *Tentara yang Gelisah: Hasil Penelitian YIPIKA tentang Posisi ABRI dalam Gerakan Reformasi*. Bandung: Mizan, 1999.

Candra, Ardan Adhi. "Dongkrak Ekonomi di Perbatasan, PLBN Juga Dilengkapi Pasar". *detikFinance*, 7 January 2018. Available at <https://finance.detik.com/

infrastruktur/3803140/dongkrak-ekonomi-di-perbatasan-plbn-juga-dilengkapi-pasar> (accessed 10 January 2018).

Chauvel, Richard. "Electoral Politics and Democratic Freedoms in Papua". In *Problems of Democratization in Indonesia: Election, Institution, and Society*, edited by Edward Aspinall and Marcus Mietzner. Singapore: Institute of Southeast Asian Studies, 2006.

Crouch, Harold. *Political Reform in Indonesia after Soeharto*. Singapore: Institute of Southeast Asian Studies, 2010.

Dwipayana, A.A.G.N. Ari. *Kelas dan Kasta: Pergulatan Kelas Menengah Bali*. Yogyakarta: Lapera Pustaka Utama, 2001.

Eko, Sutoro. "Drama Reformasi Kejayaan dan Keruntuhan Bupati I Gede Winasa di Jembrana" [Reformed Glory and the Fall of Regent I Gede Winasa in Jembrana]. PhD thesis, Universitas Gadjah Mada, 2015.

Eldridge, Philip. *NGOs in Indonesia: Popular Movement or Arm of Government?* Clayton, Vic., Australia: Centre of Southeastern Asian Studies, Monash University, 1989.

―――. *Non-Government Organizations and Democratic Participation in Indonesia*. Kuala Lumpur: Oxford University Press, 1995.

Erb, Maribeth and Priyambudi Sulistiyanto, eds. *Deepening Democracy in Indonesia?: Direct Elections for Local Leaders (Pilkada)*. Singapore: Institute of Southeast Asian Studies, 2009.

Firmanto, Danang. "Ini 10 Kepala Daerah yang Meraih Penghargaan Tempo". *Tempo*, 4 March 2017. Available at <https://nasional.tempo.co/read/852478/ini-10-kepala-daerah-yang-meraih-penghargaan-tempo> (accessed 4 April 2018).

Fox, Colm A. "Candidate-centric System and the Politicization of Ethnicity: Evidence from Indonesia". *Democratization* (2018): 1–20.

Gabrillin, Abba. "Kronologi Operasi Tangkap Tangan KPK di Pamekasan". *Kompas*, 2 August 2017. Available at <https://nasional.kompas.cosm/read/2017/08/02/22525201/kronologi-operasi-tangkap-tangan-kpk-di-pamekasan> (accessed 5 February 2018).

Gerritsen, Rolf and Saut Situmorang. "Beyond Integration? The Need to Decentralize Central-Regional/Local Relations in Indonesia". In *Central–Local Relations in Asia-Pacific*, edited by Mark Turner. London: Palgrave Macmillan, 1999.

Hadiz, Vedi R. *Dinamika Kekuasaan: Ekonomi Politik Indonesia Pasca Orde Baru*. Jakarta: LP3ES, 2005.

―――. *Localising Power in Post-Authoritarian Indonesia: A Southeast Asia Perspective*. Palo Alto: Stanford University Press, 2010.

Hamid, Abdul. "Politisasi Birokrasi dalam Pilkada Banten 2006". *Jurnal Ilmu Administrasi Negara* 11, no. 2 (2011): 97–110.

Harvey, Barbara S. *Permesta: Half a Rebellion*. Ithaca, New York: Cornell University Press, 1977.

Haryanto. *Klanisasi Demokrasi: Politik Klan Qahhar Mudzakar di Sulawesi Selatan*. Yogyakarta: PolGov, 2014.

Haryanto, Cornelis Lay, and Bambang Purwoko. "Asymmetrical Decentralization, Representation, and Legitimacy: A Case Study of Majelis Rakyat Papua". *Asian Survey* 58, no. 2 (2018): 365–86.

Ika, Aprillia. "Membangun Perekonomian Miangas Melalui Bandar Udara". *Kompas*, 17 October 2016. Available at <https://ekonomi.kompas.com/read/2016/10/17/193000326/membangun.perekonomian.miangas.melalui.bandar.udara> (accessed 5 January 2018).

Indonesian Institute – Center for Public Policy Research, The. "Ini Sebabnya Banyak Calon Kepala Daerah Berlatar Belakang Pengusaha", 26 June 2018. Available at <https://www.theindonesianinstitute.com/ini-sebabnya-banyak-calon-kepala-daerah-berlatar-belakang-pengusaha/> (accessed 26 June 2018).

Julianto, Pramdia Arhando. "Kawal Dana Desa, Mantan Petinggi KPK Jabat Ketua Satgas Dana Desa". *Kompas*, 5 July 2017. Available at <https://ekonomi.kompas.com/read/2017/07/05/140000826/kawal.dana.desa.mantan.petinggi.kpk.jabat.ketua.satgas.dana.desa> (accessed 5 January 2018)

Katadata. "Anggaran Infrastruktur 2009–2017 Terus Meningkat", 3 November 2016. Available at <https://databoks.katadata.co.id/datapublish/2016/11/03/anggaran-infrastruktur-2009-2017-terus-meningkat> (accessed 10 January 2018).

———. "3 Tahun Jokowi-JK: Hadapi Ketimpangan, Infrastruktur Daerah Digenjot", 19 October 2017. Available at <https://katadata.co.id/infografik/2017/10/19/hadapi-ketimpangan-infrastruktur-daerah-digenjot> (accessed 8 January 2018).

Kemendagri. "Pembentukan Daerah-Daerah Otonom Di Indonesia Sampai Dengan Tahun 2017". Available at <http://otda.kemendagri.go.id/CMS/Images/SubMenu/total_daerah_otonom.pdf> (accessed 17 January 2018).

Kompas. "Indonesia Selama 20 Tahun Era Reformasi", 21 May 2018, p. 2.

Lane, Max. *Decentralization and Its Discontents: An Essay on Class, Political Agency and National Perspective in Indonesian Politics*. Singapore: Institute of Southeast Asian Studies, 2014.

Lay, Cornelis. "Otonomi Daerah dan Keindonesiaan". *Jurnal Ilmu Sosial dan Ilmu Politik* 5, no. 1 (2001): 139–62.

———. "Pilkada Langsung dan Pendalaman Demokrasi". *Jurnal Ilmu Sosial dan Ilmu Politik* 11, no. 1 (2007): 63–92.

Lay, Cornelis, Hasrul Hanif, Rohman Ridwan, and Noor Rohman. "The Rise of Uncontested Elections in Indonesia: Case Studies of Pati and Jayapura". *Contemporary Southeast Asia* 39, no. 3 (2017): 439–40.

Leandha, Mei. "DL Sitorus Pengusaha yang Tak Punya Utang dan Sayang Kali Mamaknya". *Kompas*, 4 August 2017. Available at <https://regional. kompas.com/read/2017/08/04/07190241/-dl-sitorus-pengusaha-yang-tak-punya-utang-dan-sayang-kali-mamaknya> (accessed 27 April 2018).

Magenda, Burhan D. "The Surviving Aristocracy in Indonesia: Politics in Three Provinces of the Outer Islands". PhD thesis, Cornell University, 1989.

Mas'udi, Wawan. "Creating Legitimacy in Decentralized Indonesia: Joko 'Jokowi' Widodo's Path to Legitimacy in Solo, 2005–2012". PhD thesis, University of Melbourne, 2017.

Mas'udi, Wawan and Cornelis Lay, eds. *The Politics of Welfare: Contested Welfare Regimes in Indonesia*. Jakarta: Yayasan Obor Indonesia, 2018.

Mas'udi, Wawan and Nanang Indra Kurniawan. "Programmatic Politics and Voter Preferences: The 2017 Election in Kulon Progo Yogyakarta". *Contemporary Southeast Asia* 39, no. 3 (2017): 417–26.

Mietzner, Marcus. "Reinventing Asian Populism: Jokowi's Rise, Democracy, and Political Contestation in Indonesia". *Policy Studies* 72 (2015).

Padmasari, Salviah Ika. "Mendagri Sebut 237 Daerah Mengantre untuk Dimekarkan". *Merdeka*, 28 February 2017. Available at <https://www.merdeka. com/peristiwa/mendagri-sebut-237-daerah-mengantre-untuk-dimekarkan. html> (accessed 8 January 2018).

PIDmorut. "Program Inovasi Desa" [Village Innovation Programme], 3 February 2018. Available at <http://pidmorut.com/2018/02/03/program-inovasi-desa-2/> (accessed 19 February 2018).

PLOD. "Model Kerjasama Antar Daerah". Research Report. Yogyakarta: PLOD and APEKSI, 2007.

Prabowo, Dani. "Anggaran infrastruktur 2018 Naik Jadi Rp 410,4 Triliun". *Kompas*, 8 December 2017. Available at <https://properti.kompas.com/read/2017/12/08/213705121/anggaran-infrastruktur-2018-naik-jadi-rp-4104-triliun> (accessed 5 January 2018).

Pratikno and Cornelis Lay. "From Populism to Democratic Polity: Problems and Challenges in Solo, Indonesia". In *Democratization in the Global South: The Importance of Transformative Politics*, edited by Kristian Stokke and Olle Törnquist. London: Palgrave Macmillan, 2013.

Purnamasari, Desi. "Memeriksa Keterlibatan Polri dalam Pengelolaan Dana Desa". *Tirto*, 1 March 2018. Available at <https://tirto.id/memeriksa-keterlibatan-polri-dalam-pengelolaan-dana-desa-cFti> (accessed 18 January 2018).

Putsanra, Dipna Videlia. "Daftar 14 Proyek Strategis Nasional yang Dibatalkan Jokowi". *Tirto*, 20 April 2018. Available at <https://tirto.id/daftar-14-proyek-strategis-nasional-yang-dibatalkan-jokowi-cH4Z> (accessed 22 April 2018).

Republika. "Perludem: Dian Eka Nugraheny, Jumlah Calon Independen di Pilkada Semakin Menurun", 29 November 2017. Available at <http://nasional.republika.co.id/berita/nasional/politik/17/11/29/p06qvk354-perludem-jumlah-calon-independen-di-pilkada-semakin-turun> (accessed 8 January 2018).

Riwu Kaho, Josef. *Prospek Otonomi Daerah di Negara Republik Indonesia.* Jakarta: Rajawali Pers, 2002.

———. *Analisis Hubungan Pemerintah Pusat dan Daerah di Indonesia.* Yogyakarta: PolGov, 2012.

Robinson, Geoffrey. "Indonesia: On a New Course?". In *Coercion and Governance: The Declining of Political Role of the Military in Asia,* edited by Muthiah Alagappa. Stanford: Stanford University Press, 2001.

Robinson, Richard and Vedi R. Hadiz. *Reorganising Power in Indonesia: The Politics of Oligarchy in an Age of Markets.* London & New York: Routledge, 2004.

Simorangkir, Eduardo. "Jokowi Bakal Bangun 9 Pos Perbatasan Baru Lagi, Ini Lokasinya". *detikFinance,* 23 August 2017. Available at <https://finance.detik.com/berita-ekonomi-bisnis/3611995/jokowi-bakal-bangun-9-pos-perbatasan-baru-lagi-ini-lokasinya> (accessed 5 January 2018).

Sitompul, Juven Martua. "10 Bakal Calon Kepala Daerah Terkaya di Pilkada 2018". *MetroTV,* 22 January 2018. Available at <http://news.metrotvnews.com/politik/JKRlezpb-10-bakal-calon-kepala-daerah-terkaya-di-pilkada-2018> (accessed 27 April 2018).

Stokes, Susan C., Thad Dunning, Marcelo Nazareno, and Valeria Brusco. *Brokers, Voters, and Clientelism: The Puzzle of Distributive Politics.* New York: Cambridge University Press, 2013.

Suzuki, Wataru. "Indonesia Lives Dangerously with $355bn Infrastructure Drive". *Nikkei,* 23 November 2017. Available at <https://asia.nikkei.com/magazine/20171123/Politics-Economy/Indonesia-lives-dangerously-with-a-355bn-infrastructure-drive> (accessed 13 January 2018).

Tapsell, Ross. *Media Power in Indonesia: Oligarchs, Citizens and the Digital Revolution.* Lanham, Maryland: Rowman and Littlefield, 2017.

Tempo. "Mendagri Siapkan Dua Rancangan Peraturan Pemekaran Daerah", 25 July 2016. Available at <https://nasional.tempo.co/read/790143/mendagri-siapkan-dua-rancangan-peraturan-pemekaran-daerah> (accessed 8 January 2018).

Törnquist, Olle, Stanley Adi Prasetyo, and Teresa Birks. *Aceh: Peran Demokrasi Bagi Perdamaian dan Rekonstruksi.* Yogyakarta: PCD Press, 2010.

van Klinken, Gerry. "Return of the Sultans: The Communitarian Turn in Local Politics". In *The Revival of Tradition in Indonesian Politics: The Deployment of Adat from Colonialism to Indigenism,* edited by Jamie S. Davidson and David Henley. London: Routledge, 2007.

————. *The Making of Middle Indonesia: Middle Classes in Kupang Town, 1930s–1980s*. Leiden: Brill, 2014.

van Klinken, Gerry and Henk S. Nordholt, eds. *Politik Lokal di Indonesia*. Jakarta: KITLV & Yayasan Obor Indonesia, 2007.

van Klinken, Gerry and Ward Berenschot, eds. *In Search of Middle Indonesia: Middle Classes in Provincial Towns*. Leiden: Brill, 2014.

Warburton, Eve. "Jokowi and the New Developmentalism". *Bulletin of Indonesian Economic Studies* 52, no. 3 (2016): 297–320.

Wicaksana, I. Gede Wahyu. "Indonesia's Maritime Connectivity Development: Domestic and International Challenges". *Asian Journal of Political Science* 25, no. 2 (2017): 212–23.

Zuhriyah, Dewi Aminatuz. "Bentuk Satgas, Dana Desa Bisa Terawasi". *Bisnis*, 16 July 2017. Available at <http://finansial.bisnis.com/read/20170716/9/671881/bentuk-satgas-dana-desa-bisa-terawasi> (accessed 10 January 2018).

8

The Roots and Actors of Corruption in the Political Realm

Leo Agustino

Introduction

Political corruption is a major source of many problems in Indonesia. The main reason for corruption being so widespread in this sphere is the high cost that burdens politicians when attempting to be elected as members of central or district parliaments, senators, governors or mayors, and even president. I will discuss in this chapter the major examples of corruption in the election process for local leaders (*Pemilihan Kepala Daerah, Pilkada*), both prior to and after the change to direct elections for these posts. *Pilkada* cases were selected as the example for this chapter because it has been within the new electoral system that corruption has most flourished. Ironically, *Pilkada* initially was believed to be the key to the fundamental changes in local politics after the New Order era to facilitate the end of the systemic, centralistic corruption and non-democratic regime. Unfortunately, the results go in the opposite direction.

The New Order: Centralization and Political Hegemony

During the New Order, the election of heads of regional government was regulated by Law No. 5/1974 on regional government.[1]

In this law, Regional House of Representatives (*Dewan Perwakilan Rakyat Daerah*, DPRD) members were given the authority to elect heads of regional government, but the nomination and inauguration of proposed candidates were carried out by the Ministry of Home Affairs. This was the form of central government intervention into the regions and was evident in Article 15 governing the election of the governor:

> *Kepala Daerah Tingkat I dicalonkan dan dipilih oleh Dewan Perwakilan Rakyat Daerah dari sedikit-dikitnya tiga orang dan sebanyak-banyaknya lima orang yang telah dimusyawarahkan dan disepakati bersama antara Pimpinan Dewan Perwakilan Rakyat Daerah/Pimpinan Fraksi-fraksi dengan Menteri Dalam Negeri.*

(The head of the First Level Region is nominated and elected by the Regional House of Representatives from at least three people and as many as five people who have discussed and mutually agreed between the heads of the Regional House of Representatives and leaders of the factions with the Ministry of Home Affairs.)

Then, Paragraph (2) mentioned:

> *Hasil pemilihan yang dimaksudkan dalam Ayat (1) pasal ini diajukan oleh Dewan Perwakilan Rakyat Daerah yang bersangkutan kepada Presiden melalui Menteri Dalam Negeri sedikit-dikitnya dua orang untuk diangkat salah seorang di antaranya.*

(The election results referred to in Paragraph (1) of this article shall be submitted by the Regional House of Representatives to the President through the Minister of Home Affairs [recommending] at least two persons, of whom one should be appointed.)

In addition, the election of regents and mayors was prescribed in Article 16, Paragraph (1), which resembles Article 15, Paragraphs (1) and (2).

After obtaining the names of candidates selected by the Minister of Home Affairs, the leaders of the DPRD brought the list to the Parliamentary Assembly to elect a "centrally approved" candidate through *musyawarah–mufakat* (consultation-deliberation). If this failed, then the regional head was chosen by voting. During both *musyawarah–mufakat* and voting, high officials from the Ministry of Home Affairs (in gubernatorial elections) or provincial officials (in regent or mayoral elections) were often present, usually accompanied by elite military officials. This was to avoid any "defiance" by DPRD members. To secure the scenario (and to avoid any embarrassments for high officials), the voting was rehearsed the day before the actual election. Generally, this "drama" ran smoothly, without any opposition.

This centralization of power at least created two things. First, nationally, central government eliminated significant government power; second, locally, society was deliberately alienated from political mechanisms. This election system marginalized the people as holders of political sovereignty.

On top of that, to strengthen this centralization of power, the New Order regime restructured the territorial function of the army to parallel to bureaucratic structures (from central to village level). Provincial governors' activities were "supervised" by the head of the Military Regional Command (*Komando Daerah Militer*, Kodam) with the rank of major general, and frequently the commander became governor of the area after his retirement. To oversee the political dynamics of several districts or municipalities, the army also established a Military Resort Command (*Komando Resort Militer*, Korem) headed by a colonel. Below the Regional Command stood the District Military Command (*Komando Distrik Militer*, Kodim) headed by a lieutenant colonel, which took care of a district or city. Below District Military Command, the Military Rayon Command (*Komando Rayon Militer*, Koramil) supervised and controlled a region as wide as the district. On the lowest public structures, they also put a sergeant called *Babinsa* (*Bintara Pembina Desa*). Commanders of Kodam, Korem, Kodim or Babinsa could be appointed by the central government to become the heads of regional government in their territories, as governors, regents, mayors or village heads.

Reformasi: Direct Elections for Local Leaders

After the fall of the New Order in 1998, the format and pattern of local government (including local elections) were amended. Two laws on local government were passed: Law No. 22/1999 and Law No. 32/2004. One of the amended points was Article 18, Paragraph (4) of 1945 Constitution, which states: "Governors, Regents, and Mayors respectively are heads of provincial, district, and municipal governments, who are elected democratically"; "democratically" here refers to direct election.

The demand for direct elections — *Pilkada* — was very strong immediately after 1998. This reflected the desire for a change from the centralized governance of the New Order. The demand for direct elections became even stronger after the 2004 presidential election, in which both the president and vice-president were directly elected. These *Pilkada* were seen as beneficial for the development and deepening of democracy.

High Cost Politics

Despite the expected benefits of *Pilkada*, dangerous developments have also appeared. One of the dangers is corruption. Where does it come from? How does it arise and anchor so deeply in our political system? One basic reason has been the much higher cost of participating in electoral politics.

High cost politics occurs not only during the head of regional government elections, but also during the legislative elections (for central parliament, regional parliaments, senators and president).

In the past, when local leadership elections were indirect, candidates did not need as much money as is now necessary. They would need to spend money only if they decided to buy support from regional parliament members. The amount ranged between Rp 30 million and Rp 500 million per member or per vote.[2] During the indirect election of the head of local government, the average local member of parliament might receive a total from all candidates of Rp 115 million to Rp 1 billion (depending on how influential was the position of the member). This was the case when the central government did not have its own favourite candidate.

This "transactional politics" was not merely to "buy the votes" of members of parliament only, but also of other stakeholders in the region. These political transactions required solid coordination involving many parties, NGOs, local journalists, community leaders, religious leaders, and entrepreneurs. They had their own special roles. NGOs played the role of "fun-loving" providers of information about the candidate's high rating in the candidate's electoral district. Essentially, they assured that the candidate was very well known and liked by the people. Local journalists' role was to produce publicity about support from community leaders, religious leaders, and the people; their role was also that of public opinion makers. In their publications, positive statements from community leaders, religious leaders, and average people (who were part of the candidate's network) provided testimony and support for the candidate. They also convinced the candidate that the organizations under the guidance of these community and religious leaders would assemble outside the parliament during the election to show support for the candidate.

Furthermore, transactional politics involving money in the era of indirect local elections also occurred during the candidacy stage. The role of the factions in the parliament made their bargaining position very powerful. On average, each faction asked Rp 100 million to Rp 2 billion, excluding the lobbying costs, which ranged from Rp 7 million up to Rp 75 million.[3] A source even stated that they also set up pressure groups (paid demonstrators) to provide shows of support to paying candidates, or to degrade other candidates' profiles. Furthermore, candidates often utilized the charisma of community and religious leaders to influence the parliament members' decision, by conducting hearings and declaring that their communities (often thousands of people) fully supported these candidates. For these groups, the "transportation fee" was between Rp 100,000 and Rp 2 million per person (depending on their position in the group structure). Referring to all expenditures above, a candidate might spend Rp 150 million. This is far below the amount that average candidates of current *Pilkada* have to spend.

Money politics continues until the voting is completed. In the era of indirect local elections, candidates usually quarantined the legislators on the eve of voting to secure the votes away from other candidates who might be willing to pay more. Back then, there were infamous terms such as *Tim Siluman* ("stealth team") or *Tim Mawar* ("rose team"). Their job was to "kidnap" or "secure" board members so that their votes did not change during the actual voting. Normally, the candidate's outcome was predictable in the morning, according to his success or failure in securing the board members that he "shepherded". During the voting process, candidates spent Rp 100 million to Rp 1 billion (including the cost of board and lodging of members of board during their quarantine). When a candidate was finally elected, he would have to give a bonus to his support team ranging from Rp 200 million to Rp 500 million.

To sum up, to become a head of regional government during the era of indirect elections, candidates had to have hard cash between Rp 475 million and Rp 5.5 billion. This amount is very small compared to that of current *Pilkada*.

How are vote buying and money politics carried out in the era of direct elections? And how much does direct election cost provincial, district, and municipal candidates?

One thing is certain: the political costs are huge. This is because the candidacy of a political figure must not only be approved by district/city party officials but also should be recommended at the provincial level, and most importantly from the party's central leadership. The requirement for a written recommendation from provincial and central party leaders often leads to clashes over selection of candidates. Such a situation happened in Depok in 2005. All political parties, except Partai Keadilan Sejahtera (PKS), agreed to push Badrul Kamal as the mayoral candidate. After the agreement, the official written recommendation was released by each party leader. But in the middle of the process, those parties failed to come to an agreement on the vice-mayoral figure. Badrul Kamal suggested Sihabuddin Ahmad, but the parties rejected the idea and suggested different figures. The parties that did not accept Kamal's proposal departed from the coalition and aborted their support, while the supporting documents were submitted to the higher hierarchy. As a result, some parties showed formal support letters that were different from whom they were actually supporting.

Similar cases occurred to several candidates in other local elections like Sukawi Sutarip (former mayor of Semarang) in the 2005 elections. Initially, he was nominated by the Partai Demokrasi Indonesia Perjuangan (PDIP, Indonesian Democratic Party of Struggle), but then shifted to Partai Persatuan Pembangunan (PPP, United Development Party), Partai Amanat Nasional (PAN, National Mandate Party), and Partai Kebangkitan Bangsa (PKB, National Awakening Party) due to allegedly huge fees requested from the first party. The former chairman of the Komisi Pemberantasan Korupsi (KPK, Corruption Eradication Commission), Taufiequrachman Ruki, resigned from his candidacy for governor of Banten because of the huge fee that he was asked to provide. At the national level, the late Nurcholish Madjid was forced to resign from his presidential candidacy for Golkar because he did not have "nutrition" — meaning money. The high political costs of direct election of regional government heads are also partly caused by socializing costs during the campaign. Interviews with former candidates, former winning teams, supporters of former candidates, printing entrepreneurs, textile entrepreneurs, event organizers, and gamblers in West Java and other areas showed that the costs for a regent or mayoral candidate are between Rp 3 billion and Rp 25 billion; for governor candidates, the costs ranged between Rp 8 billion and Rp 200 billion (Agustino and Fitriani 2017, pp. 111–15; also see Mietzner 2011; Wibowo 2013). This enormous expenditure, inevitably, drives them to recover these costs once they are elected.

Roughly, candidates normally spend Rp 100 billion. This amount is then split into two and shared equally with their tandem. So, roughly a candidate spends Rp 50 billion. When they are eventually elected as regional government leaders, annually they have to regain at least Rp 10 billion, or Rp 834 million per month or Rp 28 million a day. The total of salary and allowances for regional government heads for five years ranges from Rp 192 million to Rp 324 million. This condition forces them to "work hard" to restore their capital and political costs of the campaign.

Corruption as a Way of Restoring and Collecting Political Capital

The question now is, how to explain the ways and mechanisms of the elected regional government head (and cronies) to restore all his political costs during the campaign as well as raising capital for the next political contest? There are many ways that can be done, one of which is trading of positions. This is justified by the former head of the Information Centre of the Ministry of Home Affairs (*Kepala Pusat Penerangan Kementerian Dalam Negeri* (*Kemendagri*)), Reydonnyzar Moenek, on 3 December 2010:

> *Praktik jual-beli jabatan di Pemda memang ada, karena kepala daerah harus mengembalikan sejumlah dana (untuk biaya Pemilukada) yang bisa saja bersifat talangan. Maka bisa dipastikan yang bersangkutan akan berupaya mengembalikannya, antara lain dengan menentukan harga kursi untuk sebuah jabatan (Jpnn.com 2010).*

(The practice of position trading in regional government does exist, because the head of regional government must recover some costs (for the *Pilkada*), which could be a debt. So it is certain that he/she will attempt to restore it, among other things by determining the price tag of a seat.)

The truth about position trading was revealed clearly when Sri Hartini, Regent of Klaten, 2016–21, was caught in the act by the Corruption Eradication Commission. The price tag was fantastic, from Rp 25 million for Echelon IV up to Rp 400 million for Echelon II (see Table 8.1).

TABLE 8.1
The Price of Echelon/Position in Klaten District
(in Education Office Circles)

No	Echelon/Position	Price
1	Echelon II (Head of Office)	Rp 400 million
2	Echelon III (Secretary and Head of Division)	Rp 100–150 million
3	Echelon IV (Head of Sub-Division and Head of Section)	Rp 25 million
4	Head of Regional Technical Implementation Unit (Unit Pelaksana Teknis Daerah, UPTD)	Rp 50–100 million
5	Administration UPTD	Rp 25 million
6	Primary School Principal	Rp 75–125 million
7	Primary School Administration	Rp 30 million
8	Junior High School Principal	Rp 80–150 million
9	Certain Functional Position (change of teachers within district)	Rp 15–60 million
10	Fixed Offices (non-mutation)	Rp 10–50 million

Source: *Koran Tempo*, 7 January 2017, p. 5.

In the provincial government of West Java, a source states that to get his current position he must give bribes of about Rp 35 million — just for Echelon IV. The money, he recalled, was given to a colleague who was very close to the vice-governor of West Java in 2008–13.

Position trading occurs not only in provincial governments but also in district and city governments. Source #2, a civil servant in Subang regency, claims that each change is targeted to generate income: around 60 per cent for the head of regional government and 40 per cent for his deputy.[4] In the district of Cirebon, position trading is done via the regent's relative. Source #3 explains that to get a "non-wet" (non-profitable) Echelon IV position, a civil servant is required to pay approximately Rp 5 million. The price tag for a "wet" position in Echelon IV such as the Office of Revenue, Permit, or Finance is around Rp 15 million to Rp 20 million. The Echelon III "non-wet" price tag is Rp 25 million while an Echelon III "wet" position needs Rp 45 million to Rp 60 million. To be the head in a "non-wet" subdistrict, the price tag is Rp 60 million while the head in the "wet" subdistrict requires Rp 100 million. The price tag for an Echelon II "non-wet" position is around Rp 100 million to Rp 130 million while that for an Echelon II "wet" position is more than Rp 200 million.[5]

Position trading also occurred in Tasikmalaya city. Interestingly here, the transaction used code words. For instance, 206 for Echelon IV. The code 20 indicates the nominal, while 6 indicates the number of zeros behind the nominal. So, the "price" for Echelon IV is Rp 20 million.[6] The use of this kind of password occurred not only in Tasikmalaya city; in Wonogiri district, last-six-digit codes are also utilized.

In addition to the island of Java, the trading of positions also resonates almost all over Indonesia since *Pilkada*. In the city of Padang, for example, to become the head of office, the mayor (through a trusted civil servant who is also the mayor's personal assistant) usually asked for a payment of around Rp 300 million, and Rp 150 million for the head of a subdistrict.[7]

Besides position trading, requests for project money from entrepreneurs getting a tender from the local government were also a common mode of political cost recovery. Agustino (2014*a*, p. 228) explains that during the reign of Ratu Atut Chosiyah in Banten province, at least 10 to 11 per cent of project valuation would be transferred to her (see Table 8.2).

TABLE 8.2
Project Fee Based on Project Classification and Source of Funds

Project Classification	Project Fee by Source of Funds (%)	
	Provincial Budget (APBD)	National Budget (APBN)
Bina Marga Project (Road)	10%	11%
Watering Project	11%	11%
Building Construction Project	10%	10%
Procurement Project	10%	10%

Source: Agustino (2014*a*, p. 228).

Social aid (*Bantuan Sosial, Bansos*) and grants (*Hibah*) are also often used as instruments for returning political fees by elected regional heads. The mechanism is simple: the local government (on direction from the head of regional government) may direct *Bansos* to any organizations or communities. The amount of grant is up to the regional head to determine. As a result, the grant can be easily manipulated and transferred to "close people" rather than to organizations or communities that really need it. This is what happened in Banten province, where the grant was directed to the governor's relatives (see Table 8.3). Its motive is, of course, to recover the political cost of *Pilkada* election.

At the national level, corruption is becoming common among politicians. This can be seen in the case of the involvement of several parties from the Koalisi Merah Putih (KMP) as well as the Koalisi Indonesia Hebat (KIH).[8] The closer they get to the government, the more open the opportunity for their parties to earn money from the state treasury.

Some cases below illustrate how ministries and state-owned enterprises (*Badan Usaha Milik Negara*, BUMN) are misused by irresponsible and corrupt officials. A case in the Ministry of Marine and Fisheries (*Kementerian Kelautan dan Perikanan*, KKP) under the leadership of Rokhmin Dahuri (2001–4) is worth noting.[9] The findings about the KKP began when the Corruption Eradication Commission (KPK) conducted regular checks at the ministry in August 2006. In the examination, the KPK found some "oddities" in Rokhmin's banking accounts and

TABLE 8.3
Flows of Bantuan Sosial to Institutions Led by the
Governor's Family (Banten)

Name of Institution/ Organization	Relation with Governor	Fund
KNPI Banten Prov	Chair: Aden Abdul Khalik (step-brother of governor)	Rp 1,850,000,000
Tagana Banten	Chair: Andika Hazrumy (son of governor)	Rp 1,750,000,000
PMI Banten	Chair: Ratu Tatu Chasanah (sister of governor)	Rp 900,000,000
PW GP Ansor	Treasurer: Andika Hazrumy (son of Gubernur Banten)	Rp 550,000,000
Himpaudi Banten	Chair: Ade Rossi Cherunnisa (daughter-in-law of governor)	Rp 3,500,000,000
P2TP2A	Chair: Ade Rossi Cherunnisa (daughter-in-law of governor)	Rp 1,500,000,000
GWKS	Chair: Ratu Tatu Chasanah (sister of governor)	Rp 700,000,000
Youth Association	Chair: Andika Hazrumy (son of governor)	Rp 1,500,000,000
Dekranas	Chair: Hikmat Tomet (husband of governor)	Rp 750,000,000
Dekopinwil	Chair: Ratu Tatu Chasanah (sister of governor)	Rp 200,000,000
Association of Banten United Forum	Chair: Ratu Tatu Chasanah (sister of governor)	Rp 500,000,000
IMI Banten	Chair: Tubagus Haerul Jaman (step-brother of governor)	Rp 200,000,000
The Coalition of Indonesian Women Politicians	Chair: Ratu Tatu Chasanah (sister of governor)	Rp 200,000,000
The Ansor Youth Movement	Chair: Tanto Warsono Arban (son-in-law of governor)	Rp 400,000,000
TOTAL		Rp 14,000,000,000

Source: Agustino and Fitriani (2017), pp. 148–49.

questioned the legitimacy of the funds he collected during his tenure, including their use and distribution. A few months later, on 27 November 2006, the KPK issued an arrest warrant against Andin Taryoto (secretary general of the KKP) on charges of using the money. Rokhmin was arrested by the KPK the following day based on Andin's acknowledgment that the use of the funds was made under Rokhmin's direction. Through examination in court, it is clear that around Rp 31 billion was lost; the funds remaining in the account of the minister were only Rp 789 million.

The question now is: where did the money go? Most of the funds ended up in party and party elites' pockets. This information was obtained from Andin's confession, which made a very clear and detailed report on the names of those who received funds from the KKP (*Tempo*, 11–17 December 2006, p. 32). The report encouraged Amien Rais, former presidential candidate and former chairman of the MPR, to urge all political party elites and former presidential candidates who received KKP funds to speak the truth. His statement is based on the fact that he himself admitted to getting Rp 200 million for his campaign in the first round of presidential election in 2004. In fact, Amien further accused Susilo Bambang Yudhoyono's campaign team of receiving the funds as well.[10] Amien Rais even said that he was ready to go to jail if others followed in his footsteps to admit receiving dirty money from the KKP. In the end, the case faded and became merely a discussion and polemic in discussion rooms.

Another case occurred in the Ministry of Agriculture during Yudhoyono's second administration (2009–14). Its player this time was a high official of PKS who tried to take advantage of the ministry chair he led as a "cash cow". According to *Tempo* (20–26 May 2013), some high officials of PKS had prepared a winning strategy for the 2014 election as early as possible. One of the discussions was the preparation of electoral funding. Interestingly, the funding was not collected from membership fees, but was sought from institutions managed by the PKS (see Figure 8.1). In Figure 8.1, at the top right side is written PKS and amounts of Rp 20 billion and Rp 2 trillion. Below that are "Luthfi" (referring to Luthfi Hasan Ishaaq, former president of PKS) and "Hilmy" (Aminuddin, former chair of Majelis Syuro PKS). There are three columns with three ministerial names: the Ministry of Communication and Informatics (with Rp 0.5 trillion written next to the ministry name), the Ministry of Agriculture (Rp 1 trillion), and

FIGURE 8.1
PKS Calculation of Potentially Acquired State Fund

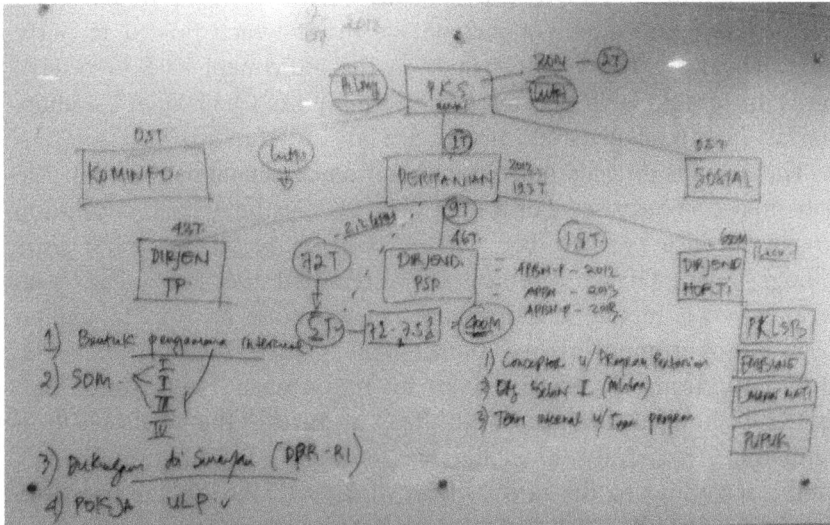

Source: Tempo, 20–26 May 2013, p. 37.

the Ministry of Social Affairs (Rp 0.5 trilion). Yudi Setiawan, a KPK justice collaborator, testified that the picture is of a funding target to be collected by the PKS for the 2014 general election, and, as show in Figure 8.1, Rp 2 trillion was to be obtained from the three ministries. How? As revealed in court in a beef import case of the Ministry of Agriculture, one mode is to sell a Letter of Import Recommendation to importers.

In addition to the party, its elites also get a share from the trading of import recommendation letters: every kilogram of meat entering the country gives them Rp 1 to Rp 3. Multiplied by the tonnage imported each year, the gain for the PKS elites will be fantastic. In 2012 alone, when the importing of 32,000 tonnes was allowed by the Ministry of Agriculture, those elites will have received Rp 32–96 billion from beef importers.

Another big corruption case involving cross-party actors is that of the electronic ID card (*elektronik-Kartu Tanda Penduduk*, e-KTP), which created a Rp 2.3 trillion loss for the state. At least 60 people were involved, ranging from civil servants and company partners to members of parliament (including party elites). In the indictment, there are three parties deeply involved: Golkar, Democratic Party (receiving Rp 150 billion), and PDIP (Rp 80 billion) (*Tempo*, 13–19 March 2017, p. 25). The figure does not include the funds which flowed to party elites. There are many elite names in the indictment said to receive funds, including Setya Novanto, Ade Komarudin, Chairuman Harahap, Markus Nari (Golkar), and Miryam S. Haryani (Hanura).[11]

The corrupt officials not only rob a number of ministries, but also state-owned enterprises. For a long time BUMNs have been corruption targets because of their big money, such as *Badan Urusan Logistik* (Bulog). *Tempo* (19–25 February 2001) reported that there had been various Bulog money disbursements of as much as Rp 71.7 billion from a government-owned bank, *Bank Umum Koperasi Indonesia* (Bukopin), from 27 August 1998 to 10 October 1999. More than Rp 53 billion of that was withdrawn during the 1999 election campaign. Around Rp 40 billion was destined for Akbar Tandjung's hands, according to the news, given directly to the Golkar treasurer. A total of Rp 10 billion flowed to the Minister of Defence (General Wiranto) for Civil Security Forces (Pam Swakarsa).[12] A remaining Rp 3 billion was used by Bulog to complete an asset swap between Bulog and Goro. This case was never revealed because political cartels prevailed in this race. Another example occurred in the next few years. In May 2000, one of the chairs of the Central Executive Board of PKB, Taufikurrahman Saleh, asked the head of Bulog, Rahadi Ramelan, to investigate rumours of Rp 35 billion in Bulog fund abuse by President Gus Dur. In court proceedings, it was found that Rahadi, indeed, had withdrawn Rp 30 billion to assist the resolution of conflicts in Aceh. Unfortunately, the funds never reached Aceh, but spread to bank accounts of people in Gus Dur's "inner circle" (one of them was Suwondo); a small portion also went to Suko Sudarso (chair of the Central Executive Board of PDIP) (Ambardi 2009, p. 311).

The same thing happened when the Democratic Party utilized the Hambalang project to fill the party's coffers. Initially, this was a government project to build a complete sports complex on a hill later known as Bukit Hambalang (many people sneered at the project as an attempt to rival Bukit Jalil in Malaysia). The project budget suddenly multiplied to twenty times that of the initial plan, which was only Rp 125 billion (*Tempo*, 4–10 June 2012, p. 31). To build the facilities alone, the Ministry of Youth and Sport (*Kementerian Pemuda dan Olahraga*, Kemenpora) budgeted Rp 1.175 trillion, of which Rp 275 billion was disbursed in 2010, around Rp 475 billion in the following year, and around Rp 425 billion in 2012. That amount was only for building construction, if funding for facilities was included, the total cost of the project was Rp 2.57 trillion (*Tempo*, 4–10 June 2012, p. 39).

The national tragedy came when some elites from Democratic Party "played" in this project which happened to be under the Ministry of Youth and Sport, which was led by Democrat elite figure, Andi Mallarangeng, the minister in 2009–12. The involvement of some Democratic Party elites became so deep that it could determine the winner of the project tender. Contractor companies had from the beginning been filtered through a process that seemed to follow formal rules, but required a fee of 18 per cent of the total project value paid in advance. The winner of the tender was P.T. Adhi Karya, who had agreed to provide a Rp 100 billion initial commitment fee. That is according to Nazarudin's testimony in the *Tindak Pidana Korupsi* (Tipikor) trial in the Hambalang case. He also stated that the funds were distributed in various directions, including into the Democratic Party, especially for the organization of the party congress which happened at that time to be electing a new chairman, Anas Urbaningrum, and Nazarudin as treasurer. According to Nazarudin's blunt testimony, the Hambalang money was for funding the victory of Anas (*Tempo*, 4–10 June 2012, p. 31). Besides the party congress, the illegal funds also went to "Senayan" as a lubricant for various other projects, and was also transferred to several high officials in the Ministry of Youth and Sport.

At least three points should be understood about corruption in the *reformasi* era. First, ministries and BUMN are not only institutions that perform their duties as public servants, but are also servants of the interests of parties and party elites, especially in recovering the political costs of becoming members of parliament. Second, the theft of state funds is not done by merely one or two parties, but by many political parties, creating a cartel party mechanism (borrowing the term from Ambardi 2009). Finally, all of the cases described above show how parties, elites, and civil servants work hand in hand to cover up their corruption.

The Corruption Eradication Commission

The rise of corruption perpetrated by many actors pushed the government to give a mandate to the KPK (*Komisi Pemberantasan Korupsi*) to eradicate corruption to its roots. Therefore, it is not surprising that the KPK arrested many actors, ranging from ministers, parliament members, bureaucrats, and party members to high-ranking military personnel and police officers.

At the ministerial level are such names as Jero Wacik (former minister of energy and mineral resources (*Energi Sumber Daya Mineral*, ESDM)), Suryadharma Ali (former minister of religious affairs), Dr Andi Mallarangeng (former minister of youth and sport), and Dr Siti Fadhilah Supari (former minister of health). At the head of regional governments (governor, regent, or mayor), some names caught in corruption cases include Ratu Atut Chosiyah (former governor of Banten), Syamsul Arifin and Gatot Pujo Nugroho (former governors of North Sumatra), Anas Makmun (former governor of Riau), Yan Anton Ferdian (former Banyuasin regent), Eep Hidayat and Ojang Sohandi (former Subang regents), and Sunaryo (former mayor of Cirebon).[13]

In both central and regional parliaments, names caught in corruption crimes included Damayanti Wisnu Putranti (member of Commission V of DPR), I Putu Sudiartana (member of Commission III of DPR), Andi Fuad Tiro (member of Commission V of DPR), Dewie Yasin Limpo (member of Commission VII of DPR), Fuad Amin (former chair of Bangkalan Regional House of Representatives (DPRD)), Muhammad Sanusi (member of DPRD DKI Jakarta), and Ali Surahman (vice-chair of Majalengka DPRD). At the bureaucratic level, there are names like Akil Mochtar (former chair of the Constitutional Court (MK)), Patrialis Akbar (former judge of MK), Emirsyah Satar (former president director of Garuda Indonesia), Burhanuddin Abdullah (former governor of Bank of Indonesia), Dr Miranda S. Goeltom (former senior deputy governor of Bank of Indonesia), Rudi Rubiandini (former head of the Oil and Gas Special Unit), Nurhadi (former secretary of the Supreme Court (MA)), and many more. Local bureaucrats are not exempt from KPK's attention: Suprapto (former head of Department of Infrastructure, Roads, Spatial Planning and Settlement of West Sumatra province), Asep Hilman (former head of Education Office of West Java province), Jamaludin (former head of Population and Civil Registry of Tasikmalaya regency), and many more.[14]

From political parties, there are names such as Luthfi Hasan Ishaaq (former president of the Prosperous Justice Party (PKS)), Patrice Rio Capella (former secretary general of the Democratic National Party (Nasdem)), Muhammad Nazarudin (former treasurer of the Democratic Party), and Siti Hartati Murdaya Poo (former member of Democratic Party Consulting Body). At the regional level, the situation is even worse. At the end of March 2018, the commission (KPK) released the names of thirty-eight North Sumatra DPRD members accused of bribery in connection with the Regional Revenue and Expenditure Budget (*Anggaran Pendapatan dan Belanja Daerah*, APBD). Among army/police officers and civil servants, there are Inspector General Djoko Susilo (former chief of Traffic Corps of the National Police (*Polri*)), Commissioner General Susno Duadji (former head of Criminal Investigation Unit of *Polri*), Brigadier General Teddy Heryadi (former finance director of Army Headquarters), Dr Abdul Rahem Faqih (lecturer at the Faculty of Fisheries and Marine Affairs, Brawijaya University), and Dr Erva Yendri (former chair of the Institute for Research and Community Service, University of Lancang Kuning) who were charged with bribery prosecution.[15]

The sheer number of corruption cases after the New Order era is a tragedy. The hope was that the *reformasi* era would provide a new political reality. But that expectation was 180 degrees contrary to reality. Unfortunately, the tragedy of corruption is being repeated before the 2019 election. The latest case of heated conversation among Indonesians is the electronic ID card (KTP-el), seemingly designed to be a feast for members of parliament and Ministry of Home Affairs (*Kemendagri*) high officials. The indictment mentions that sixty members of the DPR are allegedly involved in the case of KTP-el with state losses of up to Rp 2.3 trillion. The names of elite bureaucrats and politicians accused of receiving illicit money include Gamawan Fauzi (former minister of home affairs), Diah Anggraeni (former general secretary of the ministry of home affairs), Anas Urbaningrum (former chair of the Democratic Party), Marzuki Ali (Democratic lawmaker and former chair of the DPR), Setya Novanto (former chair of Golkar) and many more.

KPK efforts to eradicate corruption are certainly not without obstacles and challenges, the biggest being the weakening roles and duties of the KPK. The direction is to eradicate and eventually eliminate the KPK so that corrupters can easily rob state assets.

Some forms of weakening the KPK are, first, the arrest of KPK commissioners while they are dealing with major corruption cases. The first KPK commissioner arrest occurred when Commissioner General Susno Duadji (chief of the Criminal Investigation Unit (*Kepala Badan Reserse Kriminal, Kabareskrim*) of the Indonesian National Police at the time) arrested Antasari Azhar, who was designated as the murderer of Nasrudin Zulkarnaen (director of PT Rajawali Putra Banjaran) with a background infidelity in 2009.[16] The arrest of KPK commissioners also occurred when KPK investigators accused Inspector General Djoko Susilo (head of the Traffic Police Corps) as a suspect in the procurement of steering simulators worth Rp 782 billion in 2012. The weakening is clearly visible in the targeting of Novel Baswedan, leading the procurement simulator case investigation, by the police in October 2012, a few days after Djoko Susilo's arrest by the KPK. The pursuit of Novel is based on his alleged torturing to death of a prisoner when he was still serving in the Bengkulu Regional Police in 2004 (*Tempo*, 23–29 December 2013; *Tempo*, 7–13 March 2016).

The dispute between the KPK and the police is also known as *Cicak* (Gecko) v. *Buaya* (Crocodile); *Cicak* in this context refers to the small, less powerful, and new institution KPK, while *Buaya* refers to a large and very powerful police institution. The case fluctuated greatly before General Tito Karnavian was appointed chief of the Indonesian Republic Police (*Kapolri*). The latest episode of this dispute is the Abraham Samad and Bambang Widjojanto case. In mid-January 2015, after the appointment of Commissioner General Budi Gunawan, they were charged by the KPK as suspects in a bribery and gratuity affair. However, this condition has eased slightly after the appointment of General Tito Karnavian as National Police Chief, who is well known as one of the police elite who can "communicate" with the KPK.

Second, reiterating the KPK's original purpose as an ad-hoc institution that eventually could be terminated, in 2011, at a consultation between the DPR, police, attorney general, and KPK, the idea of dissolving the KPK was put forward because it was considered inefficient in dealing with corruption. The proposal stated that the KPK succeeded only in prosecuting corruption cases, but did not prevent corruption, so the agency was considered unsuccessful.

Moreover, in the same year, the then-chair of the House, Marzuki Ali, stated that the KPK was an ad-hoc institution: temporary in nature and could be dissolved at any time. The idea of dissolving the

KPK re-emerged in August 2015 at the Constitution Seminar in the parliament building when Megawati stated that ad-hoc institutions, including the KPK, could be discontinued because of their temporary nature (*Tempo*, 18 August 2015).

Third was weakening through legislation. In the observation of the author, a number of political parties in the DPR have proposed and discussed revision of the KPK law since 2011. A revised draught of the KPK law that has been circulating will certainly delegitimize the role and power of the KPK. The idea starts from letting the KPK issue SP3 (*Surat Perintah Penghentian Penyidikan*, case termination letters), restricting the recruitment of independent investigators, wiretaps requiring permission from the Board of Trustees, and limiting the life of the commission to twelve years. In addition, the House attempted to weaken the KPK through revision of the Criminal Code (*Kitab Undang-undang Hukum Pidana*, KUHP) by including corruption offences in the draught (at the time of writing, the code draft has not yet been passed by the House of Representatives). If this proposal is passed, then corruption is no longer considered an extraordinary crime, but merely an ordinary one. In fact, in the new Criminal Code, cumulative penalties do not apply and there is also a rule to reduce maximum criminal penalties by one-third for corruption.

If the weakening through regulation and the dissolution of KPK succeed, then the corrupt elites will, of course, be cheering. They will feel more free to feast on the country's wealth and it will hurt the democracy that has been nurtured since the *reformasi* era. This is also what eventually makes people feel that the New Order era was much better than the era of *reformasi*. President Joko Widodo has repeatedly tried to stop the weakening and politicians' efforts to revise the anti-corruption law. But unfortunately, politicians (whose colleagues have been jailed by the KPK) always seek ways to weaken the anti-bribery agency.

Despite the constant attacks, KPK's performance has never weakened. Even prior to the simultaneous regional elections on 27 June 2018, the KPK arrested several candidates who were caught abusing their power and cause detriment to the national interest: Zumi Zola (governor of Jambi), Mustafa (regent of Lampung Tengah, Lampung), Imas Aryumningsih (regent of Subang, West Java), Abu Bakar (regent of West Bandung, West Java), Mohammad Yahya Fuad (regent of

Kebumen, Central Java), Nyono Suharli Wihandoko (regent of Jombang, East Java), Abdul Latif (regent of Hulu Sungai Tengah, South Kalimantan), Marianus Sae (regent of Ngada, East Nusa Tenggara), and many more — all are cadres of political parties. This shows that multiple external pressures never degrade the KPK's spirit. The KPK is opening branches in regions (Aceh, Medan, Riau, Banten, Papua, and West Papua) as a manifestation of its faithful services to the country in eradicating corruption.

Conclusion

This chapter has discussed the development of politics, especially the election of heads of regional government in two eras, namely the New Order and *reformasi*. Both eras opened up opportunities for corrupters to work in their own way. Corrupt practices have increased in the *reformasi* era. Initially, we criticized the authoritarian system of Soeharto's New Order that facilitated systematic corruption. But since the New Order fell in 1998 and the democratic system began to be institutionalized, corruption has remained, becoming an endless story from the beginning of *reformasi* until Widodo's administration. The actors are also becoming more diverse than ever. Ministers, regional government heads, top officials of BUMN, and political party elites are no exceptions. The multiple corruption cases described in this chapter not only explain how difficult it is to minimize corruption but have also opened our eyes to how dangerous corruption has become, putting the future of Indonesia's democracy in danger.

NOTES

1. Since independence, Indonesia has had several laws on regional government. The first, Law No. 1/1945 (passed on 23 November 1945), states that autonomy is at the village level, where the head of local administration is elected directly by its people. The second, Law No. 22/1948 (passed on 10 July 1948), widened the autonomous region to the district and made the village a Level III District. Under the third, Law No. 1/1957, the head of regional government was elected by DPRD members at each level. After a political restructuring resulting from a 1959 presidential decree, the

government made the Presidential Stipulation (*Penetapan Presiden, Penpres*) No. 6/1959, which governed regional administration in the political construction of Guided Democracy. Based on this *Penpres*, the election of the head of regional government began to be watched by the central government. Then, this *Penpres* was replaced by Law No. 18/1965 on regional government and Law No. 19/1965 on village administration. Several years later, Law No. 5/1974 paved the way for serious intervention by the New Order at the local level. For a more comprehensive discussion on this subject, see, *inter alia*, Malley (1999a; 1999b) and Agustino (2014a).

2. Interview with former Bogor regent candidate in 1999, former Depok mayor 1997–2000, former Depok mayor 2000–5, former Depok mayoral candidate 2005 and 2011 and several speakers who refused to be named (candidates for regent, mayor and governor in some areas in West Java).

3. Interview with several candidates for regional government head who do not want to be named.

4. Interview with #2 in Bandung.

5. Interview with #3 in Cirebon.

6. Interview with #4 in Bandung.

7. Interview with #5 in Tasikmalaya.

8. The Red and White Coalition (Koalisi Merah Putih (KMP)) comprises Gerindra, PAN, PPP, PKS, and Golkar. On the other side, the Great Indonesia Coalition (Koalisi Indonesia Hebat) consists of PDIP, Nasdem, PKB, and Hanura. The Democratic Party is outside these two coalitions, although it is often closer to the KMP. This is based on (1) the similarity of military background between Yudhoyono and Prabowo and (2) competition in the election of Jakarta's governor in 2017. The outbreak of KMP is based more on the wishes of some of its component parties to join the government coalition (KIH), which is considered to help parties' survival. Therefore, Golkar, PPP, and PAN eventually joined KIH, although PAN often seems to be less committed to the coalition between the component parties in the KIH. For further discussion, see Agustino (2014b).

9. The author cites mostly from Ambardi's (2009) research results.

10. After Amien Rais issued the statement, Yudhoyono denied receiving KKP funds. When mass media mentioned the name of one of Yudhoyono's campaign team members, Munawar Fuad, Yudhoyono claimed that Munawar was not part of his campaign team (*Tempo*, 4–10 June 2007, p. 21). In the same issue, the magazine tried to find Munawar's role and his relationship with Yudhoyono. It is true that Munawar's name was not found in the list of Yudhoyono's campaign teams submitted to the Komisi Pemilihan Umum (KPU). Nevertheless, on many occasions, according to

Tempo, Yudhoyono always introduced Munawar as his special staff for social and religious affairs.

11. In a report of *Tempo* (13–19 March 2017, pp. 38–39), there are many names who received e-KTP funds: Anas Urbaningrum, Muhammad Nazaruddin (Democratic Party), Ganjar Pranowo, Olly Dodokambey (PDIP), Tamsil Linrung, Jazuli Juwaini (PKS), Rindoko Dahono Winggit (Gerindra), Abdul Malik Haramian (PKB), and many more. The receivers of these fraudulent funds were not only party elites but also civil servants such as Diah Anggraeni (former secretary general of the Ministry of Home Affairs), Sugiharto (former director of information of Population Administration), and others.

12. Pam Swakarsa is a volunteer force recruited by the army with the support of General Wiranto, the TNI commander. The number at that time reached approximately 125,000 people with the aim of strengthening the security of the General Assembly of the People's Consultative Assembly, held 10–13 November 1998. Some people have interpreted the formation of *Pam Swakarsa* as a reflection of political competition in the army organization between General Wiranto and Lieutenant General Prabowo, with *Pam Swakarsa* being aimed at matching Prabowo's moves.

13. Data obtained from online and print media, such as: *Tempo* (2014), *Tribunnews* (2016), Nugraha (2015), as well as *Tempo* magazine, *Kompas* daily, and *Koran Tempo*. For further discussion, see Agustino and Fitriani (2017).

14. Data are obtained from online media and print media, *inter alia*, such as: *detikNews* (2011), *Okenews* (2017), *Tempo* (2019), as well as *Tempo* magazine, *Kompas* daily, and *Koran Tempo*. For further discussion, see Agustino and Fitriani (2017).

15. Data are obtained through online media search as well as from printed media, *inter alia*, such as: *Tempo* (2015), *Rappler* (2016), and *Tempo* magazine, *Kompas* daily, and *Tempo* newspaper. For further discussion, see Agustino and Fitriani (2017).

16. Antasari Azhar's arrest is still controversial. In some versions, it is said that it was caused by his verdict on Aulia Pohan (father of Yudhoyono's daughter-in-law), after Pohan was allegedly responsible for a flow of funds from the Indonesian Banking Development Foundation (Yayasan Pengembangan Perbankan Indonesia (YPPI)) worth Rp 100 billion to members of parliament and the attorney officials. Aulia Pohan was convicted in the Jakarta High Court and sentenced to four and a half years in prison and Supreme Court (Mahkamah Agung (MA)) to alleviate the sentence of former deputy governor of BI to three years. Not long after that, Antasari was charged with murder.

REFERENCES

Agustino, Leo. *Politik Lokal dan Otonomi Daerah.* Bandung: Alfabeta, 2014*a*.
———. "Pemilihan Umum di Indonesia Tahun 2014". *Prisma* 33 (2014*b*): 110–25.
Agustino, Leo and Indah Fitriani. *Korupsi: Akar, Aktor, dan Locus.* Yogyakarta: Pustaka Pelajar, 2017.
Ambardi, Kuskrido. *Mengungkap Politik Kartel: Studi Tentang Sistem Kepartaian di Indonesia Era Reformasi.* Jakarta: KPG, 2009.
detikNews. "7 Jaksa Paling Populer karena Terjerat Kasus Suap Hingga Selingkuh", 23 November 2011. Available at <http://news.detik.com/berita/1773680/7-jaksa-paling-populer-karena-terjerat-kasus-suap-hingga-selingkuh>.
Emmerson, Donald K. *Indonesia's Elite: Political Culture and Culture Politics.* Ithaca: Cornell University Press, 1978.
Jenkins, David. *Suharto and His Generals: Indonesian Military Politics 1975–1983.* Ithaca: Cornell University, 1984.
Jpnn.com. "Marak Jual-beli Jabatan di Pemda", 4 December 2010. Available at <http://www.jpnn.com/read/2010/12/04/78772/Marak-Jual-beli-Jabatan-di-Pemda->.
King, Dwight Y. "'Indonesia' New Order as a Bureaucratic Polity, a Neopatrimonial Regime or Bureaucratic Authoritarian Regime: What Difference Does It Make?" In *Interpreting Indonesian Politics: Thirteen Contributions to the Debate,* edited by Benedict R. O'G. Anderson and Ruth McVey. Ithaca: Cornell University, 1982.
Koran Tempo, 7 January 2017.
Listy, Diah L. and Ayu Puspitasari. "Penyuap Bupat Klaten Dicopot". *Tempo,* 3 January 2017, p. 10.
Malley, Michael. "Regions: Centralization and Resistance". In *Indonesia Beyond Suharto: Polity, Economy, Society, Transition,* edited by Donald K. Emmerson. New York: M.E. Sharpe, 1999*a*.
———. "Resource Distribution, State Coherence, and Political Centralization in Indonesia, 1950–1997". PhD dissertation, University of Wisconsin-Madison, 1999*b*.
McVey, Ruth. "The Beambtenstaat in Indonesia". In *Interpreting Indonesian Politics: Thirteen Contributions to the Debate,* edited by Benedict R. O'G. Anderson and Ruth McVey. Ithaca: Cornell University, 1982.
Mietzner, Marcus. "Funding Pilkada: Illegal Campaign Financing in Indonesia's Local Elections". In *The State and Illegality in Indonesia,* edited by Edward Aspinall and Gerry van Klinken. Leiden: KITLV Press, 2011.
Nugraha, Rizki. "Daftar Tangkapan Terbesar KPK". *DW.com,* 26 January 2015. Available at <http://www.dw.com/id/daftar-tangkapan-terbesar-kpk/a-18214980>.

Okenews. "Mantan Kadisdik Jabar Pucat Pasi Dengar Vonis 3 Tahun, Lalu Pingsan", 6 September 2017. Available at <https://news.okezone.com/read/2017/09/06/525/1770387/mantan-kadisdik-jabar-pucat-pasi-dengar-vonis-3-tahun-lalu-pingsan>.

Rappler. "LINI MASA: Anggota DPR 2014-2019 yang terlibat korupsi", 1 July 2016. Available at <http://www.rappler.com/indonesia/138209-anggota-dpr-tersangka-korupsi>.

Rinangkit, Sukardi. *The Indonesian Military After the New Order.* Singapore: Institute of Southeast Asian Studies, 2005.

Tempo, 19–25 February 2001.

———, 11–17 December 2006.

———, 4–10 June 2007.

———, 4–10 June 2012.

———, 20–26 May 2013.

———, 23–29 December 2013.

———. "7 Elite Demokrat Ini Tersandung Kasus Korupsi", 4 September 2014. Available at <https://m.tempo.co/read/news/2014/09/04/063604384/7-elite-demokrat-ini-tersandung-kasus-korupsi>.

———. "Hampir Satu Dekade, 5 Polisi Terjerat Korupsi", 14 January 2015. Available at <https://m.tempo.co/read/news/2015/01/14/078634731/hampir-satu-dekade-5-polisi-terjerat-korupsi>.

———. "ICW Protes Pernyataan Mega Soal Pembubaran KPK", 18 August 2015. Available at <https://nasional.tempo.co/read/692969/icw-protes-pernyataan-mega-soal-pembubaran-kpk>.

———, 7–13 March 2016.

———, 31 January–5 February 2017.

———, 13–19 March 2017.

———. "OTT KPK: Sumbar Benarkan Penangkapan Kadis Prasjaltarkim", 7 February 2019. Available at <https://kabar24.bisnis.com/read/20160630/16/562689/ott-kpk-sumbar-benarkan-penangkapan-kadis-prasjaltarkim>.

Tribunnews. "Dahlan Iskan dan Daftar Menteri Era SBY yang Tersangkut Korupsi SBY yang Tersangkut Korupsi", 28 October 2016. Available at <http://www.tribunnews.com/nasional/2016/10/28/dahlan-iskan-dan-daftar-menteri-era-sby-yang-tersangkut-korupsi?page=2>.

Wibowo, Pramono A. *Mahalnya Demokrasi, Memudarnya Ideologi: Potret Komunikasi Politik Legislator-Konstituen.* Jakarta: Penerbit Buku Kompas, 2013.

9

Why Is It Really Hard To Move On? Explaining Indonesia's Limited Foreign Policy Reform After Soeharto

Ahmad Rizky Mardhatillah Umar

Introduction

The aim of this chapter is to explain the absence of fundamental change in Indonesia's foreign policy after the New Order. Most discussion of *reformasi* in Indonesia is largely dominated by national or local politics, with some limited accounts on Indonesia's foreign policy and changing international profile. Most of these accounts have been widely influenced by theories of "democratic transition" that put emphasis on democratization of foreign policy-making processes. According to these theories, the democratization process has driven foreign policy change in Indonesia since the fall of Soeharto in 1998. Another strand of argument takes into account the role of "international pressure" relating to human rights and East Timorese independence as the causes of Indonesia's foreign policy change after *reformasi*. Taking a slightly different angle, Laksmana (2011*a*) argues that *reformasi* has created Indonesia's different international profile to cope with a changing geopolitical and geostrategic landscape.

In this chapter, I shall propose a rival argument, that Indonesia's foreign policy after *reformasi* does not fully embrace broader ideational, political, and institutional transformations. Whilst the existing arguments are correct in arguing that there are some institutional changes in Indonesia's foreign policy-making, which were caused by democratization, the reform is only limited and partial. Current analyses are flawed in three senses. First, they are too narrow in understanding Indonesia's foreign policy only in terms of institutional dynamics or policy-making process. Less has been said about ideational foundations of Indonesia's foreign policy, as well as its political and ideological underpinning in the changing context of Indonesian domestic politics. Second, given the neglect of the ideational foundation, they also fail to explain the broader paradigm shift in Indonesia's foreign policy, in which the bureaucratic institutions are taken for granted as the main actor in foreign policy. Third, this literature also neglects contestation between "social forces" in the process of foreign policy-making.

These weaknesses necessitate rethinking Indonesia's foreign policy after *reformasi*. In contrast to the democratic transition literature, I argue that Indonesia's foreign policy has undergone only "limited reform". Three important factors persist in post-New Order foreign policy: (1) the "dual" capitalist-developmental and security-oriented doctrine; (2) bureaucratic elitism in decision-making; and (3) the preserved legacy of Cold War alignment in international politics, particularly at the regional level. I further argue that this "limited reform" is primarily caused by the lack of engagement of the proponents of *reformasi* with foreign policy, which reflect the partial and incomplete nature of *reformasi* that persists after twenty years.

In this chapter, I shall develop what I call "critical institutionalism" as my main theoretical framework to understand Indonesia's foreign policy change, which takes into account the ideational, institutional, and geopolitical aspects of foreign policy. By critical institutionalism, I consider foreign policy not only as an implication of elites' rational choice or a technocratic decision-making process within a particular institution, but also a form of "translation of ideas into policy", which is also affected by history or particular ideologies held by foreign policymakers. Foreign policy is, therefore, a political variable, which involves the contestations of various ideologies and "social forces" across history.

Drawing upon this approach, Table 9.1 presents a three-layered framework to understand foreign policy change, which will be applied to understand the extent to which Indonesia's foreign policy changes after the New Order. It consists of three level of analysis. First, foreign policy change derives from the dissolution of old ideas in foreign policy and the invention of new ideas that could be translated as policy framework at the bureaucratic level. Second, foreign policy change is also visible in the translation of new ideas into a new set of policies and an institutional framework that guides foreign policy-making at the institutional level. Third, this new set of policies and institutional framework also differ on the political level, where there are new set of political process to articulate the foreign policy in the international sphere, which changes the way a country aligns itself in the broader international order.

In what follows, I shall analyse the three dimensions of foreign policy change in Indonesia's foreign policy after Soeharto. Furthermore, I shall propose a concluding remark to explain why the New Order's legacy persists in Indonesia's foreign policy, and why the foreign policmakers after Soeharto failed to move on from that legacy.

TABLE 9.1
A Critical Institutionalist Framework for Foreign Policy Analysis

No.	Dimension	Characteristics	Locus of Analysis
1.	Ideational	Foreign policy is produced by "a group of intellectuals" who set a particular foreign policy doctrine to navigate the state in the international order.	Foreign Policy Doctrine
2	Institutional	Ideas that have been produced are institutionalized, in particular, bureaucratic institutions, incorporated to policy preference.	Institutional Process in either Bureucratic or Political Institutions
3	Geopolitical	The "institutionalized" ideas of foreign policy are further deepened in the international order, which changes the way a country aligns itself to major international powers in world politics.	Geopolitical Alignment in World Politics

The Persistence of Security-Developmentalist Doctrine

The New Order's foreign policy was primarily established upon the centrality of what I shall call "security-oriented" foreign policy doctrine, complemented by a capitalist-developmental approach. In contrast to analyses that sees Soeharto's foreign policy as more "nationalistic" and centred upon his cultural world view, I argue that Soeharto steered foreign policy in accordance with: (1) a capitalist-developmental doctrine of foreign policy, in which foreign policy is a tool for maintaining economic relations with a particular bloc in world politics, and (2) security-oriented doctrine, which follows Soeharto's planned and centralized economic development. These two doctrines situate Indonesia's foreign policy in the early New Order, which strived to obtain recognition from the "Western bloc" whilst dissociating itself from the Soviet Union and its allies, and at the same time securing the domestic and regional security environment after the regime transition in 1965–66.

Hence, I argue that the rise of New Order was accompanied by a set of new foreign policy preferences for peace and stability rather than contesting with the United States and its allies in the Cold War, as well as preferring capitalist development rather than a progressive nationalist approach to economic development. It led to the re-orientation of Indonesia's foreign policy, which manifests not only by what Gordon Hein referred to as "the doctrine of co-centric circles" but also the militaristic doctrine of "preserving national security". The persistence of these security-oriented concepts, whilst also shared by some civilian thinkers (such as Muhammad Yamin), was systematically developed by prominent military strategists within ABRI. Furthermore, this militaristic and security-oriented doctrine can be traced to the Army's doctrine of Catur Dharma Eka Karma (CADEK), which was developed as the military's official view of world politics and the national strategy to address geopolitical changes in the early New Order era. Even though CADEK was not a primary document for Indonesia's foreign policy, the inception of military structure in foreign policy through *dwifungsi* paved the way for partial incorporation of CADEK as a foreign policy doctrine. *Dwifungsi* linked foreign policy doctrine with broader security doctrine, such as CADEK, and was framed through an authoritarian co-centric doctrine. This re-orientation of foreign policy from a revolutionary approach centred upon anti-colonial internationalism — as practised by Sukarno — to a realist approach that put forward national stability as the core principle. Through *dwifungsi*, a security-oriented doctrine penetrated the foreign policy-making process, locating foreign policy as merely a subordinate of security policies. "Territorial unity" — more specifically understood as "Persatuan Indonesia" — frames Indonesia's foreign policy. This move has established a security-oriented approach in foreign policy and made the Foreign Ministry merely an extension and "speaker" of domestic security policies.

This realist security-oriented doctrine has been complemented by a capitalist-developmental approach to foreign economic policy. The backbone of this doctrine was to secure foreign aid and investment, combined with centralized and market-oriented development policies, backed by an intellectual group of "technocrats" educated mostly in the United States. Through aid from the United States, Japan, and their allies, Indonesia managed to achieve capitalist economic growth in a planned and state-authorized manner. Investment was initiated to boost capitalist development. A "developmental approach", as argued by Robert Cribb, emphasized the role of professional work of a group of technocrats in managing the economy, which set the technocratic basis of the New Order's policy foundations guided by a liberal economic framework. With this doctrine, Indonesia's foreign economic policies in the New Order radically departed from the "revolutionary" and nationalist policies of the Sukarno era. Soeharto preferred to maintain a close economic relationship with the United States and its allies, whilst at the same time establishing ASEAN as a regional forum for economic cooperation. In the 1990s, the growing regional economic cooperation put ASEAN at the forefront of Indonesia's economic cooperation in the global political economy.

The persistence of this "dual" capitalist-developmental and security-oriented doctrine might have altered at the edge of Soeharto's rule in the mid-1990s. However, the post-Soeharto foreign policy has failed to produce a more dynamic doctrine. Habibie's policy, for example, was to tackle international pressure on Timorese crisis and bring back economic stability after the Asian crisis. Megawati — despite her opposition towards the Soeharto regime in the 1990s — brought back this security-oriented doctrine with her military campaign in Aceh.

These failures are understandable as due to domestic constraints: both Habibie and Megawati had to deal with either "crisis recovery", which brings back the liberal technocrats and their capitalist agenda, or tackling terrorism and secessionism, which brings the military back in. Abdurrahman Wahid and Susilo Bambang Yudhoyono brought some breakthroughs in their approach to foreign policy. However, whilst Wahid established a more outward-looking approach by taking personal initiatives abroad during his short-lived presidency, his international initiatives in taking a "moderate" Islamic view abroad was constrained by his ability to steer the Foreign Ministry to support his personal initiatives and networks. Susilo Bambang Yudhoyono brought a more energetic approach, attempting to establish a good international image "Zero Enemies and Million Friends" doctrine. However, it was later seen that his foreign economic policy, along with his predecessor's policy, did not significantly depart from that of the New Order. Even though Yudhoyono's presidency was successful in democratizing Indonesia's foreign policy, "Zero Enemies and Million Friends" doctrine did not radically transform Indonesia's security and economic policies. Both "Zero Enemies and Million Friends" doctrine and Foreign Minister Natalegawa's slightly different "Dynamic Equilibrium" failed to escape from the *realpolitik* ideology centred upon national stability, even though their policies had a less militaristic approach.

Persistence of Bureaucratic Elitism

The dual security-oriented and capitalist-developmental doctrine has established a very inward-looking approach. This was also maintained by a "bureaucratic elitism" guided by a very centralistic hierarchical political order. Within this context, the role of the Foreign Ministry was pivotal in formulating the security-oriented doctrine into a policy. The origins of this bureaucratic elitism can be traced to the reorientation of the ministry with a more passive outlook and the replacement of ministry officials with former members of the military. Having seen the ministry as the ideological fulcrum of Sukarno's nationalist foreign policy, which was led by Subandrio during the "guided democracy" era, Soeharto started the "purification and cleansing" of the ministry through several presidential decrees. By 1970, as Nabbs-Keller (2013) noted, the Ministry of Foreign Affairs had been subordinated to the military's *dwifungsi* doctrine, in which military personnel were embedded in both the ministry and Indonesian embassies overseas.

The leading voices of Indonesia's foreign policy during this era became the "cleansed" Ministry of Foreign Affairs and various military institutions that aimed to put forward the security-oriented doctrine. Having been "cleansed" of Sukarno's legacy and his revolutionary policy, the ministry has been pivotal in designing foreign policy. However, two things need to be noted. First, the ministry has been staffed with military officials and provided with a security-oriented doctrine. According to Nabbs-Keller, the "cleansing" of the ministry started as early as Soeharto's taking power in 1966, when Soeharto established Tim Penertib (Team for Restoring Order) and a Special Executive Team in the ministry. After the initial process had been completed in the 1970s, the Foreign Ministry was re-established with a combination of military and civilian elites in its organizational structure.

Second, the recomposition of the Foreign Ministry in the 1970s led the institution to work within a more complex, hierarchical bureaucratic system. The ministry did not make foreign policy alone; it worked with other governmental institutions. The bureaucratic process was built upon a hierarchy and controlled by an elite group led by President Soeharto. Even though there were some contentions between the Foreign Ministry and the military on several security issues, Soeharto's centralized authority resolved the problem and directed the Foreign Ministry's work. Consequently, the bureaucratic process tended to be very complex and multi-institutional, involving the Foreign Ministry, the military, intelligence, the Trade Ministry and even the president's inner circles.

The East Timor case exemplifies the primacy of bureaucratic complexity connected to maintaining the security-oriented doctrine. In 1975, Indonesia decided to intervene forcibly in the Timorese crisis and integrate this former Portuguese colony into the country. This policy was, of course, made by security elites in Jakarta. Gordon Hein argues that this decision was driven primarily by a co-centric circles doctrine that put national and territorial unity as the core of Indonesia's foreign and security policy. Yet, Indonesia had to maintain a good image internationally as criticism was directed to this move. It is the role of foreign policy to counter criticism abroad. As Ali Alatas, the longstanding foreign minister, reflected, the Timorese case was "a pebble in the shoe" in Indonesia's foreign policy. However, whilst the move was driven by a militaristic and security-oriented approach, the Foreign Ministry was tasked to save the country's face in international fora.

The result of the complexity of the Indonesian bureaucratic polity in which the foreign policy decision was made is a high degree of elitism. Since the Foreign Ministry was tasked only to negotiate, represent, and "save" Indonesia's face abroad, it did not do much public engagement. There was no role for engagement with civil society. With the strong security orientation in foreign policy, as well as strong bureaucratic rule in the governmental structure, decision-making is top-down. Even though there were some deliberations that involved parliament, the strong co-optation by Soeharto and his powerful allies silenced any domestic opposition and resulted in the absence of civil society from foreign policy-making. There was, however, some participation from think tanks or academic institutions (such as the Center for Strategic and International Studies). However, it was not until the 2000s that civil society organizations were participating in the foreign policy process.

The process has arguably been reformed since 1998. In some areas (ASEAN, for example), the government introduced some new spaces for civil society and broader academic institutions, such as Foreign Policy Breakfast (introduced during Hassan Wirajuda's tenure), particularly on ASEAN-related issues. The Foreign Ministry also started to obtain policy "inputs" (albeit only from limited stakeholders) before going to negotiations or dealing with specific cases. However, the legacy of elitism could still be traced in some "securitized" issues such as Aceh or Papua. In the Papuan case, the foreign policy decision was made jointly with other ministries in the Coordinating Ministry for Security and Political Affairs (Kemenko POLHUKAM). For example, in order to obtain permission to conduct journalistic activities in Papua, a foreign journalist needs "clearing" by twelve government institutions in Jakarta. Indonesia's policy related to the Papuan issue has been made in a complex bureaucratic structure. Compared to policy regarding ASEAN, policy in regard to Papua did not involve much public debate or civil society participation due to its "political-security sensitivity". On some issues, bureaucratic elitism is still manifest, even after several attempts to implement reform in the Foreign Ministry.

Persistence of Cold War Alignments

Finally, the limitations of *reformasi* in foreign policy can be understood in the light of alignments in world politics. It is important to see Indonesia's alignment in world politics to understand how foreign policy doctrine, which was preserved by a strong and centralized bureaucratic institution, works. It is therefore important to understand Indonesia's foreign policy not only in terms as independent and active (as set out by Mohammad Hatta in the 1950s) but also in relation to the New Order's security-oriented doctrine, complemented by a capitalist-developmental approach, and preserved through a high degree of bureaucratic elitism.

The New Order radically reoriented Indonesia's foreign policy by cutting ties with the People's Republic of China (PRC) — although the relationship was restored in the 1990s. Indonesia also re-established its relations with the Western states. In 1967, Indonesia rejoined the International Monetary Fund after withdrawing two years before. The Inter-Governmental Group on Indonesia (IGGI) was established in the same year to coordinate the disbursing of aid. These economic policies not only helped to restructure Indonesia's foreign policy but also reoriented it to closer relations with Washington and its allies. In the same year, Indonesia also normalized relations with Malaysia (after the turbulent politics of *konfrontasi* in the early 1960s) and helped establish ASEAN along with five other states. The establishment of ASEAN thus marks a new regional "order" in Southeast Asia characterized by a strong "non-intervention". In the 1970s, coinciding with the "oil boom" that benefitted oil-exporter countries, Indonesia was set to pursue a higher stage of development fuelled by a centralized capitalistic economy and guided by authoritarian political rule.

Even though the New Order continued several "unfinished" Indonesian initiatives in world politics, such as the establishment of the Non-Aligned Movement, the way Indonesia approaches international security and international political economy is still aligned with the US-led order in world politics. There are several important signs that locate Indonesia's alignment in world politics close to the United States and its allies from the Cold War era. First, Indonesia's security cooperation has been very close to the United States and its allies. Since the 1960s, Indonesia has cooperating with the United States in security sectors. As Murphy (2010) shows, the US politics of containment made Indonesia one of US's political allies in Southeast Asia, even though Indonesia preferred to maintain a low profile in the international rivalry. The close relationship between the two states, for example, is visible in the Timorese case. Murphy argues, citing a report from Adam Schwarz:

> When it appeared that left-wing forces would assume power in the wake of Portugal's abrupt withdrawal from East Timor, the logic of containment led the US to acquiesce to Indonesia's 1975 invasion of East Timor with Secretary of State Henry Kissinger asking only that it be carried out "quickly, efficiently, and without the use of American military equipment"...

Second, in development and economic cooperation, Indonesia prefers to access foreign aid and investment from the United States, Japan, and their political allies under the IGGI. In 1967 and 1968, the United States took the lead in providing aid and assistance for the stabilization and reconstruction of Indonesia's economy. In 1972, the United States spent more than US$28 million on Indonesian technical assistance. This aid paved the way for closer ties, which were sustained in the coming years. The Foreign Investment Law in 1967 boosted foreign direct investment and served as a gateway for major multinational companies to invest in Indonesia. Japan, Australia, and the United States became Indonesia's major trade partners until the 2000s, when the PRC rose as a prominent trade partner in the wake of the global financial crisis.

Post-Soeharto foreign policy did not change this alignment, except with the closer economic ties with the PRC, which are partly due to the changes in the international order in the 1990s: economic policy change in the PRC, the dissolution of the Soviet Union, and the end of the Cold War. In security cooperation, the United States remains Indonesia's major ally, particularly in the "Global War on Terror". Indonesia has attempted to establish other security cooperation, such as with the purchase of Sukhoi airplanes from Russia during Megawati's presidency. However, the War on Terror made Indonesia the main ally in the US campaign in Southeast Asia, considered the "second front" for the global campaign. An analysis from the US Council for Foreign Relations summarizes six areas of Indonesia–US security cooperation during the War on Terror (2002–6):

1. International Military Education and Training, which was renewed in 2002 after being temporarily suspended due to

concerns about human rights abuses by the military in East Timor.

2. Anti-terrorism Assistance Program, which provides assistance to Indonesia's war on terror and to the Indonesian Special Detachment Unit (DENSUS-88).
3. Counterterrorism Fellowship Program, which provides education in counterterrorism practices and strategies for Indonesian military and intelligence officials.
4. Military spare parts for non-lethal items.
5. Foreign Military Financing, which partially assisted the Indonesian navy in maritime security.
6. More general economic support to assist legal and security enforcement.

It is thus visible that the post-Soeharto foreign policy is not radically different. The reason, however, is not necessarily that Indonesia was reluctant to shift the alignment; it was due to the reconfiguration in world politics that made realignment seem not very realistic. However, Indonesia's involvement in the Global War on Terror shows that the New Order's legacy of alignment with the United States has been preserved. Whilst Indonesia reopened ties with the PRC and maintains a closer relationship with other Asian states, preference is still given to the US camp. Indonesia is reluctant to confront the United States in its foreign policy. Even though the so-called "dynamic equilibrium" doctrine, which was coined by Foreign Minister Natalegawa (2009–14), attempted to address global political change (particularly the rise of the PRC and the global financial crisis), Indonesia is still aligned with the United States in world politics.

Limits of Democratization: Making Sense of Indonesia's Limited Foreign Policy Change

What explains the "limited reform" in Indonesian foreign policy after Soeharto? So far, I have shown that even though post-Soeharto policy-makers have attempted to embrace institutional and policy reform, it is still partial and limited. I argue that the New Order's legacy in post-New Order foreign policy has been preserved ideationally, institutionally, and politically. Ideationally, it is clear that *reformasi* does not necessarily lead to changes in foreign policy doctrine: witness the persistence of security-oriented doctrine, complemented by a capitalist-developmental approach. Institutionally, attempts have been made to reform the Foreign Ministry and democratize policy formulation. However, in some cases, such as secessionist issues, complex bureaucratic rule puts aside democratization and deliberation. Politically, whilst Indonesia aims to reorient its international alignment after Soeharto, it appears that the United States and its allies, which have been pivotal in shaping Indonesia's foreign security and economic policies since 1967, are still at the forefront of Indonesia's alignment in world politics, despite a more flexible engagement with Russia and PRC.

Furthermore, I suggest that this "limited reform" is not only related to the elite's attitude to reform. Utilizing the three-level critical institutionalist framework, I suggest that three variables significantly account for the limited reform in Indonesia's foreign policy.

First, policymakers have not yet developed an alternative doctrine that directly and systematically challenges the New Order foreign policy. Habibie and Abdurrahman Wahid were not able to embrace a particular policy approach, given their short-lived presidencies. Whilst Habibie trusted his foreign minister veteran diplomat Ali Alatas, who was focused on saving Indonesia's image in world politics amid international criticisms over human rights issues in East Timor, Alwi Shihab's tenure as foreign minister under Wahid was marred by domestic opposition over several issues, such as the idea to open trade ties with Israel and Habibie's extensive travel abroad. Megawati, similarly, faced the terrorist threat after the bombing in Bali, which put Indonesia at the centre of the Global War on Terror. Some alternative ideas, however, were developed during Yudhoyono's tenure. During his first term, he embraced the "Zero Enemies and Million Friends" doctrine, which was developed more systematically by Foreign Minister Natalegawa in his "Dynamic Equilibrium" and "Cold Peace" doctrine. However, neither "Zero Enemy and Million Friends" nor "Dynamic Equilibrium" doctrine opposed the New Order's security-oriented and capitalist-developmental approach. Development and investment remain at the forefront of Indonesia's foreign economic policies. In essence, both doctrines were built upon the New Order legacy of national security and co-centric principle, albeit with some modifications (particularly with Dynamic Equilibrium). Therefore, although there have been some innovations, the point of reference is not radically different from that of the New Order. In some politically sensitive foreign policy issues such as secessionism in Aceh or Papua, the approach returns to the security-oriented doctrine.

Second, there are some limitations on public participation in foreign policy decision-making. Whilst the Foreign Ministry endeavoured to open up participation, it was still limited to issues like ASEAN or debate over Indonesia's stance in the United Nations Security Council. This does not necessarily mean that the government closed the space for participation. It is also due to the legacy of foreign policy as a technocratic or highly elitist matter, in which the Foreign Ministry or other institutions only act as spokesperson in a particular negotiation. As a result, deliberation reaches only a limited number of stakeholders. This was evident in the public debate over Indonesia's stances in ASEAN. Whilst the government has been relatively open for policy inputs from non-state actors, it has never invited serious public debate. Participation is even less when it comes to a more technical form of cooperation, such as trade negotiation or security cooperation. Many factors account for this, including limited public knowledge on technical issues. Bureaucratic elitism after Soeharto, therefore, is not merely a product of bureaucrats' reluctance to open space for participation; it is also a result of limited public engagement and knowledge, especially among civil society organizations or broader pressure groups, which prevents a more intense public debate and participation.

Third, there is Indonesia's adaptation to the changing international order, particularly after the Cold War, which is completely different from pre-1990. When Soeharto established the New Order in 1965–66, he faced intense great power rivalry in the Cold War between the United States and the Soviet Union. With this international setting, Soeharto could easily align Indonesia with one of the major forces and obtain sufficient aid and assistance. With the end of the Cold War in 1990, the choice of alignment became more complex. Thus, when Soeharto stepped down in 1998, the government did not have much opportunity to establish an alternative political alliance in world politics, especially given the lack of power after the political crisis in 1998–99. There was, however, an attempt to establish "alternative alignment" by Abdurrahman Wahid, by proposing closer engagement with India and the PRC. However, as noted by Smith (2000), it appears that Wahid's foreign policy is more orthodox than his predecessor's. His foreign policy was never fully implemented due to his short-lived presidency. Megawati and Yudhoyono, on the other hand, chose to preserve the old pro-US alignment in their foreign policy, particularly when they had to deal with the Global War on Terror. President Jokowi, even though more flexible and eclectic in his foreign policy, has never radically differed with his predecessors over aligning with the United States, except that he started to embrace a more pro-Chinese economic policy, particularly with regard to infrastructure cooperation.

More substantial reform to foreign policy, therefore, lies not only with the government, but also with the wider civil society and pressure groups. The starting point is to consider foreign policy not only as an elitist policy ruled by only a group of diplomats, but also a public policy that is subject to public debates and scrutiny. Democratizing foreign policy by involving broader civil society in its formulation, rather than giving the authority only to diplomats and policy elites, is essential to further reform foreign policy and get rid of New Order legacies.

ACKNOWLEDGEMENT

The author would like to thank Max Lane, the book editor, for helpful suggestions in preparing this chapter, as well as Greta Nabbs-Keller, Lina Alexandra and Raditya Kusumaningprang for insightful conversations that enrich the analysis. The earlier version of this chapter has been presented at the Global Change Institute Symposium, University of Queensland, Brisbane, April 2018.

REFERENCES

Alatas, Ali. *The Pebble in the Shoe: The Diplomatic Struggle for East Timor.* Jakarta: Aksara Karunia, 2006.

Allinson, Jamie. *The Struggle for the State in Jordan: The Social Origins of Alliances in the Middle East.* London: IB Tauris, 2005.

Allison, Graham T. *Essence of Decision: Explaining the Cuban Missile Crisis.* New York: Little Brown and Company, 1971.

Alons, Gerry C. "Predicting a State's Foreign Policy: State Preferences between Domestic and International Constraints". *Foreign Policy Analysis* 3, no. 3 (2007): 211–32.

Anwar, Dewi Fortuna. *Indonesia in ASEAN: Foreign Policy and Regionalism.* Singapore: Institute of Southeast Asian Studies, 1994.

Baker, Andrew. "Varieties of Economic Crisis, Varieties of Ideational Change: How and Why Financial Regulation and Macroeconomic Policy Differ". *New Political Economy* 20, no. 3 (2015): 342–66.

Barkin, Samuel. "Realism, Prediction, and Foreign Policy". *Foreign Policy Analysis* 5, no. 3 (2009): 233–46.

Carlsnaes, Walter. "Can Perceptions Be Ideological?". *Cooperation and Conflict* 16, no. 3 (1981): 183–88.

———. "The Agency-Structure Problem in Foreign Policy Analysis". *International Studies Quarterly* 36, no. 3 (1992): 245–70.

Cox, Robert W. "Social Forces, States and World Orders: Beyond International Relations Theory". *Millennium* 10, no. 2 (1981): 126–55.

Cribb, Robert. "The Historical Roots of Indonesia's New Order: Beyond the Colonial Comparison". In *Soeharto's New Order and its Legacy: Essays in Honour of Harold Crouch*, edited by Edward Aspinall and Greg Fealy. Canberra: ANU E Press, 2010.

Davies, Matt. *Indonesia's War over Aceh: Last Stand on Mecca's Porch*. London and New York: Routledge, 2006.

Fakih, Farabi. "The Rise of the Managerial State in Indonesia". PhD thesis, Leiden University, 2014.

Fitriani, Evi. "Yudhoyono's Foreign Policy: Is Indonesia a Rising Power?" In *The Yudhoyono Presidency: Indonesia's Decade of Stability and Stagnation*, edited by Marcus Mietzner, Edward Aspinall, and Dirk Tomsa. Singapore: Institute of Southeast Asian Studies, 2015.

Hadi, Syamsul. "Indonesia, ASEAN, and the Rise of China: Indonesia in the Midst of East Asia's Dynamics in the Post-Global Crisis World". *International Journal of China Studies* 2 (2012): 151–70.

He, Kai. "Indonesia's Foreign Policy after Soeharto: International Pressure, Democratization, and Policy Change". *International Relations of the Asia-Pacific* 8, no. 1 (2008): 47–72.

Hefner, Robert W. *Civil Islam: Muslims and Democratization in Indonesia*. Princeton: Princeton University Press, 2001.

Hein, Gordon R. "Indonesia in 1981: Countdown to the General Elections". *Asian Survey* 22, no. 2 (1982): 200–211.

———. "Soeharto's Foreign Policy: Second-Generation Nationalism in Indonesia". PhD dissertation, University of California at Berkeley, 1986.

Jackson, Karl D. "Bureaucratic Polity: A Theoretical Framework for the Analysis of Power and Communications in Indonesia". In *Political Power and Communications in Indonesia*, edited by Karl D. Jackson and Lucian W. Pye. Ithaca, NY: Cornell University Press, 1978.

Jenkins, David. "The Evolution of Indonesian Army Doctrinal Thinking: The Concept of 'Dwifungsi'". *Southeast Asian Journal of Social Science* (1983): 15–30.

Kaarbo, Juliet. "Foreign Policy Analysis in the Twenty-First Century: Back to Comparison, Forward to Identity and Ideas". *International Studies Review* 5, no. 2 (2003): 155–202.

Laffey, Mark and Jutta Weldes. "Decolonizing the Cuban Missile Crisis". *International Studies Quarterly* 52, no. 3 (2008): 555–77.

Laksmana, Evan A. "The Enduring Strategic Trinity: Explaining Indonesia's Geopolitical Architecture". *Journal of the Indian Ocean Region* 7, no. 1 (2011a): 95–116.

———. "Indonesia's Rising Regional and Global Profile: Does Size Really Matter?". *Contemporary Southeast Asia: A Journal of International and Strategic Affairs* 33, no. 2 (2011b): 157–82.

Leftwich, Adrian. "Bringing Politics Back in: Towards a Model of the Developmental State". *Journal of Development Studies* 31, no. 3 (1995): 400–427.

MacDougall, John A. "Patterns of Military Control in the Indonesian Higher Central Bureaucracy". *Indonesia* 33 (1982): 89–121.

Mendiolaza, Gustavo and Cherika Hardjakusumah. "Aspects of Indonesia's Foreign, Defence, and Trade Policies: Current Developments and Future Expectations". Strategic Analysis Paper, Dalkeith, WA, Future Directions Australia, 23 July 2013.

Moravcsik, Andrew. "Taking Preferences Seriously: A Liberal Theory of International Politics". *International Organization* 51, no. 3 (1997): 513–53.

Mortimer, Rex. *Showcase State: The Illusion of Indonesia's Accelerated Modernisation.* Sydney: Angus and Robertson, 1973.

Murphy, Ann Maria. "US Rapprochement with Indonesia: From Problem State to Partner". *Contemporary Southeast Asia* 32, no. 3 (2010): 362–87.

Nabbs-Keller, Greta. "Growing Convergence, Greater Consequence: The Strategic Implications of Closer Indonesia–China Relations". *Security Challenges* 7, no. 3 (2011): 23–41.

———. "Reforming Indonesia's Foreign Ministry: Ideas, Organization and Leadership". *Contemporary Southeast Asia* 35, no. 1 (2013): 56–82.

———. "The Impact of Democratisation on Indonesia's Foreign Policy". PhD thesis, Griffith Business School, Griffith University, 2014.

O'Brien, Adam. "The US–Indonesia Military Relationship". *Backgrounder*, published by the Council for Foreign Relations, 2005.

Resosudarmo, Budy P. and Ari Kuncoro. "The Political Economy of Indonesian Economic Reforms: 1983–2000". *Oxford Development Studies* 32, no. 3 (2006): 341–55.

Robison, Richard. *Indonesia: The Rise of Capital.* Sydney: Allen and Unwin, 1987.

Robison, Richard and Vedi R. Hadiz. *Reorganising Power in Indonesia: The Politics of Power in an Age of Markets.* London and New York: Routledge Curzon, 2004.

Rodrik, Dani. "When Ideas Trump Interests: Preferences, Worldviews, and Policy Innovations". *Journal of Economic Perspectives* 28, no. 1 (2014): 189–208.

Rüland, Jürgen. "Deepening ASEAN Cooperation through Democratization? The Indonesian Legislature and Foreign Policymaking". *International Relations of the Asia-Pacific* 9, no. 3 (2009): 373–402.

Schwarz, Adam. *A Nation in Waiting: Indonesia's Search for Stability*. Boulder: Westview Press, 1999.

Sebastian, Leonard C. *Realpolitik Ideology: Indonesia's Use of Military Force*. Singapore: Institute of Southeast Asian Studies, 2006.

Singh, Bilveer. *Dual Function of the Indonesian Armed Forces*. Singapore: Institute of International Affairs, 1995.

Siregar, Sarah Nuraini. "Tinjauan Kritis Reformasi Kultural Polri (1999–2012)". *Jurnal Penelitian Politik* 11, no. 1 (2006): 1–18.

Smith, Anthony L. "Indonesia's Foreign Policy under Abdurrahman Wahid: Radical or Status Quo State?". *Contemporary Southeast Asia* 24 (2000): 498–526.

Sukma, Rizal. "The Evolution of Indonesia's Foreign Policy: An Indonesian View". *Asian Survey* 35, no. 3 (1995): 304–15.

Sulaiman, Yohanes. "The Banteng and the Eagle: Indonesian Foreign Policy and the United States During the Era of Sukarno 1945–1967". PhD dissertation, Ohio State University, 2008.

Suryodiningrat, Meidyatama. "US Rapprochement with Indonesia: From Problem State to Partner — A Response". *Contemporary Southeast Asia* 32, no. 3 (2010): 388–94.

Umar, Ahmad Rizky Mardhatillah. "A Critical Reading of Natalegawa Doctrine". *Jakarta Post*, 7 January 2011.

———. "Dari Politik Pembangunan ke Regionalisme ASEAN: Melacak Genealogi Politik Luar Negeri Indonesia Kontemporer". *Jurnal Diplomasi* 6, no. 2 (2014): 1–46.

———. "A Genealogy of Moderate Islam: Governmentality and Discourses of Islam in Indonesia's Foreign Policy". *Studia Islamika* 23, no. 3 (2016): 399–433.

———. "The Bandung Ideology: Anti-Colonial Internationalism and Indonesia's Foreign Policy (1945–1965)". *Asian Review* 30, no. 2 (2017): 24–49.

United States Agency for International Development/Indonesia. "Indonesia and US Assistance". Report, September 1972.

Vatikiotis, Michael R.J. "Indonesia's Foreign Policy in the 1990s". *Contemporary Southeast Asia* 14, no. 4 (1993): 352–67.

———. *Indonesian Politics under Soeharto: The Rise and Fall of the New Order*, 2nd ed. New York: Taylor and Francis, 2013.

Walt, Stephen M. *The Origins of Alliance*. Ithaca, NY: Cornell University Press, 1987.

Wangge, Hipolitus Yolisandry Ringgi. "Clumsy Diplomacy: Indonesia, Papua, and the Pacific". Indonesia at Melbourne, 12 July 2016.

Wangge, Hipolitus Yolisandry Ringgi and Gafur Djali. "Indonesia Must Confront its Papua Problem". *Diplomat*, 18 March 2016.

Weinstein, Franklin B. *Indonesian Foreign Policy and the Dilemma of Dependence: From Sukarno to Soeharto*. Ithaca: Cornell University Press, 1971.

Wirajuda, Muhammad. "The Impact of Democratisation on Indonesia's Foreign Policy: Regional Cooperation, Promotion of Political Values, and Conflict Management". PhD thesis, London School of Economics and Political Science, 2015.

Yalvaç, Faruk. "Strategic Depth or Hegemonic Depth? A Critical Realist Analysis of Turkey's Position in the World System". *International Relations* 26, no. 2 (2012): 165–80.s

10

Papua under the Joko Widodo Presidency

Richard Chauvel

President Joko Widodo (Jokowi) has shown more interest in Papua[1] than any of his predecessors. He campaigned in Papua as a candidate in 2014. He won a strong majority of the vote in both Papuan provinces, with levels of support among the highest in the country. As president, Jokowi has visited Papua more often than earlier presidents and he has visited Papua more frequently than any other province outside Java.

Jokowi's appeal to voters in Papua was easier to explain than his interest in Papua. During the campaign he had discussed the possibility of a political dialogue, raised the prospect of addressing human rights issues and his informal political style was thought to appeal to the voters. Jokowi also had the great advantage of not being Prabowo Subianto, his opponent in the 2014 Presidential campaign, who is remembered in Papua for his record of human rights abuses in 1996 (IPAC 2014). There was little in his background in business or as mayor of Solo and governor of Jakarta to suggest why Jokowi should show an interest in one of Indonesia's most intractable issues.

During a visit to New Zealand in March 2018, Fransiscus Orlando, a Papuan student, asked the president what motivated him to make so many visits to Papua. Jokowi related how Papua had been neglected for far too long, but it was part of the Unitary State of Indonesia (NKRI) and had to be paid attention. He recalled his visit to the highland district of Nduga in December 2015.[2]

> At the time the head of the military had advised against the visit because Nduga was the most dangerous region. I flew there by helicopter because from Wamena to Nduga required four days and nights of travel through the jungle. In the Nduga district there was not one meter of sealed road. This made me very sad. It is my motivation to develop the infrastructure and human resources to the same level as other provinces (Sekretariat Kabinet Republik Indonesia 2018).

Nduga district strongly supported Jokowi in the 2014 election, but it has come to represent many of the problems the Jokowi's government confronts in Papua, beyond the poor infrastructure noted by the president. Nduga is the poorest district in the poorest province. It has the lowest Human Development Index (27.87) in Papua (59.09), significantly lower than any other highland district (BPS 2017). At the time of the health crisis in the neighbouring district of Asmat in 2017–18, where 61 infants died from measles and malnutrition, Jokowi summoned the district heads of Asmat and Nduga as well as the governor of Papua to the Bogor Palace (*Kompas*, 23 January 2018). According to Papuan Catholic leader, Dr Neles Tebay, in a four-month period in 2017, 35 children died in one village in Nduga district (*Tabliod Jubi*, 17 January 2018). It would appear that the military advice given to Jokowi in 2015 remains relevant. On the eve of local elections in June 2018, the head of police in Papua identified Nduga as one of six volatile districts where additional police would be deployed (*KabarPapua.co*, 25 June 2018). As anticipated, there was conflict between the armed resistance, West Papua Liberation Army (TPN) and the security forces on four occasions in June and July 2018. Following the joint operation against the TPN, the *Jakarta Post* reported that some local figures including Nduga youth leader, Samuel Tabuni, and leading cleric, Lipius Biniluk, had asked the head of police to withdraw the Brimob (Police Mobil Brigade) forces as the villagers had been traumatized. Tabuni was cited as saying the government had provided special funds, but money would not solve the political conflict that dated from the 1960s (Somba 2018).

Jokowi's Nduga story suggests his good intentions about developing Papua and recognizing the scale of the challenges, but also reveals his naivety that the problems in Nduga were only isolation and extreme poverty. This chapter will examine how the president's concern has been translated into policy changes to address Papua's complex problems.

The Travelling President

It was Jokowi's second visit to Papua as president in May 2015 when he seemed to give substance to his campaign commitment to resolve the conflicts in Papua. During the visit he met with five Papuan political prisoners and announced their release. Jokowi also announced the Papuan provinces would be open to foreign journalists. It was the first time since Abdurrahman Wahid in 2000 that a president has made gestures towards Papuan grievances.

Jokowi's gestures related to the symptoms rather than the substance of the conflict, but they were framed in terms of solving the conflict. Symbolic gestures are important in a conflict where there is so much mutual distrust and misunderstanding. Jokowi hoped that clemency would be seen in the context of conflict resolution and making Papua into a "land of peace" (Suhartono 2015), adopting the language of human rights groups in Papua. The president said that foreign journalists would no longer require special permits and would be able to work in Papua without restrictions, as in other regions of Indonesia. The clearing house process that had been used to limit the access of foreign journalists would no longer operate (Mambor 2015).

Of the two issues, it was foreign journalists' access to Papua that was more sensitive, at least for the security forces. The security forces are reluctant to relinquish their control over Papua. The US Department of State noted Indonesian press freedom advocates alleged the TNI and intelligence services were still represented in an inter-ministerial that reviewed requests from foreign journalists to visit Papua (US Department of State n.d., p. 14). The security forces consider Papua to be different from the rest of Indonesia and should be treated differently.

Within a couple of days of Jokowi's announcement, a senior minister, military and police figures had qualified, if not negated the announcement. The head of police in Papua, Inspector General Yotje Mende, made it clear that foreign journalists would still have to comply with the Ministry of Foreign Affairs procedures and report to the police in Papua so that they could be kept under surveillance (*Pasific Pos.com*,

13 May 2015). He explained that conditions in Papua were different from other regions in Indonesia, as there were still armed civilian groups, and maintaining security was the responsibility of the police.

Tedjo Edhy Purdijatno, the then Coordinating Minister for Political, Legal and Security Affairs, confirmed that foreign journalists would still have to follow Papua-specific procedures, because "there are parties who deliver negative information about human rights violations in Papua". He stated that the clearing house, renamed the "foreign monitoring team of Indonesia", was essential to "preserve national interests and national sovereignty" (*Antaranews.com*, 26 May 2015). General Moeldoko, the commander of the Armed Forces, emphasized this concern about outside interference. "We must be tough", he said. "We are a sovereign nation that cannot be allowed to become a plaything for foreigners" (*Berita Satu*, 29 May 2015).

The question was whether the president's writ extends to Papua and whether his policies would be implemented by his security forces. Since 2015, the record of foreign journalists' access to Papua has been mixed. The US Department of State noted in its 2017 Report on Human Rights in Indonesia that some journalists had received permission to report in Papua, while others had experienced delays and rejections (US Department of State n.d., p. 14). The International Coalition for Papua observed that many journalists' requests were denied, while those permitted to travel, experienced obstruction, surveillance, intimidation and violence (ICP 2017, p. 3).

Two cases in 2018 involving Australian journalists illustrate the different ways the system works. During the Asmat health crisis, the BBC's Rebecca Henschke was permitted to report in Papua, but was detained and questioned by immigration officials and police after she tweeted photos of soft drinks and biscuits provided for malnourished children. The photos were thought to have offended the feelings of soldiers involved in the relief programme (Harsono 2018). In August 2018, an Australian graduate student and one-time journalist with the *Jakarta Globe* and the *Jakarta Post*, Belinda Lopez, was detained in Bali and then deported seemingly because she intended to travel to Papua to attend the Baliem Valley Festival, as part of her honeymoon. She related: "Immigration asked me if I was a journalist. Two staff members kept asking me if I had 'done something wrong to Indonesia'." (Singhal 2018). Indonesia has some way to go before Jokowi's commitment, articulated in his 2015 state address, that foreign journalists would be permitted to enter and report on Papua is realized (Rimamdi 2015).

Even releasing political prisoners was not without its complexities. The pattern of releasing political prisoners, followed by arrests of others, suggests shifting approaches to the policy of criminalizing peaceful pro-independence politics. Jokowi estimated that there were about ninety political prisoners, of which according to Papuans Behind Bars, thirty-eight are Papuans (excluding the five released). He indicated that it was his intention to release all political prisoners. The five Papuans already released – Linus Hiluka, Apotnaholik Enos Lokobal, Kimanus Wenda, Numbungga Telenggen and Yafrai Murib – had been imprisoned since 2003 for attempting to seize arms from the TNI in Wamena. The released prisoners made it clear that the offer of clemency came from the president and was not at their request (*Belau* 2018). Given the large number of Papuan political prisoners, including many imprisoned for peaceful political activities like raising the Morning Star flag, why these five were chosen for release is not clear.

Filep Karma, the best known of the Papuan political prisoners, would not be released for another six months. He was released after serving more than ten years of a fifteen-year sentence for treason. Greeted by several hundred supporters, Karma was carried shoulder high to a waiting car, then whisked off to celebrate the sixth birthday of the pro-independence National Committee of West Papua (KNPB). At the celebration, Karma said that he had dedicated his life to the independence struggle and was not going to stop now.

Karma was an example of Indonesia's policy of criminalizing peaceful pro-independence activity in Papua. He was arrested in 2004 after raising the Morning Star flag and leading a peaceful celebration on the anniversary of what Papuans consider their Independence Day, 1 December 1961. Karma was a repeat offender. He was imprisoned for his leadership of one of the first pro-independence demonstrations after the fall of President Soeharto in 1998 in Biak, where the Morning Star flag flew for four days (*CNN Indonesia*, 19 November 2015).

In August 2017, Andreas Harsono of Human Rights Watch Indonesia reported that most of the Papuan political prisoners, estimated to be about thirty-seven, had been quietly released (Harsono 2017). In marked contrast to publicity given to Jokowi personally giving five Papuans their clemency documents in May 2015, after the release of Filep Karma, the other political prisoners were released without any public ceremony or announcement. Yet, their release was consistent with Jokowi's commitment to release all the Papuan political prisoners.

In June 2018, Papuans Behind Bars reported that in the previous four months eleven Papuans had been arrested. Three of the political prisoners were young members of the pro-independence KNPB, while the others were mostly associated with armed resistance and were arrested in various regions in the highlands (Papuans Behind Bars, March–June 2018; *Jakarta Post*, 14 July 2018).

Jokowi saw his release of political prisoners and lifting of the restrictions on foreign journalists as the beginning of a process to resolve the conflict in Papua. While in Jayapura, the president requested an audience of hundreds of military and police personnel: "I want the approach in Papua to change. Not a repressive security approach, rather replaced by a development and welfare approach." While implicitly recognizing that the security approach, developed since the time of Sukarno and Soeharto, had been counterproductive, he was reluctant to acknowledge the political dimensions of the conflict. In response to a question about the dialogue desired by many Papuans, Jokowi explained that he had already talked with customary and religious leaders and heads of local governments. "Isn't that dialogue?" he said. "There is no longer a problem in Papua. What's dialogue for?"

Jokowi considers that because policies in Papua are now welfare and development orientated, there is no need for a political Jakarta–Papua dialogue (*Tabloid Jubi*, 12 May 2015). The then army commander, General Gatot Nurmantyo, expressed this understanding more explicitly. "[I]f development in Papua is smooth and rapid, the [independence] movement will disappear" (*Kompas*, 26 December 2014). The security forces' use of terms such as "armed civilian group" and "armed criminal group" to describe the pro-independence fighters is another example of how the authorities are disinclined to recognize the political and historical dimensions of the conflict.

In August 2017, Jokowi seemed to revive the dialogue approach at a meeting with Papuan adat and religious leaders. The dialogue approach was recast as "Sectoral Dialogue". Dr Neles Tebay, Wiranto, the Coordinating Minister for Political, Legal and Security Affairs, and Teten Masduki of the Presidential Office, were appointed to coordinate the dialogues. The "sectors" identified were education, health, forestry and other sectors of the economy and society. There was no mention of the political, human rights, economic and historical issues that were central to the dialogue approach earlier advocated by LIPI and JDP. Those to be involved in the sectoral dialogue included the three levels of government, academics and community institutions rather than political stakeholders (Tebay, 6 September 2017). In the context of the health crisis in Asmat, and elsewhere in the highlands, in which significant numbers of Papuan children died from measles and malnutrition, Neles Tebay advocated a sectoral dialogue on health at district level (You 2018). Whatever the merits of the revised dialogue approach there have been few if any further developments. Indeed, within a couple of months of the meeting with Jokowi, Neles Tebay reverted to his earlier approach to dialogue, arguing that none of the strategies adopted by the government to counter the armed resistance had worked. He believed that with the government's experience of successful negotiated settlements in Aceh, Ambon and Poso, a dialogue with the armed resistance, as partner rather than enemy, could address the five decades-old conflict (Tebay, 7 December 2017). There have been no signs from Jokowi's government that it is open to negotiations comparable to those that led to the resolution of the conflict in Aceh with the Helsinki MOU.

Also, during the health crisis in Asmat, Jokowi issued a presidential instruction to accelerate the development of welfare in Papua and West Papua provinces. (Inpres 9 of 2017) Jokowi's presidential instruction followed two similarly titled instructions under President Yudhoyono, issued in 2007 and 2011. Jokowi's presidential instruction with respect to education and economic development reflected an affirmative priority for indigenous Papuans that echoed the Special Autonomy Law of 2001, including the development of entrepreneurial skill of Papuans and especially "mama-mama Papua" as well as the provision of micro finance. However, this presidential instruction confirmed Jokowi's policy shift away from an interest in resolving problems in Papua, as evident in his 2015 state address and the political gestures of his early visits, to a sole focus on welfare, infrastructure and development.

The belief that providing greater welfare and economic development for Papuans would somehow make the desire for independence and concerns about human rights disappear informed the Papua policies of President Yudhoyono. Perhaps ironically, it was retired Lieutenant-

General Bambang Darmono, who led the Yudhoyono government's Unit for the Acceleration of Development in Papua and West Papua (UP4B), acknowledged the political nature of the conflict in Papua. Interviewed after Jokowi's visit to Papua in May 2015, he recalled that granting foreign journalists access to Papua and releasing political prisoners had been discussed with Yudhoyono but was politically too difficult to pursue. In any case, he did not believe these sorts of measures would solve the problem. He asserted: "The root of the problem is that activists want Papua to be independent, even though that may not be the case among the grassroots" (*Tempo*, 21 May 2015).

The nature of conflict in Papua and how it should be addressed is where Papuan opinion differ most starkly from the assumption that underpins both Yudhoyono and Jokowi's policy approach. After several of Jokowi's visits to Papua, the Baptist Church leader, Socretez Sofyan Yoman, observed: "The people of Papua don't need lots of visits from President Joko Widodo rather Jokowi has to address the substantive problems. He has to resolve the human rights problems first" (*Tabliod Jubi*, 19 October 2016).

With respect to Jokowi's presidential instruction, Paskalis Kossay, a Papuan former Golkar parliamentarian, argues that these presidential instructions, however titled, to accelerate development are not capable of resolving Papua's complex multi-dimensional problems, which were clearly identified in the Special Autonomy Law of 2001. The problems with the law and subsequent presidential instructions were matters of inconsistent implementation and contradictory policies. What Jokowi required was an evaluation of the Special Autonomy Law and its implementation (Kossay 2017).

Human Rights and Governance

President Jokowi's commitment to resolve human rights abuses in Papua has been problematic for domestic and international reasons and because the abuses invariably involve the security forces. As the discussion below suggests, the policy initiatives of the Jokowi's government have often been responses to international interest in the on-going abuses. Just a couple of weeks before Jokowi's first visit to Papua as president for Christmas 2014, the security forces fired into a crowd of demonstrators in Enarotali (Paniai district), killing four and injuring at least eleven others. Jokowi committed his government to bringing those responsible to justice (ICP 2017, p. 14). In his first state address in August 2015, the president repeated his commitment to resolve human rights cases (Rimandi 2015). The killings in Paniai have taken on an importance because of the occurrence early in Jokowi's presidency and because it was a case where the security forces had resorted to violence and killing as a means of crowd control of a demonstration that did not have a pro-independence political dimension, rather it was a protest against police ill-treatment of local children the day before.

In April 2016, Luhut Binsar Pandjaitan, Jokowi's Second Coordinating Minister for Political, Legal and Security Affairs undertook diplomatic missions to Fiji and Papua New Guinea as part of the government's strategy to counter pro-independence Papuan lobbying in the Pacific. In Jakarta the Coordinating Minister announced the establishment of an investigation team to resolve the numerous serious cases of human rights abuses in Papua, including the Paniai killings, by the end of 2016. The resolution of the human rights cases would be part of President Jokowi's "holistic" welfare approach to address the problems in Papua, including health, education and the development of infrastructure, leaving military operations as the last option (Polkam 2016). To emphasize how this initiative was related to Indonesia's diplomatic initiatives in the Pacific, the ambassadors of Fiji, the Solomon Islands and Papua New Guinea were invited to the announcement to demonstrate how committed Indonesia was to resolve the human rights issues and to counter the untruths and exaggerations propagated by the pro-independence lobbyists (Utama 2016). Nevertheless, convincing Pacific countries that Indonesia was serious about resolving human rights issues did not extend to welcoming a fact-finding mission from the Pacific Islands Forum. Luhut would welcome a visit to Papua from neighbours in the Pacific to witness the economic development there, but he rejected the proposal for a fact-finding mission about human rights abuses because this was an internal matter for Indonesia as a sovereign nation. Luhut had told Fiji and Papua New Guinea, two nations that had consistently supported Indonesia, that the Papuan provinces were an integral and irrevocable part of Indonesia (Simbolon 2016).

Internationalizing the Conflict

Pro-independence activists lobbying in the Pacific predates Jokowi's election as president, but it has gathered momentum during his administration. The Papuan activists' focus on diplomacy in the Pacific is partly a reflection of the way Papuan political identity, in distinction to Indonesian national identity, has developed a Melanesian dimension, with Papuans identifying themselves with fellow Melanesians to the east rather than with Indonesians to the west. In recent years, Papuan diplomacy has focused on the Melanesian Spearhead Group (MSG) and the Pacific Islands Forum and through Pacific island states to the UN General Assembly and Human Rights Council. Papuan applications for membership of the MSG are based on the premise that Papua is a Melanesian society with the same culture and values as the members of the MSG. One of the MSG's objectives is to support independence for all Melanesian societies, including the Kanaks of New Caledonia.

In 2013 the MSG passed resolutions that recognized Papua's right of self-determination and expressed concerns about human rights abuses. The MSG granted the umbrella organization, the United Liberation Movement for West Papua (ULMWP) "observer" status in 2015, at the same time upgraded Indonesia from "an observer" to "an associate member". These decisions make the MSG the only forum at which both Indonesia and Papua have representation. The ULMWP's campaign for full membership of the MSG has not been successful, which reflects the effectiveness of Indonesian diplomacy and differences among the MSG members (SIBC n.d.).

As important as Papuan lobbying in the Pacific has been, the willingness of Pacific Island leaders to raise Papua's right of self-determination and human rights abuses at the UN General Assembly and the Human Rights Council has been more effective in raising the international profile of Papua. Since Vanuatu Prime Minister Moana Carcasses Kalosil's speech in the General Assembly in 2013 numerous Pacific Island leaders have raised human rights and self-determination issues at the annual General Assembly meeting as well as at the Human Rights Council.[3]

Papuan diplomacy in the Pacific and at the UN has provided a new focus for pro-independence mobilization in Papua itself. Diplomacy in the Pacific and at the UN has pressured the Indonesian government in a way resistance, peaceful and armed, in Papua alone has not been able to do. Neles Tebay has tried to use the success of Papuan lobbying in the Pacific and at the UN to persuade Jokowi to open a dialogue with Papuans. He argued the longer the Papua conflict remained unresolved, the more it would become an international issue. Tebay asserts dialogue is the most effective means to resolution (*Tabliod Jubi*, 19 October 2016).

The unwelcome discussion of human rights abuses in the Pacific and at the UN has seemingly not added urgency to Luhut's investigation team. Few of the established human rights organizations were prepared to cooperate. Those organizations that did participate reported the investigation had made no progress. Indonesia's Human Rights Commission, KOMNASHAM, announced that it could not be part of Luhut's investigation team, as it was an independent institution that could not be involved with the state actors in the abuses (*Tabloid Wani*, 20 June 2016). Not surprisingly, those supporting independence, both in Papua and internationally, rejected an investigation team dominated by the security forces and intelligence agencies and understood it to be an attempt to defeat the endeavours of the ULMWP and obstruct the Pacific Island Forum's fact-finding mission. How could those involved in the abuses be part of a team investigating the abuses (*Harian IndoPROGRESS*, 14 June 2016)? In July 2017, Matius Murib, one of the Papuan activists prepared to cooperate with Lutut's team, reported that there had been no significant progress in the investigation (Pak-Ham-Papua, 9 July 2017).

In July 2018, Luhut Binsar Pandjaitan's successor as Coordinating Minister, retired General Wiranto, without any mention of the investigation established in 2016 announced another government team to address alleged serious human rights abuses (Polkam 2018). It is not possible to evaluate whether Wiranto's investigation team will be any more effective than his predecessor's. However, the announcement is implicit recognition by the government that human rights abuses in Papua is an issue it has not been able to resolve.

While the Indonesian government's attempts to investigate human rights abuses have produced no results, Amnesty International Indonesia (AII) and the International Coalition for Papua (ICP) produced detailed and highly critical reports of ongoing human rights abuses.[4] The scope and focus of the two reports is somewhat different, but the analysis is consistent, showing the continuation of a long-established pattern of human rights abuses, frequently involving the security forces. Both reports argue that the pro-independence activities have grown in influence and scale. Human rights abuses, restrictions on freedom of expression and organization are an integral part of Indonesian governance in Papua. The government restricts freedom of expression and assembly as a means to control peaceful political activity, particularly related to support for independence. The AII report observed that Papua is the only region of Indonesia where there is a peaceful and armed struggle for independence. It notes that while abuses continue in Papua, they have declined elsewhere in Indonesia (Amnesty International Indonesia 2018, p. 16). The ICP report argued that there was an increase in peaceful political civil society activities resonating with international pro-independence campaigns, while the government attempted to shrink the permissible political space in Papua (ICP 2017, section 5, p. 6).

The AII report notes the unlawful killings often occurred in political contexts when the security forces confronted flag-raising ceremonies or religious gatherings on commemoration dates in the Papuan political calendar (Amnesty International Indonesia 2018, pp. 7–8). However, some were targeted at activists, with 10 of the 95 victims of unlawful killings being members of the major pro-independence organization, the KNPB (Amnesty International Indonesia 2018, p. 42). Notable examples were the killings of Musa Mako Tabuni in Jayapura (2012) and Martinus Yohame in Sorong (2014). Budi Hernawan, an experienced analyst of human rights in Papua, estimated some forty KNPB activists had been killed by the security forces in the first eight years of the organization's existence (Hernawan n.d.). Institute for Policy Analysis of Conflict, the Jakarta-based think tank, argues that the KNPB has sought to provoke the security forces into human rights violations, in the hope of attracting international attention. It quotes one KNPB leader saying: "That's exactly what we want, lots of police abuses against us."

KNPB

The KNPB, established in 2008, is one of the important organizations in the generational transformation of the independence movement in Papua following the assassination of Theys Eluay in 2001. LIPI scholars, in updating the Papua Road Map of 2009, argued that there is a more numerous and better organized younger generation of activists, including the KNPB, who support independence through a referendum.

The younger activists had never been part of Soeharto-era politics. Unlike the older pro-independence leaders, they were less willing to work with government and the Freeport mine (Wilson 2017, p. 102). The KNPB called for a boycott of the 2014 national elections and declared that it did not support any candidate in the Governor Election of 2018. In its view: "Whoever is elected as Governor will follow instructions from Jakarta in the interests of Jakarta" (*Tabliod Jubi*, 26 June 2018). It describes the Indonesian administration in Papua as a "colonial" regime. Following the LIPI analysis, "militarism", discrimination and the violence of the security forces they had experienced and witnessed made the younger generation more radical. Given that many of the young activists were from the central highlands, they brought values associated with warfare and leadership. Many of the young highlander activists had studied in Jayapura as well as elsewhere in Indonesia (Wilson 2017, pp. 124–27).

The KNPB considered itself as continuation of the *Komite Nasional* that in October 1961 issued a "Manifesto Politiek", which asserted for the first time Papua's right of self-determination with its own Morning Star flag and anthem. Wilson argues that with the establishment of the KNPB, younger generation activists have created a vehicle of political struggle, mass organization and ideology that is relatively well organized with a leadership hierarchy down to district and town level, with the objective of independence through a referendum (Wilson 2017, pp. 133–34).

The KNPB sought to cooperate with other groups in the independence movement and to strengthen coordination between resistance groups in Papua with leaders in exile, especially Benny Wenda. It was critical in the formation of the ULMWP through the Saralana Declaration of December 2014 as the umbrella organization representing West Papua National Coalition for Liberation (WPNCL), Federal Republic of West Papua (NFPB) and the West Papua National Parliament (WPNP) for Papuan lobbying in the Pacific. Its capacity to organize demonstrations in Papua to coincide with international meetings, like in May 2016 in Jayapura to support full membership for the ULMWP in the MSG, support the meeting of the International Parliamentarians for West Papua in London and mark the anniversary of Indonesia's "annexation" of Papua in 1963. Some 1,300 of its supporters were detained by police at the demonstration (*Tabloid Jubi*, 1 May 2016;

Pojokpitu.com, 3 May 2016). The KNPB's demonstrations seek to show that the ULMWP has a strong base of support in Papua and does not simply reflect the views of the leadership in exile and diaspora communities.

Although the KNPB represents a younger generation of pro-independence activists, it has the support of established Church leaders whose congregations are mainly based in the highlands. In 2017, Dr Benny Giay, Dr Socratez Sofyan Yoman and Dorman Wandibo issued a pastoral letter in which they urged the government to cease stigmatizing, denigrating and killing the KNPB and other members of their congregations. The letter asserted the state systematically criminalizes the KNPB. The Church leaders regarded the KNPB (and the ULMWP) as children born of the "forced marriage" of Papua with Indonesia (*Tabliod Wani*, 6 March 2017).

The focus of the AII report is on unlawful killings by the security forces over the period 2010 to 2018. It provides a detailed analysis of the unlawful killings, whether the military, police or both were involved and the circumstances in which the killings took place. It also identifies the targets of the killings, with 85 of the 95 victims being Papuans. While the ICP report argues "Indigenous Papuans, particularly women, continued to have a high risk of becoming victims of human rights violations. Racist attitudes toward West Papuans among the police and military persist" (ICP 2017, p. 2).

Important in an analysis of the pro-independence movement, Amnesty notes that 41 of the 69 cases of illegal killings occurred in contexts unrelated to the campaign for independence or a referendum, which suggests the use of violence in the governance of Papua is broader than the suppression of the pro-independence movement. Amnesty argues that unlawful killings in non-political contexts reflect the excessive use of force to manage social protests, public disorder and the pursuit of criminal suspects (Amnesty International Indonesia 2018, pp. 7–8). As suggested by John Philip Saklil, the Catholic bishop of Timika, it seems the security forces prioritize the use of weapons when dealing with any problem relating to Papuans (cited in Tebay, 12 March 2018). In assessing the violence of the security forces, the general level of violence in Papuan society needs to be kept in mind. Papua has a higher level of homicides than Indonesia as a whole and within Papua, it is localized in Mimika, around the Freeport mine, and in Jayapura city (Anderson 2018).

In contrast, the ICP report has a wider focus on the political space permitted to peaceful political activity, the delegitimizing and criminalization of pro-independence organizations and the mass arrest of protesters. The focus of this report is on the first two years of President Jokowi's government, 2015–16. It follows four earlier reports. The 2017 report argues that: "... the years 2015 and 2016 were characterized by a significant aggravation of the human rights situation in West Papua compared to previous years" (ICP 2017, p. 2). The worsening human rights situation in President Jokowi's first two years in office were reflected in the sharp increase in those arrested during peaceful protests in support of the ULMWP. In 2016, some 5,361 protesters were arrested, a marked increase from 1,083 in 2015. ICP suggests a change in tactics, with many of the mass arrests being released without charge within a day. Short-term mass detention was considered as a sufficient deterrence to control political dissent (ICP 2017, p. 11). Amnesty argues that mass arrests of activists are made, paradoxically, to reduce the risk of unlawful killings (ICP 2017, p. 47). The pattern of restricted space for peaceful political protests and mass detentions, was evident in the demonstrations in early September 2018 in support of the ULMWP on the eve of the Pacific Islands Forum meeting in Nauru as well as opposition to Freeport and "militarism" (Mawel 2018; Tebai 2018).

The police responses to the AII report were revealing in the sense that they understood the killings occurred in the context of the security forces conducting what they considered their duties. The unlawful killings and human rights abuses took place in the context of the implementation of the government's "security approach" in the governance in Papua. The chief of police in Jayapura, Boy Rafli Amar, explained the purpose of the military and police was not to kill civilians but rather to carry out their state duties. Police Inspector General Setyo Wasisto argued that because so many police were Papuans, there was only a small possibility they would kill their own fellow Papuans. Police were not trained to kill people but rather to protect. Amnesty, it was argued, should also consider the police killed and civilians who would have been killed if the police had not protected them. Amnesty should not only consider activists, police and soldiers were also people (*Tabliod Jubi*, 3 July 2018a; *Tabliod Jubi*, 3 July 2018b).

Apart from the impact on the human security of the victims, the violence of the security forces, both targeted at pro-independence activists and organizations as well as that deployed in non-political contexts, is an integral component of governance in Papua. The public display of Theys Eluay and Mako Tabuni's killings were examples of what Budi Hernawan has depicted as "the theatrical brutality of the state". The killings were designed to convey a "message of terror" to the broader Papuan community, rather than simply eliminating opponents (Hernawan n.d.; Hernawan 2018).

Culture of Violence

The deployment of police and military to Papua is a measure of the importance of the security forces in the governance of the two provinces. In 2013 it was estimated that there were about 37,000 military and police deployed, with a ratio of one soldier or police officer for every 97 residents. In comparison with Indonesia as a whole, the ratio was one security personnel for every 296 citizens. Supriatma contends the security forces in Papua have substantially increased over the previous decade (Supriatma 2013, pp. 97–98). Three thousand five hundred soldiers and police were deployed to secure President Jokowi's visit in May 2017 (Siagian 2017). While the contrasting deployment of security forces between Papua and other provinces provides insights into governance of Papua, an assessment of the armed resistance is important. A 2009 Kopassus document entitled "Anatomy of Papuan Separatists" provides a detailed analysis of twenty armed groups, mainly in the highlands, led by well-known figures like Galiat Tabuni, Mathia Wenda and the late Kelly Kwalik. Kopassus estimated that these groups collectively had 1,129 personnel, 131 weapons and 4 grenades.[5] In terms of military capacity, the conflict in Papua is asymmetrical, in the extreme. The military's response to the Free Papua Movement (OPM)'s declaration of war against the Indonesian security forces in March 2018 did not suggest that the OPM presented any threat. The military commander in Papua, Colonel Muhammad Aidi, stated: "If the state commands, the TNI is ready to act at any time." Adding that no additional troops would be required, as they had many more than the OPM (*Okezone* 2018), the armed resistance poses no conceivable threat to Indonesia's control of Papua.

The armed resistance has the capacity to inflict causalities on the security forces. Between 2010 and 2014 about ninety members of the security forces were killed (Anderson 2018), which helped to create a culture of violence that permeates the way the security forces and Papuan society interact with each other and frame how each side views the other. Neles Tebay observed: "Physical violence between the security forces and Papuans still colours life in Papua and can happen anytime." Referring to the killing of two members of the security forces in February 2018, three policemen in 2015 and seven soldiers in 2013 as examples, Neles Tebay argues that the armed resistance targets members of the security forces rather than Indonesian settlers. Influenced by the memories of suffering (*memoria passionis*) inflicted by military operations since 1963, the armed resistance and many other Papuans, consider the security forces responsible for their suffering as well as being the representatives of a colonial government. Citing several killings of Papuans in Timika, around the Freeport mine, Neles Tebay observes that there are many more Indonesians living in the area than Papuans, but the only people killed by the security forces are Papuans. He asks whether this pattern of violence represents state policy. Are these acts of violence against Papuans because they are still viewed as enemies of the state (Tebay, 12 March 2018)? As noted earlier, Neles Tebay urged the government to resolve the conflicts through dialogue with the TPN. Other Church leaders assert there is a racist dimension to the security forces' violence against Papuans, especially highlanders (*Tabliod Wani*, 6 March 2017).

A survey conducted by LIPI in November 2017 confirmed the very different experience and perceptions of Papuans and non-Papuans about security, relations with the security forces and human rights. The survey found that some 60 per cent of Papuan respondents considered the situation in Papua as either "concerning" or "very concerning", while more that 60 per cent of non-Papuan residents of Papua thought the situation in Papua was "good" or "very good". The non-Papuans' sense of security was related to the protective presence of the security forces. While for Papuans the foremost problem was human rights abuses (Broek 2018; LIPI and change.org 2017).

Even the Governor of Papua, Lukas Enembe, on a visit to Port Moresby in September 2018 to mark the 43rd anniversary of Papua New Guinea's independence was critical about the behaviour of the security forces. He told Radio New Zealand:

Every day my people are being killed. That's why I think, the military of Indonesia, the police of Indonesia, they've stopped thinking about the humanity in Papua. Some people in the Highlands, and the coast, they come to me, they're crying, crying about what's happening in Papua. Humanity is very important. (Dateline Pacific – Radio New Zealand 2018).

The rationale for the deployment of so many troops is not a few resistance fighters in the jungle, but the much larger and more influential group of "political separatists", who include many of the most prominent and influential political, religious and community leaders, including senior bureaucrats and elected politicians, such as Golkar politician Yorrys Raweyai, as well as influential Church leaders like Dr Benny Giay, Rev Herman Awom and Dr Socratez Sofyan Yoman. They are feared because of their ability to mobilize support, organize demonstrations and conferences as well as lobby internationally. Presumably, this concern of the security forces has grown with establishment of the ULMWP and the emergence of a younger generation of pro-independence activists. Human rights advocates and organizations are a particular concern because they discredit the Indonesian military in international opinion. Kopassus (2009) regards the documentation of human rights abuses as a cover for promoting independence. Alleged human rights abuses have been the focus of Pacific Island leaders' speeches at the General Assembly of the UN over the past decade.

Beyond keeping the Papuan leaders, identified as "political separatists" under close surveillance and containing the small armed resistance, such a large deployment of security forces has an important demonstration effect of Indonesia's authority and control of Papua – a show of force – but carries the risk of further human rights abuses.

With the integration of the security forces in the governance of Papua, reducing their presence and curbing the patterns of violence and human rights abuses poses a difficult choice and a dilemma in the governance of provinces in which a portion of the population are opposed to Indonesian rule. Bambang Darmono's statement that the core issue was the demand of Papuans for independence reflects a fear widely held in the political and security elite in Jakarta, even if rarely expressed so clearly in public. The military leaders' response to Jokowi's attempt to remove the restrictions on foreign journalists expressed a belief that Papua needs to be governed differently.

Conclusion

In an editorial to mark Indonesian Independence Day in 2018, *Suara Papua* pondered what the day meant for Papuans. The question every year for Papuans is: "Whether we Papuans are free (*merdeka*) in the framework of NKRI?" It argued Papuans do not feel involved on 17 August because of their national history and they still do not consider themselves part of NKRI. It is not that Papuans are apathetic and do not want to celebrate, but rather the state treated Papuans as if they are not Indonesian citizens. "Papuans were like 'guests' in NKRI" (*Suara Papua*, 17 August 2018).

The implications of the discussion in this chapter is that the *Suara Papua* editorial could have been written to mark the first Independence Day of Jokowi's presidency rather than the last one of his first term. Early in Jokowi's administration, the Institute for Policy Analysis of Conflict, wrote: "Indonesia's approach to the independence movement in Papua has been to try to crush it, repress it, persuade it, co-opt it, divide it, dilute it or smother it in a process called development. Nothing has worked, and it has proved impossible to eradicate. It is too powerful an idea, backed by too much history and too many differences with the rest of Indonesia" (IPAC 2015). Jokowi's policies have all these elements of suppression, persuasion, co-option and development. After President Jokowi's early gestures about human rights abuses, political prisoners and foreign journalists along with the numerous presidential visits, there has not been any fundamental change in the central government's approach to Papua. Consistent with Jokowi's national policy approach, the emphasis in Papua has been on development, especially of infrastructure, as reflected in the 2017 presidential instruction.

There is no doubt that the development of infrastructure is much needed, especially in remote and highland areas, which are the poorest and least developed regions in the two poorest provinces. The health crisis in Asmat and other highland districts demonstrated the limited capacity of local governments to provide health and other services as well as implement the central and provincial governments' development policies.

The Jokowi's government confronts complex policy dilemmas in Papua. It is doubtful if its prioritizing of economic development infrastructure policies is compatible with the heavy reliance of the security forces in the governance of the provinces. Likewise, it is unlikely Jokowi's policies will be successful, if there is no willingness to address the political and historical issues many Papuans consider important. Armed resistance poses no threat to Indonesian control, but reliance on security approaches only serves to consolidate support for independence and Papuan alienation from the Indonesian state.

NOTES

1. Reflecting on its contested history, the western half of the island of New Guinea has had numerous names. In the last decade of Dutch rule it was known as Netherlands New Guinea. In 1961, the Dutch accepted the Papuan proposal that it be called West Papua. Under Indonesian rule, it has been known as West Irian and Irian Jaya. In 2000, President Wahid accepted the Papuan preference for Papua rather than Irian. Since 2003 the territory has been divided into two provinces – Papua and West Papua – with capitals in Jayapura and Manokwari respectively. Following common Indonesian usage, in this chapter "Papua" will be used to refer to both provinces, except where the reference is to only one of the provinces.
2. This chapter was last revised in September 2018. It does not include any discussion of the killing of construction workers and military operations in Nduga in December 2018. The author's analysis of these developments can be found in Chauvel (2019).
3. See, for example, Statement by The Right Honourable Moana Carcasses Kalosil, Prime Minister of The Republic of Vanuatu Before The High Level Segment of The Twenty Fifth Session of The Human Rights Council, Geneva, Switzerland, 4 March 2014.
4. ICP (2017). The Coalition, established in 2003, consists of the major human rights organizations represented in Papua as well as local and international faith-based organizations. See Amnesty International Indonesia (2018).
5. Kopassus (2009), p. 6. This and other Kopassus documents are discussed in Human Rights Watch (2011); Allard (2011).

REFERENCES

Media

Allard, Tom. "Under the Long Arm of Indonesian Intelligence". *Sydney Morning Herald*, 13 August 2011. Available at <https://www.smh.com.au/world/under-the-long-arm-of-indonesian-intelligence-20110812-1iqtj.html>.
Anderson, Bobby. "A New Take on Violence in Indonesian Papua". *The Interpreter*, Lowy Institute, 16 April 2018. Available at <https://www.lowyinstitute.org/the-interpreter/new-take-violence-indonesian-papua>.

Antaranews.com. "Foreign Journalists in Papua Must Abide by Indonesian Laws: Minister", 26 May 2015. Available at <https://en.antaranews.com/news/99064/foreign-journalists-in-papua-must-abide-by-indonesian-laws-minister>.

Belau, Arnold. "Kami Tidak Pernah Memohon Grasi Tapi Pemberian Grasi Ini Inisiatif Presiden". *Tabliod Jubi,* 10 May 2018. Available at <http://tabloidjubi.com/16/2015/05/10/kami-tidak-pernah-memohon-grasi-tapi-pemberian-grasi-ini-inisiatif-presiden/>.

Berita Satu. "Jurnalis Asing ke Papua Harus Lalui 'Clearing House'", 29 May 2015. Available at <http://id.beritasatu.com/home/jurnalis-asing-ke-papua-harus-lalui-clearing-house/117605>.

Broek, Theo van den. "Orang Papua Takut di Tanahnya Sendiri, Orang Migran Merasa Aman Saja". *Suara Papua,* 23 October 2018. Available at <https://suarapapua.com/2018/10/23/orang-papua-takut-di-tanahnya-sendiri-orang-migran-merasa-aman-saja/>.

CNN Indonesia. "Tapol OPM Filep Karma Mengaku Dipaksa Keluar Lapas Abepura", 19 November 2015. Available at <https://www.cnnindonesia.com/nasional/20151118192438-12-92569/tapol-opm-filep-karma-mengaku-dipaksa-keluar-lapas-abepura>.

Dateline Pacific – Radio New Zealand. "Papuan Governor Seeks to Open Up Relationship with PNG", 19 September 2018. Available at <https://www.radionz.co.nz/international/programmes/datelinepacific/audio/2018663224/papuan-governor-seeks-to-open-up-relationship-with-png>.

Harian IndoPROGRESS. "Penanganan HAM Luhut VS Perjuangan HAM Rakyat Papua", 14 June 2016. Available at <https://indoprogress.com/2016/06/penanganan-ham-luhut-vs-perjuangan-ham-rakyat-papua/>.

Jakarta Post. "NGO Lambasts Incarceration of New 'Political Prisoners' in Papua", 14 July 2018. Available at <http://www.thejakartapost.com/news/2018/07/14/ngo-lambasts-incarceration-new-political-prisoners-papua.html>.

KabarPapua.co. "Inilah Kabupaten yang Rawan di Pilkada Papua", 25 June 2018. Available at <https://kabarpapua.co/inilah-kabupaten-yang-rawan-di-pilkada-papua/>.

Kompas. "KSAD: Tak Ada Ideologi Merdeka di Papua", 26 December 2014. Available at <https://nasional.kompas.com/read/2014/12/26/23425041/KSAD.Tak.Ada.Ideologi.Merdeka.di.Papua>.

———. "Jokowi Panggil Gubernur Papua, Bupati Asmat dan Bupati Nduga ke Istana", 23 January 2018. Available at <https://nasional.kompas.com/read/2018/01/23/20072091/jokowi-panggil-gubernur-papua-bupati-asmat-dan-bupati-nduga-ke-istana>.

Kossay, Paskalis. "Inpres lagi, Jokowi Menggebu Bangun Papua". *Forum Papua,* 26 December 2017. Available at <https://www.forumpapua.com/2017/12/26/inpres-lagi-jokowi-menggebu-bangun-papua/>.

Mambor, Victor. "Mulai Besok, Minggu, Akses Jurnalis Asing ke Papua dibuka", *Tabliod Jubi,* 10 May 2015. Available at <http://tabloidjubi.com/2015/05/09/jokowi-mulai-besok-minggu-105-akses-jurnalis-asing-ke-papua-dibuka/>.

Mawel, Benny. "Demo ULMWP, total ada 79 pendemo ditangkap polisi". *Tabliod Jubi*, 4 September 2018. Available at <http://tabloidjubi.com/artikel-19165--demo-ulmwp-total-ada-81-pendemo-ditangkap-polisi.html>.

Okezone. "Kodam Cendrawasih: Bila Negara Perintahkan, Kita Siap Perang Lawan OPM", 29 March 2018. Available at <https://news.okezone.com/read/2018/03/29/340/1879636/kodam-cendrawasih-bila-negara-perintahkan-kita-siap-perang-lawan-opm>.

Pak-Ham-Papua. "Masalah HAM di Papua belum tuntas, hanya ada rapat koordinasi", 9 July 2017. Available at <https://www.pak-ham-papua.or.id/2017/07/09/masalah-ham-di-papua-belum-tuntas-hanya-ada-rapat-koordinasi/>.

Pasific Pos.com. "Jurnalis Asing Harus Terdaftar di Kepolisian Papua", 13 May 2015. Available at <https://www.pasificpos.com/item/2165-jurnalis-asing-harus-terdaftar-di-kepolisian-papua>.

Pojokpitu.com. "Demo KNPB: 1300 Orang diamankan, 60 Motor ditahan", 3 May 2016. Available at <http://pojokpitu.com/baca.php?idurut=26573>.

Siagian, Wilpret. "3.500 Personel Polri-TNI Amankan Kunjungan Jokowi ke Papua". *detikNews*, 8 May 2017. Available at <https://m.detik.com/news/berita/3494841/3500-personel-polri-tni-amankan-kunjungan-jokowi-ke-papua>.

SIBC. "M.S.G Decision On West Papua & Indonesia is to Create Dialogue: PM", n.d. Available at <http://www.sibconline.com.sb/m-s-g-decision-on-west-papua-indonesia-is-to-create-dialogue-pm/>.

Simbolon, Bob H. "Luhut tolak Tim Pencari Fakta Pelanggaran HAM untuk Papua". *Satu Harapan.com*, 4 April 2016.

Singhal, Pallavi. "Sydney Woman 'on Honeymoon' Detained in Bali". *Sydney Morning Herald*, 5 August 2018. Available at <https://www.smh.com.au/national/nsw/sydney-woman-on-honeymoon-detained-in-bali-20180805-p4zvky.html>.

Somba, Nety Dharma. "Papuans Ask Police to Withdraw from Nduga". *Jakarta Post*, 13 July 2018. Available at <http://www.thejakartapost.com/news/2018/07/13/papuans-ask-police-to-withdraw-from-nduga.html>.

Suara Papua. "NKRI tanpa West Papua", 17 August 2018. Available at <https://suarapapua.com/2018/08/17/nkri-tanpa-west-papua/>.

Suhartono. "Jokowi: Kita Ingin Papua Jadi Negeri yang Damai, Jangan Dipanas-panasi". *Kompas*, 9 May 2015. Available at <https://nasional.kompas.com/read/2015/05/09/16142551/Jokowi.Kita.Ingin.Papua.Jadi.Negeri.yang.Damai.Jangan.Dipanas-panasi>.

Tabloid Jubi. "Jokowi: Di Papua sudah tidak ada masalah, dialog untuk apa?", 12 May 2015. Available at <https://tabloidjubi.com/16/2015/05/12/jokowi-di-papua-sudah-tidak-ada-masalah-dialog-untuk-apa/>.

———. "Dilarang, KNPB Lapago Tetap Demo 2 Mei", 1 May 2016. Available at <https://tabloidjubi.com/16/2016/05/01/dilarang-knpb-lapago-tetap-demo-2-mei/>.

———. "Pater Neles Tebay: Era Jokowi konflik Papua semakin mendunia", 19 October 2016. Available at <https://tabloidjubi.com/artikel-1038-pater-neles-tebay-era-jokowi-konflik-papua-semakin-mendunia-.html>.

———. "Masalah kesehatan di Papua tanggung jawab semua pemangku kepentingan", 17 January 2018. Available at <https://tabloidjubi.com/artikel-13048-masalah-kesehatan-di-papua-tanggung-jawab-semua-pemangku-kepentingan.html>.

———. "KNPB pastikan netral dalam Pilgub Papua", 26 June 2018. Available at <http://tabloidjubi.com/artikel-17173-knpb-pastikan-netral-dalam-pilgub-papua.html>.

———. "Bantah laporan Amnesty, Polri minta Amnesty bersikap obyektif", 3 July 2018a. Available at <https://tabloidjubi.com/artikel-17362-bantah-laporan-amnesty-polri-minta-amnesty-bersikap-obyektif.html>.

———. "Kapolda: Kepolisian dan Amnesty International berbeda pemahaman", 3 July 2018b. Available at <tabloidjubi.com/artikel-17398-kapolda--kepolisian-dan-amnesty-international-berbeda-pemahaman.html>.

Tabloid Wani. "Natalius Pigai: Komnas Ham tolak Tim Penyelesaian Pelanggaran Ham Papua", 20 June 2016. Available at <https://www.tabloid-wani.com/2016/06/natalius-pigai-komnas-ham-ini-tolak-tim-penyelesaian-pelanggaran-ham-papua.html>.

———. "Forum Gereja Papua Desak Republik Indonesia Akui KNPB dan ULMWP", 6 March 2017. Available at <www.tabloid-wani.com/2017/06/forum-gereja-papua-desak-republik-indonrsia-akui-knpb-dan-ulmwp.html>.

Tebai, Bastian. "Jayapura: 93 orang masa aksi Damai ditangkap polisi dalam dua hari". Suara Papua, 5 September 2018. Available at <https://suarapapua.com/2018/09/05/jayapura-93-orang-masa-aksi-damai-ditangkap-polisi-dalam-2-hari/>.

Tebay, Neles. "Ini penjelasan Pater Neles Tebay tentang penunjukan dirinya oleh Presiden Jokowi". Tabliod Jubi, 6 September 2017. Available at <https://tabloidjubi.com/artikel-9321-ini-penjelasan-pater-neles-tebay-tentang-penunjukan-dirinya-oleh-presiden-jokowi.html>.

———. "Mengatasi Kelompok Separatis Papua". Papua Peace Network, 7 December 2017. Available at <http://www.jdp-dialog.org/kolom/perspektif-jdp/1112-mengatasi-kelompok-separatis-papua>.

———. "Mengakhiri kekerasan bersenjata di Papua". Tabliod Jubi, 12 March 2018. Available at <https://tabloidjubi.com/artikel-14485-mengakhiri-kekerasan-bersenjata-di-papua.html>.

Tempo. "Bambang Darmono: All They Want is to be Free", 21 May 2015. Available at <https://en.tempo.co/read/news/2015/05/21/241668039/Bambang-Darmono-All-they-want-is-to-be-free>.

Utama, Abraham. "Janji Luhut Selesaikan Kasus HAM Papua". CNN Indonesia, 19 May 2016. Available at <https://m.cnnindonesia.com/nasional/20160519114219-12-131881/janji-luhut-selesaikan-kasus-ham-papua?>.

You, Abeth. "Generasi Papua sangat rentan terhadap penyakit". *Tabliod Jubi*, 16 January 2018. Available at <https://tabloidjubi.com/artikel-13010-generasi-papua-sangat-rentan-terhadap-penyakit.html>.

Government and NGO Reports

Amnesty International Indonesia. "Indonesia: 'Don't Bother, Just Let Him Die': Killing with Impunity in Papua". Index number: ASA 21/8198/2018, 2 July 2018. Available at <https://www.amnesty.org/en/documents/asa21/8198/2018/en/>.

Badan Pusat Statistik (BPS). "Data Nduga 2017 (Metode Baru)". Available at <http://ipm.bps.go.id/data/kabkot/metode/baru/9429>.

Harsono, Andreas. "Jokowi's Political Prisoner Problem". *Human Rights Watch*, 9 August 2017. Available at <https://www.hrw.org/news/2017/08/09/jokowis-political-prisoner-problem>.

———. "BBC Correspondent Detained in Indonesia Now Freed: Authorities Restrict Independent Journalism in Papua". *Human Rights Watch*, 6 February 2018. Available at <https://www.hrw.org/news/2018/02/06/bbc-correspondent-detained-indonesia-now-freed>.

Human Rights Watch. "Indonesia: Military Documents Reveal Unlawful Spying in Papua: End Monitoring of Civil Society, Uphold Free Expression", 14 August 2011. Available at <https://www.hrw.org/news/2011/08/14/indonesia-military-documents-reveal-unlawful-spying-papua>.

International Coalition for Papua (ICP). *Human Rights in West Papua 2017*. Germany: ICP, 2017. Available at <http://humanrightspapua.org/hrreport/2017>.

Institute for Policy Analysis of Conflict (IPAC). "Open to Manipulation: The 2014 Elections in Papua Province". IPAC Report No. 14, 10 December 2014. Available at <http://www.understandingconflict.org/en/conflict/read/32/Open-to-Manipulation-The-2014-Elections-in-Papua>.

———. "The Current Status of the Papuan Pro-Independence Movement". IPAC Report No. 21, 24 August 2015. Available at <http://understandingconflict.org/en/conflict/read/43/The-Current-Status-of-the-Papuan-Pro-Independence-Movement>.

Kopassus. "Anatomy of Papuan Separatists", 2009 (in author's possession).

LIPI and change.org. "Hasil Survei Persepsi Warganet terhadap isu Papua", 14 December 2017. Available at <http://humanrightspapua.org/images/docs/Survei%20Papua%20Presentation%20Final%20rev%204.pdf>.

Papuans Behind Bars. "Political Prisoners on the Rise", March–June 2018. Available at <http://www.papuansbehindbars.org/?p=3734>.

Polkam, Humas. "Pemerintah Akan Melakukan Pendekatan Kesejahteraan Untuk Papua, Operasi Militer Adalah Opsi Terakhir". Polhukam, Jakarta, 31 March 2016. Available at <https://polkam.go.id/pemerintah-akan-melakukan-pendekatan-kesejahteraan-untuk-papua-operasi-militer-adalah-opsi-terakhir/>.

———. "Pemerintah Akan Bentuk Tim Gabungan Terpadu Tentang Penyelesaian Dugaan Pelanggaran HAM Berat Masa Lalu". Polhukam, Jakarta, 31 July 2018. Available at <https://polkam.go.id/pemerintah-akan-bentuk-tim-gabungan-terpadu-tentang-penyelesaian-dugaan-pelanggaran-ham-berat-masa-lalu/>.

Rimadi, Luqman. "Isi Lengkap Pidato Kenegaraan Perdana Presiden Jokowi". *Liputan6*, 14 August 2015. Available at <https://www.liputan6.com/news/read/2293713/isi-lengkap-pidato-kenegaraan-perdana-presiden-jokowi>.

Sekretariat Kabinet Republik Indonesia. "Presiden Jokowi Ceritakan Soal Papua hingga Diaspora pada WNI di Selandia Baru", 20 March 2018. Available at <http://setkab.go.id/presiden-jokowi-ceritakan-soal-papua-hingga-diaspora-pada-wni-di-selandia-baru/>.

Statement by The Right Honourable Moana Carcasses Kalosil, Prime Minister of The Republic Of Vanuatu Before The High Level Segment of The Twenty Fifth Session of The Human Rights Council Geneva, Switzerland, 4 March 2014.

US Department of State. "Indonesia 2017 Human Rights Report", n.d. Available at <https://www.state.gov/documents/organization/277327.pdf>.

Books and Articles

Chauvel, Richard. "Governance and the Cycle of Violence in Papua: The Nduga Crisis". *Asia-Pacific Journal: Japan Focus*, Volume 17, Issue 2, Number 4 (15 January 2019). Available at <https://apjjf.org/2019/02/Chauvel.html>.

Hernawan, Budi. *Torture and Peacebuilding in Indonesia: The Case of Papua*. Routledge, 2018.

———. "Why Does Indonesia Kill Us? Political Assassination of KNPB Activists in Papua". *Kyoto Review of Southeast Asia* 21, n.d. Available at <https://kyotoreview.org/issue-21/political-assassination-knpb-activists/>.

Rusdiarti, Suma Riella and Cahyo Pamungkas. *Updating Papua Road Map: Proses Perdamaian, politik Kaum Muda dan Diaspora Papua*. Jakarta: LIPI, 2017.

Supriatma, Antonius Made Tony. "TNI/Polri in West Papua: How Security Reforms Work in the Conflict Region". *Indonesia* 95 (April 2013).

Wilson. "Transformasi Gerakan Kaum Muda Papua". In *Updating Papua Road Map: Proses Perdamaian, politik Kaum Muda dan Diaspora Papua*, edited by Suma Riella Rusdiarti and Cahyo Pamungkas. Jakarta: LIPI, 2017.

11

Youth "Alienation" and New Radical Politics: Shifting Trajectories in Youth Activism

Yatun Sastramidjaja

Introduction

Young Indonesians today have a completely different political experience than previous generations. They were infants, and today's teenagers had yet to be born, when Soeharto resigned on 21 May 1998 amidst massive student protests and popular unrest. They never experienced New Order authoritarianism, and have only vague recollections of the turbulent years of reform (1998–2003) with their sharp political conflicts. They came of age in a post-*reformasi* climate that is restlessly looking forward, with little memory of the past regime and the struggles that spurred its demise. They have been educated in a neoliberal policy context that grooms them for a role as "quality human resources" — the generation that will realize the nation's technocratic aspirations — with scant encouragement to participate in political life.

And yet, this is also a young generation that is actively seeking social and political change, and that is willing to take action against perceived injustices and deprivation; this includes the deprivation they experience themselves due to the growing inaccessibility and rationalization of higher education and the increasingly insecure labour market that awaits them (Sutopo 2014). How they take action — which channels and methods they use, which issues they take up, and how they frame these issues ideologically — has important implications for the direction of political struggle, considering that political struggles in Indonesia have always been spurred by radical youth activism, and that these struggles remain relevant in the post-*reformasi* era, in which political and civic rights remain secondary to elite party interests. Will today's young people be able to pose a radical challenge to Indonesia's entrenched politics?

At first glance, there are few signs of such a radical potential. Reports indicate that the majority of young people feel disengaged and alienated from politics (Gnanasagaran 2018). Many former student activists from the 1990s further lament that young people are alienated from the agenda of "total reform" that they initiated in 1998.[1] This agenda for progressive political change has never been fully realized, but few students today seem willing to continue its cause. In post-*reformasi* Indonesia, young people's political participation seems to be mostly limited to social media activism or "clicktivism" and the ephemeral public actions it occasionally sparks (Lim 2013) — a far cry from the mass mobilizations that young activists engaged in during the 1990s and early 2000s, often joining forces with marginalized social sectors such as factory workers and peasants. These days, the only images of youth radicalism dominating the public sphere are those of masses of Islamist youth mobilized by conservative clerics with shady ties to power-hungry actors. Such images of xenophobic masses represent the opposite of the modern self-image of most young people (Azca 2011), which contributes to their distaste for mass politics.

But young people's detachment from the traditional platforms of political engagement and action does not entail abandonment of radical views and practice. In fact, there are signs of a new radical politics emerging among the younger generation, which in many ways continues the legacies of radical activism of previous generations, yet in other respects departs from them in political style, strategy, and subjectivity. While this emergent radicalism has not consolidated yet, and might not consolidate, into a cohesive new movement, it seems to share characteristics with the many flashpoints of youth protest seen worldwide in recent years, in which certain patterns stand out that indicate a relatively coherent generational consciousness and sense of collective agency. Overall, these young people tend to identify as leftist in opposing neoliberal structural injustices and demanding full political liberties and civic rights, they are quick to jump into spontaneous action due to their connectivity through new media and communication technologies, they shun traditional leadership and command structures, and they want to make an immediate impact through creative direct action (Juris and Pleyers 2009; Sloam 2014).

The question is to what extent current conditions in post-*reformasi* Indonesia spur similar trends in contemporary youth activism, and how this activism intersects and recombines with the legacies of a domestic student left. If indeed a new kind of youth activism is emerging, what kind of radical potential does it represent? To assess this potential, I will first trace the development and shifting orientations of radical youth activism[2] from the New Order era to the current Joko Widodo period, and discuss the challenges this activism faced in the context of changing regimes. I will then discuss recent cases of youth activism — focusing on a recent wave of student protests against tuition fees and campus repression, and relating this to different cases — and show how these develop from deep contradictions in the post-*reformasi* political culture, where liberalization goes hand in hand with specifically targeted suppression. The radical potential of contemporary youth activism lies precisely in exposing the systematic nature of selective suppression in present-day Indonesia, as well as its historical lineage in the New Order.

Anti-regime Resistance During the New Order

Youth radicalism in Indonesia has a long history, dating to the revolutionary politics of the early nationalist movement, which was largely driven by radical youth — the *pemuda* — who advocated popular struggle even as the older leaders favoured diplomacy (Anderson 1972; Frederick 1988; Shiraishi 1990). During Sukarno's rule, this revolutionary movement evolved into a massive political force, represented by the Indonesian National Party, the Indonesian Communist Party, and the affiliated Indonesian National Student Movement and Indonesian Student Movement Concentration. This force was capable of determining a leftist future for Indonesia, until it was crushed in 1965–66 by the counter-revolution that established the New Order. This regime then introduced "a whole new political edifice whose central pillar was the suppression of mass action" (Lane 2009, p. 89). This was accomplished through not only violent repression but also a policy of systematic depoliticization of society, as well as a total rewriting of national history to erase the memory of mass mobilization as an integral part of Indonesia's revolutionary past. In its place new national myths were constructed that glorified the role of the army as the "saviour of the nation", warranting its "dual function" in military and civic affairs (McGregor 2007), as well as the role of students in pioneering the "milestones" in the national struggle, a struggle that was proclaimed completed with the founding of the New Order (Sastramidjaja 2019*b*).

While the 1966 student movement, in "partnership" with the army, played a key role in paving the way for the New Order, and most of its leadership was quickly co-opted into New Order institutions, it also contained activist elements that continued to agitate against the new regime. These activist elements, along with the ideas of the international New Left, provided the seeds for the student movements of the 1970s, which long retained a limited licence to protest not afforded to other social groups due to the students' historical legitimacy. The regime intervened, however, once the students voiced increasingly sharp criticism of rampant corruption, structural injustices exacerbated by the New Order development policy, New Order militarism, and Soeharto's authoritarianism. Massive student movements that targeted these issues were brutally repressed; first, in 1974, with orchestrated riots in Jakarta that were blamed on student protest, then, in 1978, with military raids and occupying of campuses, both occasions accompanied by mass arrests. The subsequent abolition of student councils and banning of the critical student press, and the establishment of military surveillance on campuses, ensured that student protest was stifled throughout the 1980s. But this repressive climate only ignited a new radical outlook among students. This was nurtured through informal discussion groups, in which students enhanced their leftist ideological views based on banned literature, including Marxist works and the books of Pramoedya Ananta Toer. Meanwhile, the campus controls led student activists to turn to off-campus community organizing, focusing on labour and land disputes. The dialectics of ideological study and direct involvement with the poor, a new experience for middle-class students, laid the basis for a new radical student left, which came to lead the first serious opposition to the regime, which eventually led to Soeharto's downfall.

The new radicalism became apparent after the public re-emergence of student protest in 1989 and the years following. Benefitting from a temporary "openness" policy, students in virtually all university towns began mobilizing around social justice and human rights issues, organizing themselves in ad hoc action committees that escaped campus controls (Aspinall 1993; Aspinall 1994). High-profile mobilizations in this period (e.g., against the Kedung Ombo dam construction in Central Java) further contributed to the popularization of mass action among students as well as the populations they defended, and even repression now had the effect of galvanizing rather than deterring further protest (Aditjondro 1993). By the early 1990s, this issue-based activism had evolved into permanent organizations that explicitly targeted the regime. However, not all of these organizations survived the end of the openness policy in 1994, especially when they relied on alliances with elite actors. For example, the Indonesian Student Action Front (Front Aksi Mahasiswa Indonesia, FAMI), which allied with Sri Bintang Pamungkas, a politician from the United Development Party (Partai Persatuan Pembangunan, PPP), simply disappeared when Pamungkas was sidelined and the student leaders were jailed. In a context of increasingly harsh repression — which included the risk of not just imprisonment but also torture, as happened to students for the first time in 1993 after a joint action with farmers in East Java — other radical groups were confronted with a strategic dilemma: whether to focus on intellectual action so as to avoid provoking the regime further, or to expand the strategy of mass mobilization by building the disciplined national organizational structure needed for that (Lane 2009). In 1993, students favouring the latter strategy formed the Indonesian Student Solidarity for Democracy (Solidaritas Mahasiswa Indonesia untuk Demokrasi, SMID), which soon evolved into the People's Democratic Party (Partai Rakyat Demokratik, PRD), founded as a multi-sector union in May 1994 and declared a political party in July 1996 (Lane 2008; Miftahuddin 2004).

In the PRD's strategy, multi-sectoral mobilization — including organizing mass strikes of factory workers "to strike at the heart of the New Order capitalist means of production", as one former PRD activist explained to me — was combined with risky political demands, not only targeting the state but also taking up the sensitive issue of regional rebellions and military oppression in Aceh, Papua, and East Timor. Along with its militant tactics of confrontational action and its bold use of Marxist discourse and symbols, the PRD thus presented itself as a revolutionary force for systemic change. Yet it precluded political marginalization by simultaneously pursuing a strategy of coalition-building with reformist groups, and by 1996 it was at the front of a major opposition movement, formed around its alliance with the Indonesian Democratic Party (Partai Demokrasi Indonesia, PDI) under the leadership of Sukarno's eldest daughter, Megawati (Aspinall 2005). This opposition was sufficiently threatening to the regime to provoke counteraction. This took the form of a regime-orchestrated leadership crisis in the PDI, which on 26 July 1996 ended in riots near the PDI headquarters in Jakarta. The riots were instantly blamed on the PRD and landed many of its leaders in prison, and further provided a pretext for the suppression of the entire opposition. But the movement continued underground.

Around the May 1997 elections, the PRD and other groups mobilized massive popular rallies by the slogan "Mega-Bintang-People for Democracy", campaigning against the state party Golkar and for Megawati and Sri Bintang Pamungkas (representing the PDI and the PPP, the only two other legal political parties) as alternative candidates for the presidency and vice-presidency, while repeating the demands heard in student protests since 1993: repeal the five political laws, end the military's dual function, eliminate corruption, and investigate Soeharto's wealth. While this mass mobilization could still be framed by the regime in terms of *amok* by unruly masses, it did prepare public sentiments for the 1998 *reformasi* movement that could not be framed in such terms, since it mainly involved middle-class students who played up the mythologized role of a legitimate student struggle. As soon as these students, amidst a deepening economic crisis, began to mobilize in January 1998 — rapidly becoming a national movement of unprecedented scale and assertiveness, though this movement was largely confined to campus grounds — they became the public's champions, who seemed destined to topple the by now hugely unpopular regime (Sastramidjaja 2019*b*; McRae 2001; Aspinall 1999).

Despite the evident potential of involving non-student groups in this movement — as did happen from early May 1998 in Yogyakarta, Surabaya, and a few other university towns — in Jakarta it remained confined to students, as the radical students were outvoted by a leadership that feared more violence, considering the increasingly fierce clashes with security troops that had occurred at campus gates since April. The fears were substantiated by the deadly shooting of students at Trisakti University on 13 May, and especially the mass riots in the days after. These riots in effect suspended the radical students' efforts to build a "people power" movement against Soeharto. Instead, Soeharto was unseated amidst an event that appeared to be the climax to the student struggle: the occupation of parliament on 19–21 May, in which all non-student groups — except for elite opposition actors — were barred from participation, despite objections from those students still believing in the potential of people power. Although many student activists, not only the radicals, considered this climax to be a semi-victory that allowed the New Order elites to remain in power without having to account for their crimes, Soeharto's resignation was widely acclaimed as a "student victory", affirming the role of students as the "agents of change".

Continued Struggle and New Challenges in the Era of *Reformasi*

Soeharto's departure did bring real political change, including freedom of political organization and an end to press censorship. Moderate elements of the student movement were content with this new situation and willing to accept the current elite while continuing to control them, in line with the traditional role of students as a "moral force" (Aspinall 2012; Sastramidjaja 2019*a*). But others rejected the new Habibie government as an illegitimate product of the New Order and strove for a total break with the New Order elite by replacing it with a popular transitional government; the PRD and others allied in the National Committee for Democratic Struggle (Komite Nasional untuk Perjuangan Demokrasi, KNPD) had campaigned since January for the establishment of a people's council. After Soeharto's departure, however, the elite opposition leaders quickly abandoned this idea. Furthermore, when students pressured the key symbolic opposition leaders — Megawati, Amien Rais, and Abdurrahman Wahid — to draft a plan for a transitional government, these leaders refused to heed the students' call for "total reform". This "elite betrayal", as the students saw it, convinced them that mass action remained needed.

During the special session of the People's Consultative Assembly in November 1998, students staged massive marches in Jakarta, and for the first time since May 1997 they were joined by thousands of urban poor residents, who also protected the students from attacks by the police and pro-government militia. This popular participation had been anticipated by the PRD and other radical student groups, who used the experience of the May 1997 mobilization to leaflet key urban poor areas along the planned routes to the parliament. The tactic worked, and initial worries among students that they would not be able to control the masses quickly made way for a powerful sense of "real collective action", as one initially hesitant student leader from the University of Indonesia told me, proving that the promise of people power was not just a fantasy (Sastramidjaja 2019b). But the promise was shattered with the deadly shooting of protesters in the Semanggi area near the parliament on 13 November. What is more, it was shattered by the deadly silence of the main opposition leaders, who now distanced themselves from the student movement, leaving the students all the more vulnerable to repression. In October 1999, when Semanggi became the scene of another deadly clash following mass student protests against the emergency bill, the students again received little elite support, which made them all the more distrustful, disoriented, and isolated, though not discouraged from continuing the struggle against the remnants of the New Order.

In 2000 and 2001, the PRD and other radical groups continued to mobilize against Golkar, in an attempt to prevent the reconsolidation of power by the New Order elite. The comeback of New Order forces became evident in their concerted efforts to impeach then President Wahid, whose liberal–progressive policies (including his intent to lift the ban on Marxism and to reconcile with the victims and their descendants of the anti-communist killings of 1965–66) provoked their ire. Although the PRD and other radical groups were also protesting Wahid's concessions to the IMF's demands to reduce the subsidies on fuel prices, they decided to ally with Wahid's supporters to defend him against the political attack. In the first months of 2001, this attack was reinforced by massive anti-Wahid protests staged by those student groups affiliated to Wahid's opponents, especially the Student Executive Bodies and the Indonesian Muslim Student Action Front (Kesatuan Aksi Mahasiswa Muslim Indonesia, KAMMI). The role of these students, who claimed to continue the legacy of "moral struggle", helped to legitimize the political scheme against Wahid, which eventually led to his impeachment in July 2001.

By then, though, students on all sides were left with the uneasy feeling that their alliances with elites, on either side of the power struggle, had distracted them from the unfinished struggle for comprehensive political change. Hence, during the presidency of Wahid's successor Megawati, the students no longer focused on allying with "neo-New Order" elites, but rather on building broad activist coalitions. In varying compositions, these coalitions held intense discussions and staged a series of mass rallies in 2002 and 2003, with the ultimate intent of toppling Megawati and establishing a progressive, if not revolutionary, government (Sastramidjaja 2019b). Once a symbol of the opposition, Megawati was a logical target for these activist coalitions, since she sided with Golkar and the army, did little to tackle corruption, proved intolerant to protest, and furthermore launched a neoliberal economic policy that hurt her own constituency among the urban poor and represented a structural direction which activists across the spectrum vehemently opposed.

However, as happened around the 1999 elections, and would happen again around the 2009 elections, the 2004 elections led the opposition to shift strategic focus to electoral party politics. After the disappointing experience of the PRD's ambivalent bid in the 1999 elections (with the slogan: "Boycott the Elections, or Vote PRD!"), many PRD activists and other former student activists now registered as legislative candidates for one of the elite parties — from Megawati's PDI-P, to the new parties founded by former generals (Mietzner 2013; Mietzner 2016). While they justified this move as a strategic means to use these parties' bases and infrastructure to influence the political system from the inside with the "real means of power", it led to a fragmentation of the entire movement, especially on the left. Indeed, the turn to party politics had the effect of devaluing the strategy of mass mobilization, and for ideological and historical reasons many activists did not agree with abandoning this strategy. The PRD split over this issue in 2007, when the majority that accepted the parliamentary course joined the National Liberation Party of Unity (Partai Persatuan Pembebasan Nasional, Papernas), and those activists who were expelled from the organization for refusing to abide by this course went on to build the PRD-Poor People's Political Committee (Komite Politik Rakyat Miskin-PRD, KPRM-PRD). Given the key role of the PRD in political struggle since the 1990s, despite its relatively small size, this split had detrimental effects on the political capacity of the entire radical opposition.

The effects were also felt on the student left, although the student movement experienced its own political processes. For one thing, the repeated factional splits over political strategy within the PRD and other groups since 1999 opened the way for the rise of a new generation of radical national student organizations. In the period between the 1999 and 2004 elections, several new organizations emerged that remain active today. Among the largest are the National Student League for Democracy (Liga Mahasiswa Nasional untuk Demokrasi, LMND), founded in 1999 by student groups close to the PRD or the PDI-P;[3] the Indonesian Youth Struggle Front (Front Perjuangan Pemuda Indonesia, FPPI), founded in 2000 by the Jakarta-based Student Action Front for Reform and Democracy (Front Aksi Mahasiswa untuk *reformasi* dan Demokrasi, Famred)[4] and groups from the former FAMI network close to Nahdlatul Ulama and the liberal Islamic parties; and the National Student Front (Front Mahasiswa Nasional, FMN), a Maoist-oriented organization founded in 2003 from an alliance of pre- and post-1998 radical Sukarnoist and Marxist groups. Similar organizations were founded during the presidency of Susilo Bambang Yudhoyono (2004–14), such as the Trotskyist-oriented Indonesian Student Union (Serikat Mahasiswa Indonesia, SMI) and the Populist Student Federation (Federasi Mahasiswa Kerakaytan, FMK), which claims inspiration from the Chilean student movement, and numerous other local organizations.

Many of these post-New Order student organizations emerged from a sense of disappointment with the failure of the 1998 student movement to push through radical change. The legacy of the student left of the 1990s is evident in these organizations. Each states commitment to building a political movement for national liberation from neoliberal capitalism, and they follow similar strategies oriented towards multi-sectoral mass mobilization, focusing on students as well as labourers, peasants, urban poor, and other oppressed groups. While differing in degrees of organizational discipline and centralization — the federation-type of organization (such as FMK) allowing for more autonomy of local branches than the unitary organizations — they commonly provide ideological and practical training to their membership, often with the use of materials from the previous student left. Their programmes and rhetoric, too, bear resemblances with those of the previous student left, as well as, strikingly, with the revolutionary politics of Sukarno. Indeed, many of these post-New Order student activists appear to take inspiration from Sukarno's "unfinished ideological struggle" against "neocolonial and imperialist forces". This Sukarnoist legacy is evident, for example, in the LMND's recent stance (echoing the recent stance of the PRD) as explained to me by its 2017 leadership: to "return to the true meaning of the 1945 Constitution, based on the original [not the New Order] anti-imperialist orientation of the Pancasila ideology". But for the LMND (as for the PRD), the key strategy to achieving this was "institutional revolution" first and mobilization second. This allowed it to strike alliances with other student organizations pursuing a similar strategy (including the traditional national student organizations known as the Cipayung forum),[5] but alienated other radical student groups that put mobilization first.

The student left, then, continues to develop and diversify in the post-*reformasi* era. But despite the proliferation of national and local radical student organizations, it has become increasingly difficult for them to regenerate in the normalizing atmosphere of democratization. While these organizations have waxed and waned though continued to persist in most university towns, they generally struggle to sustain their membership and their representation at the key public universities. Hence, compared with the prominent political role that their seniors played in the 1990s and early 2000s, this generation of radical students has led an increasingly marginalized existence. However, new opportunities are arising for them to make themselves all the more relevant for contemporary times, just as recent political and structural conditions appeared to spell the end of radical politics.

No Longer the Era for Radical Activism?

After the fragmentation of the left in the period between the 2004 and 2009 elections, the presidency of Joko Widodo (popularly known as "Jokowi") further complicated the radical politics of the activist elements that supported him in 2014. Many of these activists have since been absorbed into Jokowi's administration, or have otherwise remained part of the "Jokowers" network formed in 2013 for his electoral campaign, the National Secretariat of the Network of Indonesian Citizen Organizations and Communities (Sekretariat Nasional Jaringan Organisasi dan Komunitas Warga Indonesia), or "Seknas Jokowi". This network includes many former PRD members and other former activists from the student left of the 1990s, whose anti-establishment criticism has now been muted for the sake of the "greater cause" that Jokowi's populist and democratic image and credentials represent. To them, Jokowi's rise to power represents a real political opportunity to establish a clean and just democratic government with an eye for the needs of the people, signifying that their previous struggle has not been in vain. Furthermore, to his supporters, Jokowi represents a modern leader, a fresh actor untainted by the clientelist politics of the past, and a youthful leader whose identification with popular symbols of rebellion (e.g., the rock heroes Iwan Fals, Slank, and Metallica, once banned by New Order) adds to his recalcitrant aura. At the same time, the continuous threat to Jokowi's position posed by anti-democratic forces — represented by Islamist groups rallied around his contender Prabowo Subianto (a former general and Soeharto's son-in-law, who was allegedly behind the abduction and disappearance of PRD activists, the Trisakti killings, and the May riots in 1998) and other New Order figures — compels Jokowi's supporters to close ranks.

Thus, they have remained loyal supporters even as Jokowi's image was contradicted by his neoliberal, technocratic economics and his occasionally repressive policies — from his heavy-handed "war on drugs" to the draconian Electronic Information and Transaction (ITE) Law that many considered a setback to freedom of expression, and the Law on Mass Organizations, which allows authorities to disband organizations deemed threatening to national unity, which led to the banning of Hizbut Tahrir. Moreover, there has been little public criticism of Jokowi's recent anti-communist rhetoric and concomitant flirting with the army, symbolized by his attendance of an army screening of the anti-communist New Order propaganda film *The Treason of G30S/PKI* on 30 September 2017, while recommending an "updated version for the millennial generation" so that they also will understand "the dangers of communism". His supporters' justification for this move, as a clever way of taking the wind out of his opponents' sails following allegations of his "communist background", made those radical activists who were not co-opted in the "Jokower" tribe all the more cynical.

According to these critical activists, "Jokowism" has become like a "religion" for many of their former comrades; as one of them said to me, "It's ironic: once they were Marxists, now they are the evangelists of false consciousness." Yet even these (former) activists have been hesitant to express their criticism too openly, not only for fear of electoral repercussions, concerned that a weakening of Jokowi's position will benefit his conservative contenders in the 2019 elections, but also because they lack the political channels and organizational vehicles to do so, since the Jokowers network reaches into virtually all established channels of the former student left. The Jokowist chorus further encompasses the "1998 generation"; in July 2018, these former activists of the 1998 student movement collectively stated their support for Jokowi in the 2019 elections, regardless of their current political affiliation. With the channels for progressive politics thus homogenized, the few remaining platforms for radical ideological and mobilizational struggle are the unions and other organized groups on the far left, but these groups have also suffered from the narrowing space for dialogue between competing groups, making consolidation all the more difficult. And so, public political criticism is increasingly limited to radical Islamist groups (which explains their growing popularity among students)[6] and a handful of controversial public intellectuals whose critical commentary amounts to little more than political diversion.[7]

In this context, it is not surprising that the majority of young people have turned their back on politics altogether, even though Jokowi's electoral success in 2014 can partly be attributed to this first digital generation in Indonesia, whose support through social media turned many otherwise apolitical young voters to his favour. The weakness is that once Jokowi won the presidential race, this young support base returned to their normal lives. For political observers, a key question is whether this "youth vote" will again make the difference in the 2019 elections, given that young voters (below the age of thirty) will constitute approximately 50 per cent of the electoral demography in 2019. Yet, it remains to be seen whether political parties can benefit from this youth vote. According to a 2017 survey on the electoral preferences of university students, one-third support PDI-P, which bodes well for Jokowi (Prabowo's party Gerindra comes second at 15 per cent), but the majority are likely to become swing voters, if they bother to cast their votes at all (Prihatini 2018). Less than half of the young voters turned out to vote in the 2014 legislative elections (a decline from the two preceding elections), and this voter apathy is generally viewed as a threat to Indonesia's fragile democracy. However, the issue might not be growing apathy among the youth but rather disillusionment with the state of democracy post-*reformasi*, as a 2010 study on the political outlook of Indonesian youth also indicates (Chen and Syailendra 2014). Young voters, that is, tend to be critical rather than apathetic; many simply do not feel represented by any of the contending parties.

It is this disappointment with politics that the new Indonesian Solidarity Party (Partai Solidaritas Indonesia, PSI) seeks to counter by offering an alternative political platform for the "millennial generation". Founded in 2013 by young journalists, this new contender in the 2019 legislative elections presents itself as a vehicle for a novel kind of politics that "is no longer hostage to old political interests, bad track records, historical legacies and bad images from previous parties".[8] In contrast, it claims to represent "progressive, open-minded youth" — though this seems to refer mainly to the higher educated segment of this demographic — and accordingly, the party makes good use of social media, the political tool of these youth, to propagate its anti-corruption, anti-intolerance, and pro-pluralism message. This is similar to Jokowi's rhetoric, and indeed the PSI avidly supports Jokowi for a second term. However, the PSI's claim of tolerance was tainted in March 2018 by an anti-LGBT statement made by its head of office in Depok, and previously by its uncritical support for the Law on Mass Organizations. Critics further doubt its commitment to distance itself "from the domination of transactionalism and predatory politics" (Mudhoffir 2018), given the inclusion on its advisory board of controversial political figures known for their dealings with elite parties or their involvement in corruption. The PSI's alliance with the Ansor Youth Movement (the mass youth base of the traditional Islamic Nahdlatul Ulama), to make up for its weak organizational basis, further illustrates its pragmatic stance. Thus, the PSI appears to be symptomatic of the contradictory post-*reformasi* political culture, in which a neoliberal discourse of "progressive open-mindedness" combines with entrenched transactionalism and clientelism in politics; and young people are "very much part of this new state of affairs, encumbered between an old precedent and a new vision" (Chen and Syailendra 2014, p. 3).

A related contradiction is evident in the changing landscape of higher education, where the acceleration of neoliberal reform, manifested in increasing commercialization and privatization of educational facilities and institutions, has diminished democratic space for critical action. As

a result, while radical activism has always been limited to a minority
of the student population — with larger numbers only participating in
times of political crisis (including crises provoked by student activism)
— post-*reformasi* it has become more difficult for even this activist
minority to persist, let alone to mobilize a national mass student
movement as in 1998. This diminished mobilizational capacity is
partly due to the "divisive diversification" that neoliberal restructuring
of higher education brings about, as the previous experience of
post-authoritarian Latin America demonstrates (Levy 1991), which in
other Asian contexts, too, has contributed to a delegitimation of the
political role of students and thus weakened their position "as a
strategic political group" (Aspinall and Weiss 2012, p. 17). This
delegitimation is also reflected in the growing intolerance of student
protest on the part of campus authorities, who actively discourage
students from political action and are quick to suppress it when it does
occur on campus. In general, tighter curricula, stricter requirements for
student performance, shorter graduation periods, and other manifestations of neoliberal efficiency in higher education greatly diminish
opportunities for political engagement, while rising tuition fees make
the university less accessible to non-elite youth. Further interfering
with students' critical thinking, the university's increasingly common
cooperation with big corporations turns it into "a site of capitalist
propaganda", as Eko Prasetyo from the Social Movement Institute put it,
during a discussion on "the problem of the populist student movement
today" in August 2016.[9]

Consequently, the majority of students have turned away from the
intense and time-consuming type of radical activism and organization of
previous generations. Yet they have not abandoned activism altogether,
nor is this activism completely reduced to "clicktivism". Rather, many
of today's students focus on a different kind of activism as an expression of their social concern, committing to various kinds of volunteer
work for communities in need. However, according to critics, this trend
of "volunteerism" is not activism at all but rather a symptom of the
prevailing pragmatism among students. As Prasetyo stated during the
aforementioned discussion:

> In the end, rather than engaging in struggle as an act of resistance,
> students are more enthusiastic about tackling natural disasters. So we
> see a flourishing of what is known as philanthropy. Whenever a disaster
> occurs ... students are quick to react. From creating emergency posts on

campus to collect money, food, and clothes, to organizing fund-raising concerts. The student movement becomes a charity movement that is practically identical to bourgeois philanthropy. Just collect money and goods, visit the affected area, hand out aid boxes, greet the victims, take a photo, click, and upload it on social media.[10]

Prasetyo explicitly linked this trend to the current condition of the university, which encourages volunteerism as an expression of "bourgeois values" — or put differently, neoliberal subjectivity — and discourages "struggle as an act of resistance". But other participants in the discussion also pointed to the failure of campus activist groups to attract these students, who are apparently willing to dedicate their time to social causes and hence are likely to develop a disposition for active involvement in social change and possibly political change. As one student activist noted, "internal factors" are as much to blame, including "misorganization" and the "monoculture" of radical activist communities; that is, a failure to diversify and innovate recruitment, propaganda, and action tactics, as well as to create a more welcoming and inclusive atmosphere at activist gatherings for those students who might be repelled by the typical nightly meetings in a room filled with chain-smoking, shabby-dressing, disorganized, macho radicals.[11] If it is no longer the era for this particular manifestation of student radicalism of the past, so one former activist also told me, "these activist organizations should make more serious efforts to mend themselves; they have to modernize, to become 'jaman now'" — a popular youth slang expression for "contemporary". What, then, could a radical activism for the contemporary era look like?

Radical Activism for the Contemporary Condition

Being "contemporary" might be mistaken for nurturing a "modern" or "trendy" image, for example, through the stylish social media campaigns that the PSI and other parties exploit in an attempt to attract the youth vote. However, the proper meaning of "contemporary" is more politically relevant than that, signifying radical relevance to the political experience of the present. In post-*reformasi* Indonesia this experience is marked by deep contradictions, as the reformist politics of the past two decades has proven not only to be ineffective in tackling socio-economic and political injustices and corruption, but in fact to thrive on the entrenched transactionalism and clientelism in politics, as noted above, as well as on another legacy of the New Order political culture: the oppression, suppression, and repression of counter-hegemonic or "deviant" values and voices. In the era of democratization, with its freedom of political expression and organization (a real accomplishment of the 1998 movement, making Indonesia the most democratic country in Southeast Asia), this suppression is much less evident than before since it has become more selective, targeting specific groups and issues. Consequently, resistance to suppression has also become more sporadic and thereby less visible, hence making less of a political impact than the high-profile, all-out struggle against a dictatorship did previously. Yet, it is this resistance to selective suppression that contains radical contemporary relevance.

For students, the most acutely relevant experience of repression is that targeted at student protests on campus. These protests have been increasing in recent years despite the decline of the larger student movement, especially since the introduction of the Singular Tuition Fee (Uang Kuliah Tunggal, UKT) at public universities in 2013–14, which requires students to pay a fixed semester fee, replacing the previous system of smaller entry fees and various additional charges. While the UKT technically did not increase the tuition fee, and was said to increase financial transparency and to benefit equal opportunity with the provision of different levels based on the student's economic capacity, students criticized it as an increased burden that in practice did raise the costs of higher education. Student protests against the regulation thus started even before its implementation, and as it turned out that many students indeed had to quit their studies since they could no longer bear the costs, and furthermore many irregularities surfaced (for example, of rich students categorized at lower-fee levels, indicating corruption), the protests began to snowball at campuses across the country in the following years. Mobilized by the generally moderate Student Executive Bodies as well as the radical activist organizations, these protests often involved hundreds and occasionally a few thousand students, thus reviving scenes of "student struggle" not seen for years. As the protests grew larger and more brazen, repression also became harsher. For example, in August 2017 some 2,000 students at Sriwijaya University in Palembang attempted to occupy the rectorate building, which ended in a clash with the police and security forces.[12] But the most common form of repression consisted of academic sanctions, suspension, or expulsion from university. Moreover, the growing intolerance to student protest came with a lowering threshold for repression.

In January 2018, for example, two students at the Hasanuddin University in Makassar received a sanction of a one-year suspension merely for hanging posters on campus with the text: "Campus Feels like a Factory". From the students' perspective, this and many other cases of unfair suspension or expulsion at other universities indicated increasing criminalization of student protest — not much different, then, from the repressive climate of the New Order, although few students seemed to make this historical link. Rather, students commonly linked the rising tuition fees and the repression of protests against it — in tandem with the concurrent semi-privatization of many public universities — to the contemporary neoliberal policy in higher education. As two alumni of the Hasanuddin University put it in a solidarity statement (the alumni association has also strongly condemned the disproportionate sanction), this suppression of even small acts of student resistance is a symptom of "the penetration of Neoliberalism in public universities, which we cannot keep silent about", and the statement continues:

> The measure taken by the Hasanuddin University against two of its students reflects the will of the institution (read: the University authorities) to dominate the consciousness of its students. [Paolo] Freire [in his book *Pedagogy of the Oppressed,* a common reference for student activists since the 1970s] states that "the interest of the oppressor lies in the changing of consciousness of the oppressed". The given sanction is merely a method, the underlying agenda being subjection (to *Obedience*). ... The decision of suspension was taken because the University cannot accept the reality that the campus does feel like a factory. Rather than engaging in a dialogue with these two students as an educator should, the University showed its *power* as an *oppressor*. ... It is not surprising that "Campus Feels like a Factory" is becoming a tagline [for student protest] everywhere— what for? So that you become conscious of the fact that higher education of *jaman now* increasingly resembles a factory with one mould. ... Clearly, the university's anti-criticism stance against "freedom of opinion" reflects a regression in the educational system in Indonesia. At the higher level, the Indonesian Government is ever more blatantly restricting the rights of expression and organization of students.[13]

As this statement suggests, the issue at hand is deeply relevant to the contemporary condition — the *jaman now* of higher education — which not only affects those students who have been suspended or expelled, or those students forced to drop out, but all students and indeed all critical minds, since it involves a fundamental abuse of power that is indicative of broader systems of oppression, reaching all the way up to the national government. Hence, these student protests against tuition fees, which have thus far been mainly targeted at unresponsive and repressive campus authorities, have the potential to develop into a broader struggle for not just a university but also "a country free from oppression", as part of a popular slogan of the student movement of the 1990s went,[14] and it is this potential that the radical student organizations have started to tap into.

The student left has always focused on education, in particular the higher education in which it operates, as a critical node in the larger chain of capitalism, with such slogans as: "Free education for all the people", and "Democratic education oriented towards the interests of the people". But the recent surge in student protest allows these organizations to rally a broader segment of the student population behind a larger resistance against neoliberal policies, in both higher education and other sectors in present-day society. While these policies are not new, they become a relevant issue for a student resistance of the *jaman now* precisely due to the contemporary experience of repression. Moreover, this experience is amplified because it not only affects students protesting tuition hikes, but also students engaging in other activities, on and off campus, that deviate from the hegemonic political culture.

One type of activity that stands out as prone to repression is student re-engagement with the legacy of the mass killings of 1965–66, which was triggered especially by the internationally acclaimed documentary films *The Act of Killing* (2012) and *The Look of Silence* (2014) by Joshua Oppenheimer. The films caused a controversy in Indonesia, with various groups calling for a ban, using "the same jargon from the previous military regime ... that they are communist propaganda, that they threaten the social harmony of Indonesian society, that they twist the 'formal' history of the nation, are not suitable for airing in public, and are a form of 'divide and conquer' politic to create social friction and conflict" (Sutopo 2017, p. 240). The controversy also raised students' curiosity, and screenings of the films became popular. But the act of watching and discussing them only gained deeper relevance to the students' political experience once it met with repression, ranging from the same sanctions as those befalling student protesters on campus (hence Eko Prasetyo, in the aforementioned discussion, categorized them in the same category of campus repression), to intimidation and violent attacks by militant groups. This made it a radical experience. The rediscovery of "1965" as a contemporary issue was further spurred by the International People's Tribunal 1965 — held in The Hague in 2015, with the judges' verdict released in 2016 — which popularized the idea of the need to break the taboo of 1965 and to hold the responsible authorities accountable, as a condition for justice in Indonesia. The issue has since been taken up by radical student organizations and human rights groups,[15] and the fact that their gatherings and other events focusing on the issue are frequently disturbed by militias has again exposed the post-*reformasi* pattern of selective suppression, indicating the lasting legacy of the New Order system of oppression, which was also confirmed by Jokowi's recent anti-communist statements.

Besides the continued demonization of anything related to "1965" and the criminalization of student protest, the recent political stigmatization of the LGBT community is another indicator of this pattern of selective repression, and there are other relevant cases. Each is provoking its own form of radical resistance, with the potential to link the specific wrongs to systemic causes that require systemic responses. But for the radical potential to be realized, it is necessary also to connect the different current manifestations of this repression, and to build bridges between the various groups affected by it. The organizations that follow the footsteps of the previous student left, while still playing an important role in the ideological socialization of students, might not be the most suitable vehicle for this purpose, since they are tied to relatively strict organizational structures and programmes that are largely inherited from the past. To tackle the contemporary condition, more flexibility and experimentation might be needed in the forms of resistance.

NOTES

1. The 1998 student movement's "vision for reform" included the following six demands: constitutional amendment; revocation of the dual function of the armed forces; supremacy of law; far-reaching regional autonomy; a rational and egalitarian democratic culture; an end to corruption, and putting Soeharto and his cronies on trial. Of these demands, only regional autonomy has been realized. Although the military's dual function has

been revoked, the underlying demand for an end to military meddling in politics has been anything but fulfilled. Corruption still runs rampant, and the political culture remains clientelist and elitist rather than rational and egalitarian, both of which also continue to thwart the supremacy of law.

2. While this term mainly refers to student activism, in this chapter I use the term "youth" to account for the recent graduates and university dropouts who often remain involved in this activism despite no longer carrying the status of student. With "radical" I refer to those groups on the left (mainly Marxist, though to varying degrees and with different orientations) that aim for systemic political change.

3. Due to its close association with the PRD, especially after its 2002 congress, LMND has since suffered from the same factional splits, with a majority joining Papernas in 2007, and a dissident minority moving on to found LMND–PRM, PRM standing for Poor People's Politics (Politik Rakyat Miskin).

4. FAMRED was the largest splinter group from the City Forum (Forum Kota, Forkot) that formed the militant core of the 1998 student movement in Jakarta.

5. These include the Indonesian National Student Movement (Gerakan Mahasiswa Nasional Indonesia), Indonesian Islamic Student Association (Perhimpunan Mahasiswa Islam Indonesia), Indonesian Catholic Student Movement (Pergerakan Mahasiswa Katolik Republik Indonesia), Indonesian Christian Student Movement (Gerakan Mahasiswa Kristen Indonesia), and Islamic Student Association (Himpunan Mahasiswa Islam). The LMND struck an alliance with this "Cipayung Front" in 2015.

6. According to a 2017 survey, almost 25 per cent of high-school and university students support the ideas of Islamist radicalism, including implementation of sharia and the need for *jihad* for this purpose. See <http://interfidei.or.id/detail-87-survei-1-dari-4-pelajar-indonesia-terkontaminasi-radikalisme.html>.

7. One such controversial intellectual is Rocky Gerung, University of Indonesia professor and former 1990s Democracy Forum activist, who has also criticized former activists who were incorporated into the Jokowi administration. See Rocky Gerung, "Pasca-1998: Surplus Fanatisme, Defisit Akal", *Tirto.id*, 21 May 2018, available at <https://tirto.id/pasca-1998-surplus-fanatisme-defisit-akal-cKRo>.

8. See the PSI website, <https://psi.id>.

9. My translation, "Permasalahan Gerakan Mahasiswa (Kerakyatan) Hari Ini", *Arah Juang*, 2 September 2016, available at <http://www.arahjuang.com/2016/09/02/permasalahan-gerakan-mahasiswa-kerakyatan-hari-ini/>.

10. Ibid.

11. Ibid.

12. Dwi Apriani, "Ribuan Mahasiswa Unsri Protes Kenaikan Uang Kuliah Tunggal", *Media Indonesia*, 3 August 2017, available at <http://mediaindonesia.

com/read/detail/115983-ribuan-mahasiswa-unsri-protes-kenaikan-uang-kuliah-tunggal>.

13. My translation (of the quote), Himahi, "Skorsing Mahasiswa Cacat Prosedur: Fenomena Neoliberalisme Pendidikan Tinggi Dan Antipati Media Di Universitas Hasanuddin", *HIMAHI FISIP UNHAS*, 5 February 2018, available at <https://himahiunhas.org/index.php/2018/02/05/skorsing-mahasiswa-cacat-prosedur-fenomena-neoliberalisme-pendidikan-tinggi-dan-antipati-media-di-universitas-hasanuddin/>.

14. The full slogan is an adaptation of the legendary 1928 Youth Oath (Sumpah Pemuda), which in the activist version of the 1990s went as follows: "We, the people and students of Indonesia, acknowledge one country: a country free from oppression; We, the people and students of Indonesia, acknowledge one nation: a nation devoted to justice; We, the people and students of Indonesia, acknowledge one language: the language of truth."

15. Kirta Braja, "Sekali Lagi Tentang Peristiwa 65: Apa Yang Harus Diperjuangkan?", *Arah Juang*, 30 September 2016, available at <http://www.arahjuang.com/2016/09/30/sekali-lagi-tentang-peristiwa-65-apa-yang-harus-diperjuangkan/>.

REFERENCES

Aditjondro, George J. "The Media as Development Textbook: A Case Study of Information Distortion in the Debate about the Social Impact of an Indonesian Dam". PhD thesis, Cornell University, 1993.

Anderson, Benedict R. O'G. *Java in a Time of Revolution: Occupation and Resistance 1944–1946*. Ithaca, NY: Cornell University Press, 1972.

Aspinall, Edward. "Student Dissent in Indonesia in the 1980s". Working Paper 79, Centre of Southeast Asian Studies, Monash University, Clayton, Australia, 1993.

———. "Students and the Military: Regime Friction and Civilian Dissent in the Late Suharto Period". *Indonesia* 59 (1994): 21–45.

———. "Student and the Military: Regime Friction and Civilian Dissent in the Late Suharto Period". *Indonesia* 59 (1995): 21–44.

———. "The Indonesian Student Uprising of 1998". In *Reformasi: Crisis and Change in Indonesia*, edited by Arief Budiman, Barbara Hatley, and Damien Kingsbury. Clayton, Vic.: Monash Asia Institute, 1999.

———. *Opposing Suharto: Compromise, Resistance, and Regime Change in Indonesia*. Stanford: Stanford University Press, 2005.

———. "Indonesia: Moral Force Politics and the Struggle against Authoritarianism". In *Student Activism in Asia: Between Protest and Powerlessness*, edited by Meredith L. Weiss and Edward Aspinall. Minneapolis: University of Minnesota Press, 2012.

Aspinall, Edward and Meredith L. Weiss. "Conclusion: Trends and Patterns in Student Activism in Asia". In *Student Activism in Asia: Between Protest and Powerlessness*, edited by Meredith L. Weiss and Edward Aspinall. Minneapolis: University of Minnesota Press, 2012.

Azca, M. Najib, ed. *Pemuda Pasca Orba: Potret Kontemporer Pemuda Indonesia*. Yogyakarta: Youth Studies Centre, 2011.

Chen, Jonathan and Emirza Adi Syailendra. "Old Society, New Youths: An Overview of Youth and Popular Participation in Post-*reformasi* Indonesia". RSIS Working Paper, No. 269. Singapore: Nanyang Technological University, 2014.

Frederick, William H. *Visions and Heat: The Making of the Indonesian Revolution*. Athens: Ohio University Press, 1988.

Gnanasagaran, Angaindrankumar. "Will Indonesian Youths Vote for Change?". *ASEAN Post*, 9 June 2018.

Juris, Jeffrey and Geoffrey Pleyers. "Alter-Activism: Emerging Cultures of Participation among Young Global Justice Activists". *Journal of Youth Studies* 12 (2009): 57–75.

Lane, Max. *Unfinished Nation: Indonesia Before and After Suharto*. London: Verso, 2008.

———. "Mass Mobilisation in Indonesian Politics, 1960–2001: Towards a Class Analysis". PhD thesis, University of Wollongong, 2009.

———. "50 Years since 30 September, 1965: The Gradual Erosion of a Political Taboo". *ISEAS Perspective* 2015, no. 66 (2015).

Levy, Daniel. "The Decline of Latin American Student Activism". *Higher Education* 22 (1991): 145–55.

Lim, Merlyna. "Many Clicks but Little Sticks: Social Media Activism in Indonesia". *Journal of Contemporary Asia* 43, no. 3 (2013): 636–57.

McGregor, Katherine. *History in Uniform: Military Ideology and the Construction of Indonesia's Past*. Leiden: KITLV Press, 2007.

McRae, Dave. *The 1998 Indonesian Student Movement*. Clayton, Vic.: Monash Asia Institute, 2001.

Mietzner, Marcus. "Fighting the Hellhounds: Prodemocracy Activists and Party Politics in Post-Suharto Indonesia". *Journal of Contemporary Asia* 43 (2013): 28–50.

———. "Coalitional Presidentialism and Party Politics in Jokowi's Indonesia". *Contemporary Southeast Asia* 38, no. 2 (2016): 209–32.

Miftahuddin. *Radikalisasi Pemuda: PRD Melawan Tirani*. Depok: Desantara, 2004.

Mudhoffir, Abdil Mughis. "Millennials Won't Rescue Indonesia". *New Mandala*, 2 May 2018.

Prihatini, Ella S. "Mapping the 'Political Preferences' of Indonesia's Youth". *Conversation*, 12 February 2018.

Sastramidjaja, Yatun. "From Vanguard to Orphan: Student Movements and Indonesia's Democratic Transition". In *Activists in Transition: Contentious Politics in the New Indonesia*, edited by Michele Ford and Thushara Dibley. Ithaca, NY.: Cornell Southeast Asia Program, 2019*a*.

———. *Playing Politics: Power, Narrative, and Agency in the Making of the Indonesian Student Movement*. Leiden: Brill, 2019*b*.

Shiraishi, Takashi. *An Age in Motion: Popular Radicalism in Java, 1912–1926*. Ithaca, NY.: Cornell University Press, 1990.

Sloam, James. "'The Outraged Young': Young Europeans, Civic Engagement and the New Media in a Time of Crisis". *Information, Communication & Society* 17 (2014): 217–31.

Sutopo, Oki Rahadianto. "Social Generation, Class and Experiences of Youth Transition in Indonesia". *Asian Journal of Social Sciences & Humanities* 3, no. 3 (2014): 126–32.

———. "The Act of Killing and the Look of Silence: A Critical Reflection". *Crime, Media, Culture* 13, no. 2 (2017): 235–243.

Weiss, Meredith L., Edward Aspinall, and Mark R. Thompson. "Introduction: Understanding Student Activism in Asia". In *Student Activism in Asia: Between Protest and Powerlessness*, edited by Meredith L. Weiss and Edward Aspinall. Minneapolis: University of Minnesota Press, 2012.

Index

Note: Page numbers followed by "n" refer to endnotes.

www.ingramcontent.com/pod-product-compliance
Lightning Source LLC
Chambersburg PA
CBHW050408280326
41932CB00013BA/1782